Survival

GLOBAL POLITICS AND STRATEGY

Volume 58 Number 2 | April–May 2016

'Nearly every *de jure* Arab state had at least one counter-state lurking in its shadow. These aspiring players pointed to the inconsistency between promise and practice. They claimed to correct the historical mistakes of the past and promised a more just, stable and legitimate form of statehood.'

Ariel I. Ahram and Ellen Lust, The Decline and Fall of the Arab State, p. 12.

'The modern challenge to the ascendancy of liberalism is two-headed: it entails a rejection not just of the liberal-democratic model at home by right-wing populists, but also of the international order built by the United States at the end of the Second World War.'

Michael J. Boyle, The Coming Illiberal Order, p. 36.

'Donald Trump was also associated with an important political idea: that Barack Obama did not legitimately occupy the office of the presidency. The reason, never coherently stated, was nonetheless obvious.'

Dana H. Allin, Donald Trump's America, p. 221.

Survival
GLOBAL POLITICS AND STRATEGY
Volume 58 Number 2 | April–May 2016

Contents

Cover: Jabin Botsford/Washington Post/Getty

On the cover
Republican presidential candidate Donald Trump takes questions, alongside his former rival New Jersey Governor Chris Christie, left, during a campaign press event in Florida on 1 March 2016.

On the web
Visit www.iiss.org/publications/survival for brief notices on new books on Politics and International Relations, the Middle East, the United States, and War, Conflict and the Military.

***Survival* editors' blog**
For ideas and commentary from *Survival* editors and contributors, visit www.iiss.org/politicsandstrategy.

German Questions

Review Essays

Closing Argument

Survival
GLOBAL POLITICS AND STRATEGY

The International Institute for Strategic Studies
2121 K Street, NW | Suite 801 | Washington DC 20037 | USA
Tel +1 202 659 1490 Fax +1 202 659 1499 E-mail survival@iiss.org Web www.iiss.org

Arundel House | 13–15 Arundel Street | Temple Place | London | WC2R 3DX | UK
Tel +44 (0)20 7379 7676 Fax +44 (0)20 7836 3108 E-mail iiss@iiss.org

14th Floor, GBCorp Tower | Bahrain Financial Harbour | Manama | Kingdom of Bahrain
Tel +973 1718 1155 Fax +973 1710 0155 E-mail iiss-middleeast@iiss.org

9 Raffles Place | #51-01 Republic Plaza | Singapore 048619
Tel +65 6499 0055 Fax +65 6499 0059 E-mail iiss-asia@iiss.org

Survival Online www.tandfonline.com/survival and www.iiss.org/publications/survival

Aims and Scope *Survival* is one of the world's leading forums for analysis and debate of international and strategic affairs. Shaped by its editors to be both timely and forward thinking, the journal encourages writers to challenge conventional wisdom and bring fresh, often controversial, perspectives to bear on the strategic issues of the moment. With a diverse range of authors, *Survival* aims to be scholarly in depth while vivid, well written and policy-relevant in approach. Through commentary, analytical articles, case studies, forums, review essays, reviews and letters to the editor, the journal promotes lively, critical debate on issues of international politics and strategy.

Published for the IISS by
Routledge Journals, an imprint of Taylor & Francis, an Informa business.

About the IISS The IISS, a registered charity with offices in Washington, London, Manama and Singapore, is the world's leading authority on political–military conflict. It is the primary independent source of accurate, objective information on international strategic issues. Publications include *The Military Balance*, an annual reference work on each nation's defence capabilities; *Strategic Survey*, an annual review of world affairs; *Survival*, a bimonthly journal on international affairs; *Strategic Comments*, an online analysis of topical issues in international affairs; and the *Adelphi* series of books on issues of international security.

SUBMISSIONS

To submit an article, authors are advised to follow these guidelines:

- *Survival* articles are around 4,000–10,000 words long including endnotes. A word count should be included with a draft. Length is a consideration in the review process and shorter articles have an advantage.
- All text, including endnotes, should be double-spaced with wide margins.
- Any tables or artwork should be supplied in separate files, ideally not embedded in the document or linked to text around it.
- All *Survival* articles are expected to include endnote references. These should be complete and include first and last names of authors, titles of articles (even from newspapers), place of publication, publisher, exact publication dates, volume and issue number (if from a journal) and page numbers. Web sources should include complete URLs and DOIs if available.
- A summary of up to 150 words should be included with the article. The summary should state the main argument clearly and concisely, not simply say what the article is about.
- A short author's biography of one or two lines should also be included. This information will appear at the foot of the first page of the article.
- *Survival* has a strict policy of listing multiple authors in alphabetical order.

Submissions should be made by email, in Microsoft Word format, to the Managing Editor, Matthew Harries, survival@iiss.org. Alternatively, hard copies may be sent to *Survival*, IISS–US, 2121 K Street NW, Suite 801, Washington, DC 20037, USA. Please direct any queries to Matthew Harries.

The editorial review process can take up to three months. *Survival*'s acceptance rate for unsolicited manuscripts is less than 20%. *Survival* does not normally provide referees' comments in the event of rejection. Authors are permitted to submit simultaneously elsewhere so long as this is consistent with the policy of the other publication and the Editors of *Survival* are informed of the dual submission.

Readers are encouraged to comment on articles from the previous issue. Letters should be concise, no longer than 750 words and relate directly to the argument or points made in the original article.

ADVERTISING AND PERMISSIONS

For advertising rates and schedules

USA/Canada: The Advertising Manager, Taylor & Francis Inc., 325 Chestnut Street, 8th Floor, Philadelphia, PA 19106, USA Tel +1 (800) 354 1420 Fax +1 (215) 625 2940.

UK/Europe/Rest of World: The Advertising Manager, Routledge Journals, Taylor & Francis, 4 Park Square, Milton Park, Abingdon, Oxfordshire OX14 4RN, UK Tel +44 (0) 207 017 6000 Fax +44 (0) 207 017 6336.

SUBSCRIPTIONS

Survival is published bi-monthly in February, April, June, August, October and December by Routledge Journals, an imprint of Taylor & Francis, an Informa Business.

Annual Subscription 2016

Institution	$787	£449	€661
Individual	$216	£128	€175
Online only	$689	£393	€578

Taylor & Francis has a flexible approach to subscriptions, enabling us to match individual libraries' requirements. This journal is available via a traditional institutional subscription (either print with online access, or online only at a discount) or as part of the Strategic, Defence & Security Studies Collection or Conflict, Security & Strategic Studies Library. For more information on our sales packages please visit http://www.tandfonline.com/page/librarians.

All current institutional subscriptions include online access for any number of concurrent users across a local area network to the currently available backfile and articles posted online ahead of publication.

Subscriptions purchased at the personal rate are strictly for personal, non-commercial use only. The reselling of personal subscriptions is prohibited. Personal subscriptions must be purchased with a personal cheque or credit card. Proof of personal status may be requested.

Dollar rates apply to all subscribers outside Europe. Euro rates apply to all subscribers in Europe, except the UK and the Republic of Ireland where the pound sterling rate applies. If you are unsure which rate applies to you please contact Customer Services in the UK. All subscriptions are payable in advance and all rates include postage. Journals are sent by air to the USA, Canada, Mexico, India, Japan and Australasia. Subscriptions are entered on an annual basis, i.e. January to December. Payment may be made by sterling cheque, dollar cheque, euro cheque, international money order, National Giro or credit cards (Amex, Visa and Mastercard).

Survival (USPS 013095) is published bi-monthly (in Feb, Apr, Jun, Aug, Oct and Dec) by Routledge Journals, Taylor & Francis, 4 Park Square, Milton Park, Abingdon, OX14 4RN, United Kingdom.

The US annual subscription price is $676. Airfreight and mailing in the USA by agent named Air Business Ltd, c/o Worldnet Shipping Inc., 156-15, 146th Avenue, 2nd Floor, Jamaica, NY 11434, USA. Periodicals postage paid at Jamaica NY 11431.

US Postmaster: Send address changes to Survival, C/O Air Business Ltd / 156-15 146th Avenue, Jamaica, New York, NY11434.

Subscription records are maintained at Taylor & Francis Group, 4 Park Square, Milton Park, Abingdon, OX14 4RN, United Kingdom.

ORDERING INFORMATION

Please contact your local Customer Service Department to take out a subscription to the Journal: **USA, Canada:** Taylor & Francis, Inc., 325 Chestnut Street, 8th Floor, Philadelphia, PA 19106, USA. Tel: +1 800 354 1420; Fax: +1 215 625 2940. **UK/Europe/Rest of World:** T&F Customer Services, Informa UK Ltd, Sheepen Place, Colchester, Essex, CO3 3LP, United Kingdom. Tel: +44 (0) 20 7017 5544; Fax: +44 (0) 20 7017 5198; Email: subscriptions@tandf.co.uk.

Back issues: Taylor & Francis retains a three-year back issue stock of journals. Older volumes are held by our official stockists: Periodicals Service Company, 11 Main Street, Germantown, NY 12526, USA to whom all orders and enquiries should be addressed. *Tel* +1 518 537 4700 *Fax* +1 518 537 5899 *e-mail* psc@periodicals.com *web* http://www.periodicals.com/tandf.html.

The issue date is April–May 2016.

The print edition of this journal is printed on ANSI conforming acid free paper.

The Decline and Fall of the Arab State

Ariel I. Ahram and Ellen Lust

In May 2015, the last border outpost between Syria and Iraq still controlled by the regime of President Bashar al-Assad fell to the mujahideen of the Islamic State.[1] The Islamic State, also known as ISIS or ISIL, has long intended to erase what it claims are artificial boundaries, and to topple the ill-conceived states that mar the Arab world. It is not alone in that aim. From the Kurdish Democratic Union Party in Syria and Kurdistan Regional Government in Iraq, to the secessionist al-Hirak in southern Yemen and the Cyrenaican separatists in Libya, political actors across the region are mounting claims to states of their own. For the second time in a century, the map of the Arab world is on the brink of radical revision.

To some, this crisis comes as little surprise. For Arab nationalists, pan-Islamist activists and Washington DC insiders alike, reimagining the regional map is something of a pastime.[2] They have long assumed that the Arab state system was tenuous. They recount how imperial conspiracies, invasions and occupations erected borders and imposed systems of rule badly out of touch with the identities and aspirations of the region's people.[3] While Arab states enjoyed the privileges of recognition abroad, they faced a perilous dearth of legitimacy at home. In the end, popular resentments would surely sweep aside such political artifice.

Yet, even if we accept the premise that sovereignty was a sham, that Arab states were doomed from birth, and that the current crisis was therefore

Ariel I. Ahram is an Associate Professor in the School of Public and International Affairs, Virginia Tech. **Ellen Lust** is a Professor in the Department of Political Science, University of Gothenburg.

 DOI 10.1080/00396338.2016.1161897

inevitable, there are still important questions left unanswered. The first set of questions pertains to timing: why were the long-standing vulnerabilities of the Arab states exposed now, and how had these defective states been able to survive for so long? The second set concerns the aspiring successor states. Why have the challengers to sovereignty taken the particular form that they have? Do any of them offer a chance for a more stable and peaceful political order?

The Arab struggle has taken place in a wider global context in which notions of statehood and sovereignty have changed dramatically since the end of the Cold War. Domestic battles may have triggered the sudden collapse of Arab states, but changes at the regional and international levels created permissive conditions for political-opposition movements to destabilise existing states, manoeuvre toward statehood and potentially challenge the state system. Structural change at the global level made dramatic realignment at the state and regional levels possible.[4] Instability and uncertainty in the institutional rules of sovereignty affected the ways in which Arab states could respond to internal challengers, simultaneously hamstringing existing Arab states and emboldening their opposition.

The state and its competitors in the Arab world

Sovereignty, as the American political scientist Stephen Krasner famously put it, has always been a form of organised hypocrisy.[5] In part, this is because sovereignty is inextricable from international hierarchy. Sovereign states are presumed equal, but some are more equal than others. Acting self-interestedly and amorally, states exert power over others and often violate norms of sovereignty in pursuit of higher principles.[6] But hypocrisy stems also from the sheer girth of the concept itself. Sovereignty has multiple definitions, and many dimensions that are often incompatible. At the international level, sovereignty entails recognition and admission to the community of states. Once admitted, sovereignty provides for territorial inviolability and autonomy under international law. At the domestic level, sovereignty involves untrammelled control over specific territories and peoples. In other words, a sovereign state *rules*. Sovereignty is also closely tied to legitimacy. Particularly in a democratic age, sovereign states derive their legitimacy by embodying the popular will to self-rule.[7]

In practice, the meaning of sovereignty has varied over time, and changed with the evolution of state practices.[8] In 1914, the noted international jurist Robert Lansing wrote that:

> Political mastery depends upon the physical power to coerce ... The legal right to exercise the supreme will over a community fail[s] to confer upon its legal possessor a real supremacy, unless the possessor of the physical power permits such exercises.[9]

Customs dating back to the Peace of Westphalia had demonstrated that law alone was an insufficient basis upon which to derive sovereignty. Lansing was appointed the United States' secretary of state the year after he wrote about sovereignty, serving through the First World War and at the Paris peace talks of 1919. But his preference for power above law would quickly seem antiquated.

President Woodrow Wilson himself came to Paris with a radically different agenda, calling for a system of sovereignty premised on national self-determination, derived from international law, and adjudicated and enforced by international society through the League of Nations.[10] Lansing would eventually resign in disgust. This post-war moment marked the beginning of a critical period of uncertainty and fluidity in which the institutions of sovereignty would undergo drastic revision. By 1945, the rules of sovereignty had changed, but so too had its judges.[11] Sovereignty was conferred, not possessed as Lansing had posited. Sovereign states could therefore be formed by the initiative of the international community in collaboration with the population itself. Seemingly primitive peoples could be tutored until ready for self-governance. The sovereign states would then represent the will of the people.[12] The elimination of recognised states from the system was prohibited; territorial integrity was ensured not just by a national army in defence of the state, but by the international community as a whole in defence of a system.[13]

American ascent was crucial to the solidification of the mid-twentieth-century understanding of sovereignty. The United States emerged after the First World War as the only major power with its military and economy intact. By the end of the Second World War, the US possessed the world's only nuclear weapons and half the world's industrial capacity.[14] The formation of the United Nations and the start of decolonisation after 1945 saw the rules of sovereignty become steadily more institutionalised. Britain and France sought at first to rein in the anti-imperialist impulse, but eventually had to concede to American primacy. The USSR was initially sceptical of the entire idea of international law and society, but gradually came to see an opportunity to weaken imperial powers and, at the same time, confirm its own standing in the international system.[15] The American notion of sovereignty had symbolic and moral appeal as well. Leaders of anticolonial movements across the globe – including Egyptian nationalist Sa'd Zaghlul and the aspiring king of Syria, Faisal bin Hussein, as well as the leaders of China's May Fourth Movement and India's Rowlatt Satyagraha – embraced it as a route to national liberation.[16]

The US and USSR propped up regional proxies

Of course, the great powers continued to control and intervene in subordinate states.[17] Many post-colonial states appeared deliberately misconstrued. Colonially inscribed borders seemed to foment ethno-sectarian infighting, hamper state-building and ensure long-term dependence on foreign powers. Still, there remained a strong commitment on practical, if not moral, grounds to preserving even dysfunctional states. Both the US and the USSR funnelled arms and aid to prop up regional proxies whose domestic sovereignty was contested. Allowing a state to splinter could set a dangerous precedent, emboldening secessionist movements worldwide and eventually threatening the entire state system.[18] The international community would rarely countenance the birth of new successor states, nor would they declare a state dead, even if its physical power was moribund.[19]

These new rules played a crucial role in shaping the Arab state system. European powers vied with one another and, to a lesser extent, with indigenous players over the spoils of the Ottoman domains.[20] Across North Africa and the Middle East, states emerged as bricolages of colonial and indigenous institutions of rule. European colonial administrations encapsulated pre-existing political administrations in Egypt, North Africa and the Persian Gulf in the early twentieth century. At the end of the First World War, mandatory control was established over Iraq and the Levant, effectively launching entirely new political entities.[21]

Newly enshrined Arab rulers used the idea of sovereignty to manipulate their great-power sponsors and the international community as a whole. The military arsenals provided by outside patrons were often put to ulterior purposes of internal suppression or to vie for regional supremacy. Arab states tried repeatedly to gain leverage in the international system by threatening to withhold oil exports from Europe and the US, although the 'oil weapon' was never as effective as promised.[22] Still, those Arab states that had oil resources had the ability to trade petrodollars for security guarantees from outside powers or other Arab states.

Though the Arab League gestured rhetorically toward Arab unity, it served in fact as an institutional anchor, ensuring the persistence of sovereignty for member states.[23] Indeed, Arab leaders often turned the normative impulse for Arab unification into a tool to delegitimise opponents both in the domestic and the inter-state arenas.[24]

Arab autocrats claimed credit for attaining, defending and augmenting national self-determination. Sovereignty (*as-siyada*) became a totem, as individual rulers were indelibly imprinted in official nationalist discourse.[25] Schools, media, military services and banal tokens such as postage stamps and currency became vehicles for the leaders' cults of personality.[26] Basing legitimacy on the idea of self-determination, though, worked both ways. While rulers portrayed themselves as embodying national independence, the opposition ridiculed them as puppets of neo-imperialism.

In return for political acquiescence, states also promised expansive programmes of social protection and redistribution. Ensuring national food security was a top priority. These arrangements were especially generous in oil-rich states, but were evident even in resource-poor Egypt and Jordan, and elsewhere.[27] Yet these authoritarian bargains were often slipshod, with neglected rural peripheries and teeming urban slums hovering at the edge of the state's reach. Residents ate subsidised bread while pirating electricity and squatting on state-owned lands. Such bargains became progressively more tenuous in periods of economic liberalisation beginning in the 1970s. Acceding to the economic reforms required by the World Bank, the IMF and foreign investors made it impossible for rulers to keep up the domestic spending necessary to maintain the broad-based authoritarian bargain. In place of populism, narrower coalitions of crony capitalists ruled the day, further alienating the common citizenry.[28]

Few Arab states could make the transition from brutal and despotic force to administrative and infrastructural authority. When persuasion faltered, repression was at hand. Ready access to military funding and support sometimes made rulers over-confident in their ability to suppress opposition, as with the defunct Hashemite monarchy in Iraq.[29] The institutional organs of surveillance and violence, the secret police and the army, remained the mainstays of stability and governance, making Arab states fierce but weak.[30] In sum, securing internal order was less a matter of negotiation than of imposition, and remained accordingly fragile.

Nearly every *de jure* Arab state had at least one counter-state lurking in its shadow. These aspiring players pointed to the inconsistency between promise and practice. They claimed to correct the historical mistakes of the past and promised a more just, stable and legitimate form of statehood. Some, such as the Shi'ites under Saddam Hussein, demanded different forms of political order within existing territorial boundaries. Others, such as the Kurds, sought territorial adjustments and the establishment of entirely new structures of statehood. When states foundered, challengers seized the opportunity to establish a territorial base and exercise real authority, becoming, in effect, de facto states, as discussed below. But no matter their actual hold on power, depth of popular support or validity of historical grievance, these state aspirants were never welcomed into the international community. Historians and international-relations scholars treated them as momentary disruptions, dead ends in the region's evolution. But they are indicative of how populations themselves imagined alternative versions of nationhood and sovereignty.[31]

Taken as a group, the de facto states in the Middle East mirrored the weaknesses and deficiencies of the parent states they tried to supplant. They, too, derived their fiscal means from primary (and sometimes illicit) commodity exports. They, too, were often on the dole, dependent on external patrons for military, financial and diplomatic support. The Kurdish Republic of Mahabad of 1946–47 and the All-Palestine Government of 1948 quickly collapsed after their international sponsors deserted them.[32] The various Palestinian 'states within a state' that appeared in Jordan and Lebanon were eager recipients of monetary and military support from fellow Arab rejectionists and the Soviet Union. During the Lebanese Civil War, Palestinian factions (like nearly all other belligerents) used drugs and arms smuggling to finance their war-making operations.[33] The Western Sahara gained a measure of recognition through the African Union, but it was shut out by the Arab League and unrecognised by most of international society. The Polisario Front's foothold would be nearly impossible without its umbilical connection to Algeria.[34]

Despite the jeremiads of commentators and politicians alike about the impending breakdown of regional order, Arab states endured and the state system as a whole prevailed for half a century. When state power faltered, as in Yemen and Oman in the 1960s, Jordan before the 'Black September' of 1970–71 or Lebanon in 1958 and 1975, neighbours and great powers tended to fill the voids of authority through proxy wars or direct military involvement. State death or even territorial reappropriation remained anathema. Lebanon retained its seat at the United Nations despite 30 years of obvious failure and civil war, and Syria's hegemony over its neighbour was accepted in practice but never formalised by international law. Israel's control over the occupied territories has been widely judged inadmissible. Most emphatically of all, Iraq's invasion and annexation of Kuwait in 1990 was rebuffed by a coalition of Western and Arab states.[35] The political map of the Arab world might have been a fiction, but it was a useful fiction.

Global dissensus and regional ramifications

If the Gulf War represented a high-water mark in the international community's effort to preserve the territorial integrity of states, there was an undercurrent forming. Overshadowed by the Iraq–Kuwait crisis was another momentous event in the history of the Arab-state regional system: the unification of the Yemens in May 1990. The Republic of Yemen's shotgun marriage to the People's Democratic Republic of Yemen (PDRY) marked the first internationally accepted adjustment to the Arab map since the Syrian–Egyptian unity scheme of 1958.[36]

The changes in Yemen were a small part of a contentious and much larger transformation in the rules of sovereignty. The causes of these changes were both ideological and material. With the USSR collapsing, Soviet clients like the PDRY had no choice but to beggar their neighbours. Old states dissolved. Sovereignty was bestowed virtually overnight to successor states, beginning with the former Soviet republics and extending to secessionist states in the former Yugoslavia and, most recently, East Timor and South Sudan.[37]

Sovereignty itself seemed, in certain circles, obsolete. The transition towards a European Union represented an ambitious programme to pool – or perhaps surrender – sovereign powers.[38] It was some of these same states, not by coincidence, that championed the argument that the international community had a 'responsibility to protect' (R2P) civilians and might abrogate sovereignty to prevent humanitarian disasters.[39] Yet many actions ostensibly undertaken under the R2P mantle ultimately became measures meant to help build up effective state power, essentially saving sovereignty from itself.[40] The effort to fix frail and failing states proved financially and militarily exorbitant, sapping the will to intervene.[41]

As a consequence, the new rules of sovereignty remained inchoate. Who was entitled to statehood? And what did international recognition entail in terms of rights, entitlements and obligations? The implosion of the Soviet Union represented what the American political scientist Philip Roeder calls a 'nation-state crisis', in which the chances for change in the configuration of states increased dramatically.[42] But the crisis was not limited to the post-Soviet sphere.[43] Returning to the Wilsonian spirit of 1919, national self-determination re-emerged as a criterion upon which sovereignty rested. The international community backed the conferral of statehood to groups that suffered repression, and revoked the sovereignty of states that seemed to block the desire for self-rule. But ensuring statehood for every aspiring

Who was entitled to statehood?

nationalist movement, or congruence between national identity and territorial boundaries, remained a practical impossibility.[44] The gap between physical control and legal entitlement grew more glaring. The newest states tended to be fragile, prone to civil war and internecine violence, and dependent on the international community.[45] Bosnia, East Timor and Kosovo each functioned under international protectorates *after* gaining independence.

Accompanying this spike in the recognition of new states, moreover, was a dramatic increase in de facto states, built by separatist movements which declared independence and managed to maintain a more or less consolidated territorial and administrative base.[46] De facto states such as Somaliland and Abkhazia carved out footholds from territories that newly recognised parent states proved incapable of controlling, despite their ostensible sovereignty. Like their parents, de facto states depend heavily on foreign patronage for economic and military support.[47] The persistence of de facto states and the weakness of ostensibly sovereign new states demonstrated the increasingly questionable worth attached to sovereignty as a whole.[48]

American equivocation, particularly but not exclusively over the fate of Iraq, added to ambiguity about sovereignty.[49] After crushing Iraq in 1991, the United States pushed the UN Security Council to impose draconian economic sanctions and an invasive weapons-inspection programme. A no-fly zone, ostensibly used to defend the Iraqi people from recriminations by Saddam's troops, abetted the formation of the Kurdish de facto state in the north. At the same time, the US feared Iraq's potential Balkanisation and sought to preserve its territorial integrity. The 2003 invasion of Iraq deepened the confusion. The US described its actions as an intervention motivated by the principle of preserving peace and stability, not conquest. But invasion and regime change was an obvious breach of the rules of sovereignty. Other countries came to appropriate US rhetoric, as American scholar Tanisha Fazal put it, 'to justify interventions that turn into occupation that turn into conquest'.[50]

Though critical of the US invasion and neurotic about anything that could threaten its own sovereignty, Russia used precisely this rhetoric in its wars with Georgia in 2008 and Ukraine from 2014.[51] Anticipating a future in which they could exercise such prerogatives, rising powers such as Brazil,

India and China similarly came to support selective and self-serving notions of intervention, even as they defended traditional sovereignty.[52] Disorder among the greater powers had ramifications within regional subsystems. Iran, like Nigeria, South Africa and other would-be regional powers, saw the opportunity to exert its own hegemonic designs in the Middle East, starting with Iraq, putting further stress on fragmented regional order.[53]

Accompanying changes in the international system were technological developments that promised to change how power could be generated and projected.[54] From drone strikes to cyber attacks to financial warfare, new instruments of power transcended territorial boundaries.[55] Unlike the atom bomb, or the dreadnought before that, these capabilities were not confined to a handful of states but became widely accessible to actors in the international system, including non-state actors. In the Middle East in particular, information technologies granted relatively small states such as Qatar and non-state organisations such as al-Qaeda, Hamas and Hizbullah an outsized voice that could effectively set regional agendas.[56] Instability within the international hierarchy made the search for a coherent replacement to the mid-twentieth-century version of sovereignty exceedingly difficult.

The 2011 revolutions and the search for new rules

The protests that erupted in Tunisia, Egypt, Bahrain, Yemen and elsewhere in 2011 did not begin with demands for new states. Yet they confronted Arab regimes at a common weak point – their facile claims to embody sovereignty as national self-determination and popular will. The ubiquitous slogan of protest, 'The people want the downfall of the regime' (*ash-sha'ab yurid isqat an-nizam*), demolished this pillar of regime legitimacy. Protesters adopted common tactics for confronting authoritarian power, appropriating the state's own slogans and emblems of patriotism and national identity. Egyptian protesters, for instance, hijacked National Police Day to stage their demonstrations. New information technologies, such as SMS, Twitter and satellite television, diffused political messages at an unprecedented rate. This was uniquely challenging for Arab republican regimes precisely because they staked so much of their legitimacy on channelling popular will and defending national integrity from foreign domination. National armies could not easily fire on protesters draped in the national flag, even if it was to protect the president.[57] Moreover, the army, police and intelligence services harboured their own institutional agendas regarding access to money and power, which overrode the duty to defend the leader at all costs.[58]

With the state's coercive grip suddenly weakened, all kinds of political movements came forward to make claims. Some opposition movements sought to upend regimes while laying claim to the entirety of the existing unitary states.[59] Others tried to carve out new territorial foundations for statehood or reinstate previously discarded ones. Split between Iran, Iraq, Syria and Turkey, Kurdish factions were eager to make up for the diplomatic and military shortfalls that they had experienced after the First World War. In Yemen, al-Hirak was initially wary of the protest movement in Sana'a and the possibility of brutal government suppression, but then launched its own 'Day of Rage' in Aden on 11 February 2011.[60] Libya's breakdown has yielded two distinctive state aspirants. In the east, partisans of al-Barqa (Cyrenaica) refused to recognise the standing of the transitional government and demanded significant regional autonomy based on the pre-1951 constitution.[61] In the south, Tuareg fighters who had been recruited into the service of Muammar Gadhafi formed the core of the Mouvement national de libération de l'Azawad (MNLA) and seized control of northern Mali. The MNLA declared Azawad's independence on 1 April 2012, a move that had reverberations across the Sahel.[62] ISIS similarly exploited sites of localised administrative weakness in Iraq, Syria, Egypt and Libya to establish its territorial foothold. Whether secessionist or unitarian, all of these groups found themselves in the position of would-be state-builders, mimicking, recreating and appropriating the infrastructure of state power. In the absence of functional state authority, they extorted taxes, construed legal orders and, to varying degrees, imposed bureaucratic control over populations.

The beleaguered *de jure* states reflexively turned to patrons in the regional and international system for their defence. Counter-terrorism imperatives had long implied a need for strong, or at least well-armed, states in the Middle East. Reasserting and reaffirming statehood was particularly important in the face of pan-Islamic actors such as al-Qaeda, which challenged both individual state sovereignty and international society as a whole. Vacuums of state power, it was presumed, invited infestation by radicals, necessitating a flow of foreign arms and aid to help states maintain and expand their writ.[63] But these commitments were no longer assured. Misadventures in Iraq and Afghanistan and the stress of economic recession rendered the United States wary of overextension.[64] Moreover, Wilsonian sympathy for self-determination made it difficult to oppose movements that seemed geared toward democracy and national liberation.[65] As the US and Western powers played Hamlet, Saudi Arabia became Fortinbras, leading a counter-revolutionary coalition that included the Gulf states, Jordan, Algeria, Morocco and General Abdel Fattah el-Sisi's Egypt.

For their part, the rebels likewise appealed to international norms and specific great-power patrons for support. De facto states sought to use their hold over cities and towns, border crossings and transit routes, mineral, hydrological and oil infrastructure to enhance their claim to juridical sovereignty, in effect to gain membership in international society itself.[66] The Libyan opposition, trapped in its Benghazi beachhead in 2011, successfully lobbied the US, Europe, and even China and Russia to intervene to avert humanitarian disaster. The ensuing air campaign did more than prevent slaughter; it enabled the rebels to march on Sirte and oust Gadhafi. Five years later, the rival Libyan factions continue to seek support from the US and European powers on the basis of their efforts to fight the expansion of radical groups like al-Qaeda and ISIS, and their ability to stem the tide of refugees and migrants crossing the Mediterranean to southern Europe.[67]

The Syrian opposition, too, vied for patronage and support from the West and from Sunni Arab states. But unlike in Libya, Russia and China refused to countenance full international intervention, leading to an even more prolonged and still undefined endgame. In the province of Hasakah in eastern Syria, the Kurdish Democratic Union Party, closely affiliated with the Kurdistan Workers' Party (PKK) in Turkey, has assumed administrative functions, providing fuel, seed crops and electricity, and has beat back military encroachment by Islamist forces to establish Rojava, the state of Western Kurdistan. Rojava touts itself as a model of participatory democracy, open to all ethnic and religious groups and an outpost of women's liberation, but has remained hemmed in by hostility from the Turkish government.[68]

Perhaps the most elaborate case of an extroverted de facto state is the Kurdish Regional Government (KRG) in Iraq. The KRG holds itself up as a pro-US outpost of stability and liberal democracy in a sea of chaos, despite corruption and violence on the part of the ruling Kurdistan Democratic Party–Patriotic Union of Kurdistan (PUK) duopoly. The 2005 Iraqi constitution granted the KRG formal federal status and considerable autonomy. Yet the KRG has always sat precariously. Turkey has consistently opposed the prospect of an independent Kurdistan. Erbil and Baghdad have sparred for years over the allocation of oil revenue and control over the oil-rich region of Kirkuk.[69] In the midst of the ISIS onslaught of 2014, Kurdish forces not only launched a counter-attack (of middling success) but also seized disputed territory around Kirkuk. The Kurdish leadership tried to barter access to oil in return for international sponsorship of its secession and a permanent divorce from Iraq. Secret agreements granted Turkey privileged access to KRG oil fields and allowed the Kurds to use the Turkish pipelines in Ceyhan. Tankers laden with Kurdish oil steamed to Israel's Mediterranean ports.[70] Ultimately, though, the US rebuffed these efforts and the Kurds were forced back into their unhappy marriage with Baghdad.[71] In many ways, such state aspirants are trying to turn their physical control into juridical sovereignty. It remains to be seen whether the simulacra of sovereignty will someday be mistaken for the real thing.

ISIS looks and acts the state

One seeming exception to such eagerness to engage with international society is the Islamic State. ISIS has shown nothing but contempt for international borders and the underlying norms of sovereignty. Its vision of a caliphate would seem to preclude any territorial boundaries at all.[72] Yet ISIS does much to look and act the state. Indeed, the Islamic State has adopted many of the characteristics typical of governance in the Arab world.[73] Witnesses from Mosul and Raqqa describe ISIS-designated jurists meting out rulings, police apprehending and punishing criminals, and tax inspectors scouring for contraband. Proceedings from legal cases are posted on the internet, as supposed evidence of the virtues of the ISIS justice system.[74] There are even reports of ISIS-issued currency.[75] Oil smuggling provides a significant revenue stream. Engineers and technocrats oversee the subsidisation and distribution of water, electricity, foodstuffs and gasoline. A skeletal welfare system offers healthcare and pensions for mujahideen and their dependents.[76] In fact, polemicists specifically highlight the superiority of the Islamic State's welfare provision to that of the Gulf regimes.[77] Internally, ISIS functions normally – at least by regional standards – even as it purports to revive a mediaeval Islamic empire. Like other revolutionary states before it,[78] ISIS thumbs its nose at international law but appeals directly to the (Muslim) masses for recognition and legitimation. The more migrants, recruits, followers and financial backers the Islamic State's propaganda attracts, the more legitimate its claim to embody the caliphate.

Assad has wielded norms of sovereign immunity

As state aspirants clamoured for international recognition of their gains on the ground, embattled *de jure* states hoped to use their standing in the international community to augment their feeble control on the ground. Backed by Russia and China, Assad's regime in Syria has wielded norms of sovereign immunity and non-intervention as a shield, systematically blocking international observers and relief agencies from accessing rebel-held territories.[79] Bahrain and Yemen invited Saudi military intervention to beat back what they saw as Iranian encroachment on their sovereignty. Iraq maintains a close military alliance with Iran, allowing members of the expeditionary Iranian Revolutionary Guard Corps to direct the military campaigns against ISIS. In all of these cases, though, the appeal to outside powers to shore up internal control came at the cost of ultimate diminution within the global and regional hierarchy of states.

States have also made appeals abroad to funnel economic resources into particular 'useable' spaces within the rump state.[80] As peripheral zones like Sinai and Upper Egypt, the Sahel, and the Jazeera and Syrian deserts slipped from the state's grip, heavily fortified capitals (and Erbil, a de facto capital)[81] experienced real-estate bubbles and construction booms catalysed by an inflow of international aid and foreign direct investment. In the Maghreb, state authorities clung to the coastal cities and hunkered down around the far-flung oil fields and mineral deposits, pipelines and petrochemical facilities in the interior. Egypt announced intentions to build an entirely new capital city, funded by Gulf investors, somewhere in the desert east of Cairo. Tellingly, the plan was unveiled at a well-guarded south Sinai beach resort, while the peninsula's interior regions became a redoubt for smugglers, criminals and terrorists.[82]

In Iraq and Syria, the focus on useable space amounts to a retreat to defensible boundaries. Iraqi plans to retake Mosul from the Islamic State seem to have been postponed indefinitely.[83] Yet Iraq's southern oil fields, which hold nine-tenths of the country's reserves, produce at full tilt, attracting billions in foreign investment. The arrival of internally displaced people and the relocation of financial capital to government-controlled territories precipitated runs in the housing market, a boon for regime-aligned profiteers.[84] In Syria, the military and political situation is even more tenuous. In July 2015, Assad stressed the importance of Syrian independence and criticised Western powers that sought to re-impose 'imperialism' on the Syrian people by backing international 'terrorists'. 'Each part of Syria is precious and invaluable', he said, but 'war has its conditions, strategies, and priorities'. Accordingly, 'vital areas must be held as to prevent other areas from falling', while less important regions, particularly where the population appeared to side with the rebels, would be effectively vacated.[85] Yet, as in Iraq, capital and population are re-concentrating in government-held zones in Damascus and along the coast, lending the regime a measure of permanence.[86] Although Syria's relatively modest eastern oil fields quickly fell to rebel hands, Russian financing allowed new off-shore drilling rigs to go online, literally beyond the reach of rebels.[87]

Still, no clear boundaries divide state- and rebel-held domains, and no stark distinction between state and non-state power exists. Beside the formal security apparatus, states have built alliances with all kinds of armed non-state actors, including tribes, religious groups and mafias, in order to augment their coercive power. Sometimes these forces are charged with inflicting maximum damage on civilians with minimal blame for the regime itself. Iraq's Popular Mobilisation Units and Syria's National Defence Units have each been implicated in civilian massacres. Other militias function as free agents, allying alternatively with the state or rebels depending on local circumstances. In the early years of the civil war, Damascus fought mercilessly against Jabhat al-Nusra and the Free Syrian Army, but government forces typically left ISIS positions unscathed. Reciprocally, ISIS largely refrained from targeting Syrian state forces and instead preyed on other rebel factions.[88] Such state-organised crime undercuts the assumption that states will pursue and retain a monopoly over the use of force, a key dimension of internal sovereignty.

Alongside political and military collusion, patterns of economic exchange have sewn together state- and rebel-held territories. Smuggling of foodstuffs, fuels, cigarettes and migrant labourers has been a critical part of the Sahel's political economy for decades, if not centuries. In the last decade, Latin American drug cartels began shipping cocaine through the region to Europe. Rebels collaborated with, taxed and took over these criminal networks outright. And yet all of this exchange is facilitated by military and government officials across the region; they have taken bribes, issued fraudulent licences and visas, opened up transit centres and ports, provided protection and granted diplomatic cover to these criminals-cum-rebels.[89]

The seams between rebel- and state-held territory in Syria and Iraq have similarly evolved into zones of arbitrage. Oil, arms, narcotics and slaves readily circulate between rebel-held areas, the KRG, Turkey, Syria and Iraq.[90] ISIS has systematically seized weapons and resources intended to help the Western-backed Free Syrian Army or the Iraqi security services and siphoned off the salaries of police officers, judges and civil servants within its domain.[91] Weapons and funds provided by international intervention have become booty in an illicit parallel to the flow of aid and investment within the state-held zones. Rather than pit states and unrecognised state aspirants in perpetual conflict, these interactions have helped push them toward coexistence.

The end of Arab sovereignty?

The breakdown of Arab states since 2011 has reflected uncertainty about how international society should respond to claims of sovereign statehood. The initial protests in 2011 may have emerged unexpectedly,[92] but the subsequent course the Arab opposition movement took, with so many challengers to sovereignty around the region, was a result of the permissiveness of the global system. Previous generations of would-be state-makers in the Arab world had run up against an international consensus about the immutability of international borders, the impossibility of state death and the impermissibility of state birth. In 2011, none of these obstacles seemed as formidable.

In this sense, the breakdown of Arab regional order is but the latest case in a string of crises that has been enveloping parts of Africa, the Balkans and post-Soviet Eurasia for two decades. *De jure* states such as Bahrain, Syria, Tunisia, Iraq and Yemen are trying to use their status in the international system to gain the tangible and symbolic resources necessary to defend and expand control on the ground. State aspirants such as the KRG, Rojava, the Libyan General National Congress (GNC) and, idiosyncratically, the Islamic State all seek to translate physical control into symbolic standing on the global stage. The outcomes of these contests will be determined largely in the context of an international hierarchy in which Arab states, generally, are weak.

In the coming years, one possible scenario is a return to sovereign dominance, either with the existing two dozen regional states or some higher number. Some de facto states might well break through by diplomatic guile and military might. The Kurds in Iraq are today the strongest candidate. Given the weakness of the state in Libya and Yemen, though, secession is also a possibility there too. The international community might confer sovereignty upon these state aspirants, re-drawing and re-aligning regional maps to accommodate them. The vast majority, though, will probably be excluded diplomatically and, eventually, defeated militarily. With resources dwindling, petitions for international relief will fall on deaf ears. Ultimately, some form of Arab statehood will congeal, hastened by outside powers interested in maintaining the status quo.

A second scenario is that statehood and sovereignty lose their purchase entirely. The existing models of territorial statehood might be rejected. It may be easy to point to ISIS as a singular harbinger of such change. Yet for all of its utopian rhetoric, the interior of the Islamic State is remarkably state-like. Moreover, like those of other kinds of internal challengers, the Islamic State's transgressions of sovereignty have elicited a response that has helped to augment states' coercive power. Jordan, Israel, Turkey, Egypt and Saudi Arabia have collaboratively built up their arsenals and further militarised their borders in anticipation of an ISIS challenge. In this sense, statehood is hardly in retreat. On the contrary, it is being aggressively reasserted.

A far greater challenge to statehood in the Arab world comes from international society itself. If the major powers conclude that sovereignty is indeed dispensable, then the faux states of the Arab world are likely candidates to see their statehood dismantled. Terrorism, humanitarian crises, mass population outflows and threats to global energy supply may all spur outside actors to commit greater resources and troops to the region. Interventions *can* become occupations, and occupations can become the basis for neo-trusteeships or even outright annexation.[93] Though unlikely, a return to this kind of neo-imperial domination is not inconceivable.[94]

Between these two extremes is a third scenario, in which sovereign and non-sovereign political entities in the Middle East come to an uneasy coexistence. Instead of insisting on sovereignty's ultimate supremacy or its complete dismantling, the international community can find ways to engage with both recognised states and unrecognised state aspirants. This would amount to diluting the value of sovereignty itself. Key resources that the international community had reserved for recognised states, such as multilateral aid, would be allocated more flexibly. Blanket commitments to territorial integrity would be voided.[95] Frail states would tacitly concede pockets where their physical control was demonstrably nil. De facto states would give up the desire for international recognition that would, in effect, fracture existing states. Spatially, *de jure* and de facto states would sit not just side by side, but in a kind of patchwork, with de facto states pockmarking nominally sovereign territory.[96]

Some of these changes are already in evidence on the ground. In Syria, for instance, local truces and ceasefires have offered respite to civilians caught in horrendous humanitarian disasters.[97] Governance within the Middle East has frequently been conducted through negotiation with local power holders, be they tribal leaders, religious figures or other embedded societal actors.[98] These arrangements point to the possibility of pragmatic accommodation, instead of unceasing war between state and non-state actors. They could become foundations for long-term conflict management. But conceding the permanence of de facto states may require abandoning the hope of full resolution and national integration – a necessary step toward freezing otherwise bloody and protracted conflicts.[99]

From the perspective of international society, adopting such a stance toward unrecognised states would be more a change in degree than a fundamental reordering of international order. Despite a normative commitment to uphold sovereign states' territorial integrity, global powers have worked with unrecognised entities such as Somaliland, Abkhazia and other de facto states on issues such as refugees, piracy and terrorism.[100] In terms of security, development and democratisation, de facto states tend to be no worse than their estranged parents. Lack of international recognition does not necessarily doom a place to become a black hole filled by criminals, terrorists and violence.[101]

For the Arab world, dilution of an already diminished form of sovereignty will be a bitter pill. For the last 80 years, the rulers of sovereign states and their rivals have promised that sovereignty would solve persistent problems of political, economic and social backwardness. And yet, on most of these counts, statehood must be judged a disappointment. Finding ways to stabilise the relationships between *de jure* and de facto power-holders in the Arab world may be the only way to reach a level of governance sufficient for preserving human life and promoting modest economic development. Considering the historical record and the current catastrophic violence, 'good enough' may be a worthy goal.[102]

Admittedly, some of these scenarios may today appear far-fetched. Yet a mere five years ago, the suggestion that Egypt would have experienced two changes of regime or that Tunisia would be in the midst of a democratic transition would also have seemed preposterous.[103] The purposeful designs of any single actor in the Middle East, whether state or non-state, regional or great power, will not be enough to reshape the map of sovereignty and statehood. This many-sided, multilayered battle for sovereignty will yield political structures of unforeseen form and stature.

Notes

1 'Islamic State "Seizes Key Syria–Iraq Border Crossing"', BBC News, 22 May 2015, http://www.bbc.com/news/world-middle-east-32840508.

2 See Robert Kaplan, 'The Ruins of Empire in the Middle East', *Foreign Policy*, 25 May 2015, http://foreignpolicy.com/2015/05/25/its-time-to-bring-imperialism-back-to-the-middle-east-syria-iraq-islamic-state-iran/; Robin Wright, 'Imagining a Remapped Middle East', *New York Times*, 28 September 2013, http://www.nytimes.com/2013/09/29/opinion/sunday/imagining-a-remapped-middle-east.html; and Ralph Peters, 'Blood Borders', *Armed Forces Journal*, 1 June 2006, http://www.armedforces-journal.com/blood-borders/.

3 See Benjamin Miller, 'Balance of Power or the State-to-Nation Balance: Explaining Middle East War-Propensity', *Security Studies*, vol. 15, no. 4, 2006, pp. 658–705; and Michael C. Hudson, *Arab Politics: The Search for Legitimacy* (New Haven, CT: Yale University Press, 1977).

4 Hillel David Soifer, 'The Causal Logic of Critical Junctures', *Comparative Political Studies*, vol. 45, no. 12, 2012, pp. 1572–97.

5 Stephen D. Krasner, *Sovereignty: Organized Hypocrisy* (Princeton, NJ: Princeton University Press, 1999).

6 David A. Lake, 'The New Sovereignty in International Relations', *International Studies Review*, vol. 5, no. 3, 2003, pp. 303–23.

7 Neal McFarlane and Natalie Sabanadze, 'Sovereignty and Self-Determination: Where Are We?', *International Journal*, vol. 68, no. 4, 2013, pp. 609–27.

8 See Robert Jackson, 'Sovereignty in World Politics: A Glance at the Conceptual and Historical Landscape', *Political Studies*, vol. 47, no. 3, 1999, p. 433; and Luke Glanville, 'The Myth of "Traditional" Sovereignty', *International Studies Quarterly*, vol. 57, no. 1, 2013, pp. 79–90.

9 Robert Lansing, 'A Definition of Sovereignty', *Proceedings of the American Political Science Association*, vol. 10, 1914, p. 65.

10 Allen Lynch, 'Woodrow Wilson and the Principle of "National Self-Determination": A Reconsideration', *Review of International Studies*, vol. 28, no. 2, 2002, pp. 419–36.

11 Robert H. Jackson, *Quasi-States: Sovereignty, International Relations and the Third World* (New York: Cambridge University Press, 1993), p. 23.

12 Gerard Kreijen, *State Failure, Sovereignty and Effectiveness: Legal Lessons from the Decolonization of Sub-Saharan Africa* (Leiden: Martinus Nijhoff Publishers, 2004), p. 151.

13 Sharon Korman, *The Right of Conquest: The Acquisition of Territory by Force in International Law and Practice* (New York: Oxford University Press, 1996).

14 Michael H. Hunt, *The American Ascendancy: How America Gained and Wielded Global Dominance* (Chapel Hill, NC: University of North Carolina Press, 2007), p. 154.

15 See David Armstrong, *Revolution and World Order: The Revolutionary State in International Society* (New York: Oxford University Press,

1993), pp. 120–60; and Teddy J. Uldricks, *Diplomacy and Ideology: The Origins of Soviet Foreign Relations, 1917–1930* (Thousand Oaks, CA: Sage Publications, 1979).

16 See Erez Manela, *The Wilsonian Moment: Self-Determination and the International Origins of Anticolonial Nationalism* (New York: Oxford University Press, 2007), Chapter 4; and Zeine N. Zeine, *The Struggle for Arab Independence: Western Diplomacy and the Rise and Fall of Faisal's Kingdom in Syria* (Beirut: Khayat's, 1960), pp. 202–3.

17 See Barry Buzan and George Lawson, *The Global Transformation: History, Modernity and the Making of International Relations* (New York: Cambridge University Press, 2015), p. 211; Tanisha M. Fazal, *State Death: The Politics and Geography of Conquest, Occupation, and Annexation* (Princeton, NJ: Princeton University Press, 2011), p. 229; Korman, *The Right of Conquest*, p. 305.

18 See James Mayall, *Nationalism and International Society* (New York: Cambridge University Press, 1990), p. 123; and Lea Brilmayer, 'Secession and Self-Determination: A Territorial Interpretation', *Yale Journal of International Law*, no. 16, 1991.

19 Fazal, *State Death*.

20 Carl L. Brown, *International Politics and the Middle East: Old Rules, Dangerous Game* (Princeton, NJ: Princeton University Press, 1984), pp. 83–9. See also Fred Halliday, *The Middle East in International Relations: Power, Politics and Ideology* (New York: Cambridge University Press, 2005), pp. 75–130.

21 Importantly, though, there were discernible expressions of national identity in these areas even before European control. See Reidar Visser, *Basra, the Failed Gulf State: Separatism and Nationalism in Southern Iraq* (New Brunswick, NJ: Transaction Press, 2005); and Rashid Khalidi, *Palestinian Identity: The Construction of Modern National Consciousness* (New York: Columbia University Press, 2013).

22 Fuad Itayim, 'Strengths and Weaknesses of the Oil Weapon', *IISS Adelphi Paper*, 1975, pp. 1–7; Roy Licklider, 'The Power of Oil: the Arab Oil Weapon and the Netherlands, the United Kingdom, Canada, Japan, and the United States', *International Studies Quarterly*, vol. 32, no. 2, 1988, pp. 205–26.

23 See Clovis Maksoud, 'Diminished Sovereignty, Enhanced Sovereignty: United Nations–Arab League Relations at 50', *Middle East Journal*, 1995, pp. 582–94; and Gamil Matar and Ali al-Din Hilal, *Al-nizam al-iqlimi al-arabi* (Beirut: Dar al-Mustaqbal al-Arabi, 1983).

24 See Michael N. Barnett, *Dialogues in Arab Politics: Negotiations in Regional Order* (New York: Columbia University Press, 1998); and Malik Mufti, *Sovereign Creations: Pan-Arabism and Political Order in Syria and Iraq* (Ithaca, NY: Cornell University Press, 1996).

25 Roger Owen, *The Rise and Fall of Arab Presidents for Life: With a New Afterword* (Cambridge, MA: Harvard University Press, 2014), p. 15.

26 See Sami Zubaida, 'The Fragments Imagine the Nation: The Case of Iraq', *International Journal of Middle East Studies*, vol. 34, no. 2, 2002, pp. 205–15; and Donald Malcolm Reid, 'The

Postage Stamp: A Window on Saddam Hussein's Iraq', *Middle East Journal*, 1993, pp. 77–89.

27 See Steven Heydemann, 'Social Pacts and the Persistence of Authoritarianism in the Middle East', in Oliver Schlumberger (ed.), *Debating Authoritarianism: Dynamics and Durability in Non-Democratic Regimes* (Stanford, CA: Stanford University Press, 2007); and Eckart Woertz, *Oil for Food: The Global Food Crisis and the Middle East* (New York: Oxford University Press, 2013).

28 Oliver Schlumberger, 'Structural Reform, Economic Order, and Development: Patrimonial Capitalism', *Review of International Political Economy*, vol. 15, no. 4, 2008, pp. 622–49.

29 Sean Yom, *From Resilience to Revolution: How Foreign Interventions Destabilize the Middle East* (New York: Columbia University Press, 2015).

30 Nazih N. Ayubi, *Over-Stating the Arab State: Politics and Society in the Middle East* (New York: I.B. Tauris, 1996); Jason Brownlee, '… And Yet They Persist: Explaining Survival and Transition in Neopatrimonial Regimes', *Studies in Comparative International Development*, vol. 37, no. 3, 2002, pp. 35–63.

31 David Siddhartha Patel, 'Remembering Failed States in the Middle East', Project on Middle East Political Science, 4 May 2015, http://pomeps.org/2015/05/04/remembering-failed-states-in-the-middle-east/.

32 See William Eagleton, *The Kurdish Republic of 1946* (New York: Oxford University Press, 1963); and Avi Shlaim, 'The Rise and Fall of the All-Palestine Government in Gaza', *Journal of Palestine Studies*, 1990, pp. 37–53.

33 See Rex Brynen, 'The Politics of Exile: The Palestinians in Lebanon', *Journal of Refugee Studies*, vol. 3, no. 3, 1990, pp. 204–27; Cheryl A. Rubenberg, 'The Civilian Infrastructure of the Palestine Liberation Organization: An Analysis of the PLO in Lebanon Until June 1982', *Journal of Palestine Studies*, 1983, pp. 54–78; Jonathan Marshall, *The Lebanese Connection: Corruption, Civil War, and the International Drug Traffic* (Stanford, CA: Stanford University Press, 2012); and Yazid Ṣayigh, *Armed Struggle and the Search for a State: The Palestinian National Movement, 1949–1993* (New York: Oxford University Press, 1997), pp. 458–9, 559.

34 See Anour Boukhars, 'Simmering Discontent in the Western Sahara', Carnegie Endowment for International Peace, 12 March 2012, http://carnegieendowment.org/2012/03/12/simmering-discontent-in-western-sahara; and David Lynn Price, *The Western Sahara* (Beverly Hills, CA: Sage Publications, 1979), p. 30.

35 See Boaz Atzili, *Good Fences, Bad Neighbors: Border Fixity and International Conflict* (Chicago, IL: University of Chicago Press, 2011); and Ian S. Lustick, 'The Absence of Middle Eastern Great Powers: Political "Backwardness" in Historical Perspective', *International Organization*, vol. 51, no. 4, 1997, pp. 653–83.

36 See Fred Halliday, 'The Third Inter-Yemeni War and Its Consequences', *Asian Affairs*, vol. 26, no. 2, 1995, pp. 131–40; and Robert D. Burrowes, 'The

Republic of Yemen: The Politics of Unification and Civil War, 1989–1995', in Michael C. Hudson (ed.), *Middle East Dilemma: The Politics and Economics of Arab Integration* (New York: Columbia University Press, 1999).

37 Bridget Coggins, *Power Politics and State Formation in the Twentieth Century: The Dynamics of Recognition* (New York: Cambridge University Press, 2014).

38 See Bruno de Witte, 'Sovereignty and European Integration: The Weight of Legal Tradition', *Maastricht Journal of European and Comparative Law*, no. 2, 1995; and Tania F. Aalberts, 'The Future of Sovereignty in Multilevel Governance Europe – A Constructivist Reading', *Journal of Common Market Studies*, vol. 42, no. 1, 2004, pp. 23–46.

39 The idea of abrogating sovereignty to save humanity is not new, but substantiated in the 'responsibility to protect' doctrine, it enjoyed more power than it ever had before. See Alex J. Bellamy, 'The Responsibility to Protect and the Problem of Military Intervention', *International Affairs*, vol. 84, no. 4, 2008, pp. 615–39; and Phil Orchard, 'The Evolution of the Responsibility to Protect: At a Crossroads?', *International Affairs*, vol. 88, no. 2, 2012, pp. 377–86.

40 See Buzan and Lawson, *The Global Transformation*, p. 212; and Toby Dodge, 'Intervention and Dreams of Exogenous State-Building: The Application of Liberal Peacebuilding in Afghanistan and Iraq', *Review of International Studies*, vol. 39, no. 5, 2013, pp. 1,189–212.

41 Henry Kissinger, *World Order* (New York: Penguin Press, 2014), pp. 369–70.

42 Philip G. Roeder, *Where Nation-States Come From: Institutional Change in the Age of Nationalism* (Princeton, NJ: Princeton University Press, 2007), p. 163.

43 For a discussion about its implications for Africa, see Lee J.M. Seymour, 'Sovereignty, Territory and Authority: Boundary Maintenance in Contemporary Africa', *Critical African Studies*, vol. 5, no. 1, 2013, pp. 17–31.

44 Georg Sørensen, 'After the Security Dilemma: The Challenges of Insecurity in Weak States and the Dilemma of Liberal Values', *Security Dialogue*, vol. 38, no. 3, 2007, pp. 357–78.

45 Mikulas Fabry, *Recognizing States: International Society and the Establishment of New States Since 1776* (New York: Oxford University Press, 2010), p. 180.

46 See Adrian Florea, 'De Facto States in International Politics (1945–2011): A New Data Set', *International Interactions*, vol. 40, no. 5, 2014, pp. 788–811. Note that this does not include the most recent de facto states of the Middle East.

47 Pål Kolstø and Helge Blakkisrud, 'Living with Non-Recognition: State- and Nation-Building in South Caucasian Quasi-States', *Europe–Asia Studies*, vol. 60, no. 3, 2008, pp. 483–509.

48 Daniel Byman and Charles King, 'The Mystery of Phantom States', *Washington Quarterly*, vol. 35, no. 3, 2012, p. 44.

49 Amitav Acharya, 'State Sovereignty after 9/11: Disorganised Hypocrisy', *Political Studies*, vol. 55, no. 2, 2007, pp. 274–96. For US equivocation on the break-up of the USSR, see Stuart

Elden, *Terror and Territory: The Spatial Extent of Sovereignty* (Minneapolis, MN: University of Minnesota Press, 2009), pp. 150–1.

50 Fazal, *State Death*, p. 238.

51 Roy Allison, *Russia, the West, and Military Intervention* (New York: Oxford University Press, 2013).

52 See Philip Rotmann, Gerrit Kurtz, and Sarah Brockmeier (eds), 'Major Powers and the Contested Evolution of a Responsibility to Protect', *Conflict, Security and Development*, special issue, vol. 14, no. 4, 2014; Miles Kahler, 'Rising Powers and Global Governance: Negotiating Change in a Resilient Status Quo', *International Affairs*, vol. 89, no. 3, 2013, p. 718.

53 On Iran, see Joel S. Migdal, *Shifting Sands: The United States in the Middle East* (New York: Columbia University Press, 2014), pp. 196–208. On the more general rise of regional powers, see Buzan and Lawson, *The Global Transformation*, p. 297.

54 Buzan and Lawson, *The Global Transformation*, p. 303.

55 See, for instance, the influential consulting firm Eurasia Group's 2015 top risks report. Eurasia Group, 'Top Risks 2015', 5 January 2015, http://s3.amazonaws.com/toprisks2015/Top+Risks+2015.pdf.

56 See Marc Lynch, *Voices of the New Arab Public: Iraq, Al-Jazeera, and Middle East Politics Today* (New York: Columbia University Press, 2006); and Morten Valbjørn and André Bank, 'The New Arab Cold War: Rediscovering the Arab Dimension of Middle East Regional Politics', *Review of International Studies*, vol. 38, no. 1, 2012, pp. 3–24.

57 Claudia Derichs and Thomas Demmelhuber, 'Monarchies and Republics, State and Regime, Durability and Fragility in View of the Arab Spring', *Journal of Arabian Studies*, vol. 4, no. 2, 2014, pp. 180–94.

58 See Albrecht Holger, Aurel Croissant and Fred H. Lawson (eds), *Military Engagement in Mobilizing Societies: Armies and the Arab Spring* (Philadelphia, PA: University of Pennsylvania Press, forthcoming); and John Gledhill, 'Assessing (In)security After the Arab Spring', *PS: Political Science and Politics*, vol. 46, no. 4, 2013, pp. 709–15.

59 Glen Rangwala, 'The Creation of Governments-in-Waiting: The Arab Uprisings and Legitimacy in the International System', *Geoforum*, vol. 66, November 2015, pp. 215–23.

60 See Stephen W. Day, *Regionalism and Rebellion in Yemen: A Troubled National Union* (Cambridge: Cambridge University Press, 2012), p. 280; and Susan Dahlgren, 'The Snake with a Thousand Heads: The Southern Cause in Yemen', *Middle East Report and Information Project*, no. 256, 2015, http://www.merip.org/mer/mer256/snake-thousand-heads.

61 Sean Kane, 'Al-Barqa Reborn? Eastern Regionalism and Libya Political Transition', in Peter Cole and Brian McQuinn (eds), *The Libyan Revolution and Its Aftermath* (New York: Oxford University Press, 2015).

62 See Yvan Guichaoua, 'Tuareg Militancy and the Sahelian Shockwaves of the Libyan Revolution', in Cole and McQuinn (eds), *The Libyan Revolution and Its Aftermath*; and Douglas Livermore, 'The Case for

Azawad: Rectifying the Past to Save the Future in Northern Africa', *African Security Review*, vol. 22, no. 4, 2013, pp. 282–93.

63 Barak Mendelsohn, *Combating Jihadism: American Hegemony and Interstate Cooperation in the War on Terrorism* (Chicago, IL: University of Chicago Press, 2009).

64 Robert J. Lieber, *Power and Willpower in the American Future: Why the United States Is Not Destined to Decline* (New York: Cambridge University Press, 2012), pp. 132–3, 139–40.

65 Pierre M. Atlas, 'U.S. Foreign Policy and the Arab Spring: Balancing Values and Interests', *Digest of Middle East Studies*, vol. 21, no. 2, 2012, pp. 353–85.

66 Zachariah Cherian Mampilly, *Rebel Rulers: Insurgent Governance and Civilian Life During War* (Ithaca, NY: Cornell University Press, 2011), p. 43; Nina Caspersen, *Unrecognized States: The Struggle for Sovereignty in the Modern International System* (Malden, MA: Polity, 2013), p. 51.

67 Brian Klaas and Jason Pack, 'Talking with the Wrong Libyans', *New York Times*, 14 June 2015, http://www.nytimes.com/2015/06/15/opinion/talking-with-the-wrong-libyans.html?smid=fb-share&_r=0.

68 See Erika Solomon, 'Special Report: Amid Syria's Violence, Kurds Carve out Autonomy', Reuters, 22 January 2014, http://www.reuters.com/article/2014/01/22/us-syria-kurdistan-specialreport-idUSBREA0L17320140122; E. Aretaios, 'The Rojava Revolution', OpenDemocracy, 14 March 2015, https://www.opendemocracy.net/arab-awakening/evangelos-aretaios/rojava-revolution; and Meredith Tax, 'The Revolution in Rojava', *Dissent*, 22 April 2015, http://www.dissentmagazine.org/online_articles/the-revolution-in-rojava.

69 Denise Natali, *Kurdish Quasi-State: Development and Dependency in Post-Gulf War Iraq* (Syracuse, NY: Syracuse University Press, 2010).

70 'Iraqi Kurdistan's Texas Oil Tanker Unloads in Israel', *Jerusalem Post*, 27 February 2015, http://www.jpost.com/Middle-East/Iraqi-Kurdistans-Texas-oil-tanker-unloads-in-Israel-392427.

71 Marina Ottaway and David Ottaway, 'How the Kurds Got Their Way', *Foreign Affairs*, May/June 2014, http://www.foreignaffairs.com/articles/141216/marina-ottaway-and-david-ottaway/how-the-kurds-got-their-way.

72 See Richard Nielson, 'Does the Islamic State Believe in Sovereignty?', *Washington Post*, 6 February 2015, http://www.washingtonpost.com/blogs/monkey-cage/wp/2015/02/06/does-the-islamic-state-believe-in-sovereignty/; and Hope Bielat, 'Islamic State and the Hypocrisy of Sovereignty', E-IR, 20 March 2015, http://www.e-ir.info/2015/03/20/islamic-state-and-the-hypocrisy-of-sovereignty/.

73 James Fromson and Steven Simon, 'ISIS: The Dubious Paradise of Apocalypse Now', *Survival*, vol. 57, no. 3, June–July 2015, pp. 7–56.

74 Andrew March and Mara Revkin, 'The Caliphate of Law: ISIS's Ground Rules', *Foreign Affairs*, 15 April 2015, http://www.foreignaffairs.com/articles/143679/andrew-f-march-and-mara-revkin/caliphate-of-law.

75 Amre Sarhan, 'Source: ISIS Began Trading with Its Own Currency on Limited Scale in Mosul', IraqNews, 24 June 2015, http://www.iraqinews.com/features/source-isis-began-trading-currency-limited-scale-mosul/.

76 See 'Islamic State of Iraq Personnel Records', CTC Harmony Project, document MNFT-2007-005315; 'A Roster of Personal Information of 20 ISI Personnel', MNFV 2007-000364, https://www.ctc.usma.edu/programs-resources/harmony-program; and 'Analysis of the State of ISI', CTC, September 2013, p. 25, https://www.ctc.usma.edu/v2/wp-content/uploads/2013/09/Analysis-of-the-State-of-ISI-Translation.pdf.

77 Al-Khanssaa Brigade, 'Women of the Islamic State: A Manifesto', translation by Charlie Winter, pp. 38–40, available at http://www.quilliamfoundation.org/wp/wp-content/uploads/publications/free/women-of-the-islamic-state3.pdf.

78 Armstrong, *Revolutionary and World Order*, p. 97.

79 See 'Syrian Leader Blames "Foreign Interference"', Al-Jazeera, 10 January 2012, http://www.aljazeera.com/news/middleeast/2012/01/2012110977499290.html; and Steve Heydemann, 'Assad's Hollow Mandate', *Foreign Policy*, June 2014, http://foreignpolicy.com/2014/06/02/assads-hollow-mandate/.

80 James Ferguson, 'Seeing Like an Oil Company: Space, Security, and Global Capital in Neoliberal Africa', *American Anthropologist*, vol. 107, no. 3, 2005, pp. 377–82.

81 Geetika Rudra, 'Malibu Meets Iraq in Erbil McMansions', ABC News, 4 November 2014, http://abcnews.go.com/International/malibu-meets-iraq-erbil-mcmansions/story?id=26680771.

82 See Ishaan Tharoor, 'Egypt's Strange $45 Billion Plan to Abandon Cairo as Its Capital City', *Washington Post*, 14 March 2015, http://www.washingtonpost.com/blogs/worldviews/wp/2015/03/16/egypts-strange-45-billion-plan-to-abandon-cairo-as-its-capital-city/; and Mohammad Hassan Shaban, 'Egypt Declares "New" State of Emergency in North Sinai', *Asharq al-Awsat*, 26 April 2015, http://www.aawsat.net/2015/04/article55343110/egypt-declares-new-state-of-emergency-in-north-sinai.

83 Michael Knights, 'Anbar First, Mosul Never?', *Foreign Affairs*, 27 May 2015, https://www.foreignaffairs.com/articles/iraq/2015-05-27/anbar-first-mosul-never.

84 See Jack Fairweather, Aziz Alwan and Zaid Sabah, 'Baghdad Mansions Sell for $1 Million as Militants Near', Bloomberg News, 4 November 2014, http://www.bloomberg.com/news/articles/2014-11-03/baghdad-mansions-sell-for-1-million-with-islamic-state-at-gates; and Molly Hennessey-Fiske and Nabih Bulos, 'Baghdad's New Mall Is a Haven, and a Symbol of an Improving Economy', *Los Angeles Times*, 4 December 2014, http://www.latimes.com/world/middleeast/la-fg-baghdad-mall-20141220-story.html.

85 For the complete speech, see 'Ar-rais Assad: al-Mu'arika mu'arika mu'hawar mutakamil yu-mathil manhija min al-istiqlaliyya wa al-karama', Syrian Arab News Agency,

26 July 2015, http://sana.sy/?p=245771. See also Aron Lund, 'Falling Back, Fighting On: Assad Lays Out His Strategy', Carnegie Endowment for International Peace, 27 July 2015, http://carnegieendowment.org/syriaincrisis/?fa=60857; and 'Assad Regime "To Accept Syria's De Facto Partition"', Agence France-Presse, 25 May 2015, http://www.arabnews.com/world/news/751681.

86 See Reyta al-Ahmady, 'Syria's Housing Crisis Widens', Al-Monitor for al-Hayat, 8 March 2015, http://www.al-monitor.com/pulse/business/2015/03/syria-housing-rent-social-gap.html; 'Syria: Foreign Aid Will Keep War Economy Afloat', Oxford Analytica, 15 July 2013; 'Syria Economy: Regime Talks up Reconstruction', Economist Intelligence Unit, 14 July 2014; and Rashad Khattan, 'Mapping the Ailing (But Resilient) Syrian Banking Sector', *Syrian Studies*, vol. 7, no. 3, 2015, pp. 1–33.

87 James Stafford, 'Syria Signs First-Ever Offshore Oil Deal, with Russia', OilPrice.com, 26 December 2013, http://oilprice.com/Energy/Energy-General/Syria-Signs-First-Ever-Offshore-Oil-Deal-with-Russia.html.

88 Aymenn Al-Tamimi, 'The Assad Regime and Jihadis: Collaborators and Allies?', SyriaComment, 11 February 2014, http://www.joshualandis.com/blog/assad-regime-jihadis-collaborators-allies/.

89 See Wilfram Lacher, 'Organized Crime and Conflict in Sahel–Sahara Region', Carnegie Endowment for International Peace, September 2012, http://carnegieendowment.org/files/sahel_sahara.pdf; Ricardo René Larémont, 'Al Qaeda in the Islamic Maghreb: Terrorism and Counterterrorism in the Sahel', *African Security*, vol. 4, no. 4, 2011, pp. 242–68; and Jessica M. Huckabey, 'Al Qaeda in Mali: The Defection Connections', *Orbis*, vol. 57, no. 3, 2013, pp. 467–84.

90 See Sam Jones, 'New EU Syria Sanctions Reveal Regime Collusion with Isis', *Financial Times*, 7 March 2015; Ahmed Rasheed, 'Oil Smuggling Finances ISIS's New "Caliphate"', Reuters, 23 July 2014, http://english.alarabiya.net/en/business/energy/2014/07/23/Oil-smuggling-finances-Islamic-State-s-new-caliphate.html; Ewen MacCaskill and Martin Chulov, 'Isis Apparently Takes Control of US Weapons Airdrop Intended for Kurds', *Guardian*, 22 October 2014, http://www.theguardian.com/world/2014/oct/22/isis-us-airdrop-weapons-pentagon; C.J. Chivers, 'Where the Islamic State Gets Its Weapons', *New York Times Magazine*, 27 April 2015; and April Mona Mahmood and Ian Black, 'Free Syrian Army Rebels Defect to Islamist Group Jabhat al-Nusra', *Guardian*, 8 May 2013, http://www.theguardian.com/world/2013/may/08/free-syrian-army-rebels-defect-islamist-group.

91 Peter Taylow, '"It's God's gift": Islamic State Fills Coffers with Iraqi Government Cash', *Guardian*, 21 April 2015, http://www.theguardian.com/world/2015/apr/22/isis-fills-coffers-with-iraqi-government-cash.

92 Jason Brownlee, Tarek Masoud and Andrew Reynolds, *The Arab Spring: Pathways of Repression and Reform*

(New York: Oxford University Press, 2015), p. 42.

93 James D. Fearon and David D. Laitin, 'Neotrusteeship and the Problem of Weak States', *International Security*, vol. 28, no. 4, 2004, pp. 5–43.

94 See Steven R. David, *Catastrophic Consequences: Civil Wars and American Interests* (Baltimore, MD: Johns Hopkins University Press, 2008), Chapter 2.

95 Stephen D. Krasner, 'Sharing Sovereignty: New Institutions for Collapsed and Failing States', *International Security*, vol. 29, no. 2, 2004, pp. 85–120.

96 John Sidaway, 'Topography of Sovereignty', *Geopolitics*, vol. 18, no. 4, 2013, pp. 961–6.

97 Rim Turkani et al., 'Hungry for Peace: Positives and Pitfalls of Local Truces and Ceasefire in Syria', October 2014, http://www.lse.ac.uk/newsAndMedia/PDF/Syriareport.pdf.

98 See Philip Shukry Khoury and Joseph Kostiner, *Tribes and State Formation in the Middle East* (Berkeley, CA: University of California Press, 1990); Shelagh A. Weir, *Tribal Order: Politics and Law in the Mountains of Yemen* (Austin, TX: University of Texas Press, 2009); and Katherine Blue Carroll, 'Tribal Law and Reconciliation in the New Iraq', *Middle East Journal*, vol. 65, no. 1, 2011, pp. 11–29.

99 See Eiki Berg, 'Examining Power-Sharing in Persistent Conflicts: De Facto Pseudo-Statehood Versus De Jure Quasi-Federalism', *Global Society*, vol. 21, no. 2, 2007, pp. 199–217; and Dov Lynch, *Engaging Eurasia's Separatist States: Unresolved Conflicts and De Facto States* (Washington DC: U.S. Institute of Peace Press, 2004), pp. 8, 112–13.

100 See James Ker-Lindsay, 'Engagement Without Recognition: The Limits of Diplomatic Interaction with Contested States', *International Affairs*, vol. 91, no. 2, 2015, pp. 267–85; and Pegg Scott and Eiki Berg, 'Lost and Found: The WikiLeaks of De Facto State–Great Power Relations', *International Studies Perspectives*, May 2014.

101 See Stewart Patrick, '"Failed" States and Global Security: Empirical Questions and Policy Dilemmas', *International Studies Review*, vol. 9, no. 4, 2007, pp. 644–62; and Bartosz H. Stanislawski, 'Para-States, Quasi-States, and Black Spots: Perhaps Not States, But Not "Ungoverned Territories", Either', *International Studies Review*, vol. 10, no. 2, 2008, pp. 366–96.

102 Merilee S. Grindle, 'Good Enough Governance Revisited', *Development Policy Review*, vol. 29, supplement 1, 2011, pp. s199–s221. See also Susan Woodward, 'State-Building for Peace-Building: What Theory and Whose Role', in Richard Kozul-Wright and Piergiuseppe Fortunato (eds), *Securing Peace: State-Building and Economic Development in Post-Conflict Countries* (New York: Bloomsbury Publishing, 2011), p. 93.

103 See Marc Morjé Howard and Meir R. Walters, 'Explaining the Unexpected: Political Science and the Surprises of 1989 and 2011', *Perspectives on Politics*, vol. 12, no. 2, 2014, pp. 394–408; and Eva Bellin, 'Reconsidering the Robustness of Authoritarianism in the Middle East: Lessons from the Arab Spring', *Comparative Politics*, vol. 44, no. 2, 2012, pp. 127–49.

The Coming Illiberal Order

Michael J. Boyle

In a July 2014 speech in Băile Tuşnad, Romania, recently re-elected Hungarian Prime Minister Viktor Orbán declared that it was time for Hungary to 'abandon liberal methods and principles of organizing society' and to embark upon a project of building a new 'illiberal state'.[1] Citing China, Russia, Singapore, India and Turkey as models, Orbán argued that the liberal-democratic model had performed poorly compared to authoritarian states and illiberal democracies during the financial crisis in 2008.[2] Throughout that crisis, he noted, it was illiberal states – as he put it, 'systems that are not Western, not liberal, not liberal democracies, maybe not even democracies' – which proved more successful in responding to global economic turmoil. While he acknowledged that liberal values retained a degree of attractiveness, Orbán argued that it was important for states to cut themselves loose of the legal restrictions imposed by liberal democracy and to engage in a new type of economic nationalism to ensure that their interests were protected in the global economy.

At the time, Orbán's remarks were met by fierce criticism across the European Union, as many member states expressed concerns about Hungary's slide into paranoid, illiberal politics.[3] Yet over the last 18 months it has become clear that Orbán was a forerunner of a deeper shift against liberal values in Europe. The persistent economic woes of the eurozone, the missteps of the EU in managing Greece's financial crisis and the mass-scale

Michael J. Boyle is an Associate Professor of Political Science at La Salle University and a Senior Fellow at the Foreign Policy Research Institute in Philadelphia, PA. He is the author of *Violence after War: Explaining Instability in Post-Conflict States* (Baltimore, MD: Johns Hopkins University Press, 2014).

Survival | vol. 58 no. 2 | April–May 2016 | pp. 35–66 DOI 10.1080/00396338.2016.1161899

migration of refugees from Syria and elsewhere has inflamed right-wing populist sentiment and challenged those parties seen as defenders of traditional European values. Many right-wing parties are now openly questioning the liberal-democratic model and attacking those institutions, notably the EU, wedded to that model. The fraying of European liberalism can be seen in the rise of neo-Nazi parties in Greece, Switzerland, Sweden, Austria and Germany, and in the modest electoral successes recorded by right-wing populist parties, such as Marine Le Pen's National Front in France and the UK Independence Party.[4] The October 2015 victory of the Law and Justice Party in Poland's parliamentary elections – and its ensuing promise to wipe Poland clean of the 'diseases' of 25 years of 'liberal indoctrination' – only confirmed the depth of the crisis of liberal values in Europe.[5]

This assault on liberal values and democratic governance is not confined to Europe. There is growing evidence that the world is in the midst of an 'authoritarian resurgence', with more countries sliding backwards towards authoritarian rule and other forms of illiberal governance.[6] According to Freedom House, there has been a decade-long decrease in global freedom, with 105 countries seeing some sort of reversal during that period.[7] The scale of this anti-democratic reversal is growing: in 2015, 72 countries showed some sign of decline in political freedom, the largest number in ten years. Even the United States has not been immune to this trend. It is hard to see the xenophobic nationalism of Donald Trump and other Republican contenders as anything other than a symptom of the corrosion of the liberal-democratic character of American society.

The challenge facing liberalism is much greater than the sense of exhaustion and disillusionment that pervades politics in Europe and the US.[8] The modern challenge to the ascendancy of liberalism is two-headed: it entails a rejection not just of the liberal-democratic model at home by right-wing populists, but also of the international order built by the United States at the end of the Second World War. Far more than is often realised, the domestic and international fortunes of liberalism are linked; this is because historically the institutions of global order have mirrored the domestic structures of the most powerful states in the system. The early-twentieth-century dominance of the US and UK gave a liberal-democratic sheen to the earliest global institutions.

As Stanley Hoffmann put it, many of the earliest institutions were 'little more than a projection of domestic liberalism on a world scale'.[9] Indeed, a British critic noted that the League of Nations was merely an attempt 'to apply the principles of Lockean liberalism to the building of a machinery of global order'.[10] While chastened by the failure of the League, the architects of the UN were nonetheless motivated to import elements of a democratic, even American, political order – notably a written constitution, the separation of powers and the practice of a veto – into international institutions such as the UN. Other post-Second World War global institutions, such as the IMF and World Bank, were designed to reflect American hegemony, and the priorities and liberal values of the United States and its allies.[11] A world rapidly moving away from those values at home will naturally be one in which the legitimacy of such institutions will come under question.

Foundations of the international order are under attack

Today, the foundations of the international order are under attack from a growing number of rising, often illiberal, states that do not see a US-created order as consistent with their interests or reflective of their power. Speaking in Munich in 2007, Russian President Vladimir Putin asserted that the growing economic strength of India, China, Russia and others called for the creation of a 'multipolar world' to replace the unipolar system dominated by the United States.[12] Since then, Moscow has consistently warned that the days of Russia simply accepting Western preferences as inevitable are over.[13] Similarly, China has called for a multipolar world since 1992, though it has proceeded cautiously to avoid antagonising the United States with its self-styled 'peaceful rise'.[14] Yet China's ambitions are growing rapidly: it is becoming more strident in its calls for new regional-security and economic institutions in Asia, and its footprint is growing in Africa, the Middle East and South America. One prominent Chinese commentator recently described the US-built international order as 'an adult in children's clothes', adding, 'it is failing to adjust'.[15] Although they remain divided on exactly what kind of order they would prefer, many rising powers are clear that a universalisation of the Western liberal order is something they wish to avoid.[16]

For the United States, this poses a serious challenge. The demise of the liberal order is an outcome that US President Barack Obama has staked much of his presidency on avoiding. He has steadfastly maintained that the 'rise of the rest' need not be a zero-sum game – that states including China, Russia, India, Brazil and others can take their seats at the table in the new global institutional architecture of the twenty-first century. In a speech to the British Parliament in 2011, Obama predicted that the liberal-democratic order could survive even as 'more nations take on the responsibilities of global leadership' provided that the US and Europe created structures that recognised their due share of power and provided them a voice in setting the rules of the international system.[17] The world, according to Obama, had moved on from the winner-take-all power politics of the nineteenth century, becoming one of joint gains and shared prosperity. This view was made particularly clear when Secretary of State John Kerry described Russia's seizure of Crimea as reflecting outmoded 'nineteenth century thinking'.[18] Most of the Obama administration's early efforts at multilateral engagement were premised on the view that the United States could embed and socialise Russia, China, India and other rising states into the existing liberal order.

Rising powers have joined forces

As Obama's second term draws to a close, it is clear that many of his efforts have come to ashes. Although he offered several rising powers a greater role in the existing international institutions, they have instead joined forces in the form of a new grouping, BRICS, to propose an alternative global currency and to develop financial systems free from the influence of the United States.[19] Amidst this concerted effort to build a new institutional order, Obama's second term has been marked by an array of foreign-policy setbacks: the counter-revolutions that have destroyed most of the positive developments to emerge from the Arab Spring; the dismembering of Ukraine by a resurgent Russia; the sabre-rattling from China in extending its Air Defence Identification Zone further into East Asia; the collapse of Libya into chaos; the horrific civil war in Syria; and the rise of the Islamic State (also known as ISIS or ISIL). In each of these cases, America's opponents view the situation in exactly the kind of zero-sum terms that

Obama hoped to avoid. Whether they seek global rivalry (Russia and China), survival (Syria) or the overthrow of existing governments (ISIS), many key actors are driven more by the cold logic of power and interest than by the promise of shared gains. The ultimate lesson of Obama's second term may be that refusing to play a zero-sum game in foreign policy means little if one faces opponents who, like Vladimir Putin, see things in exactly those terms.

Given the change in the distribution of power in the international system, the US will have to take more seriously the preferences of illiberal states, either as competitors or potential allies.[20] The fact that the US will have to accommodate these states in ways that it is unaccustomed to doing will gradually change the character of the international system, no matter how its structure evolves. The world is moving away from a system governed by the US (and its democratic allies) and dominated by liberal values, and becoming a tiered, multipolar order in which the interests and values of illiberal states are seen as equal, if not more important, to global public opinion. The character of the new order will become more illiberal as the views of authoritarian states and weak or illiberal democracies become more influential in multilateral forums.

The coming illiberal order will not replicate the dog-eat-dog character of European great-power politics prior to 1914, nor will it lead to the complete dismantling of all of the structures that the US has supported since 1945. The past is no prologue: the US is unlikely to face a replay of either the unstable multipolarity of pre-Second World War Europe or the stable bipolarity of the Cold War. Prescriptions based on either scenario – particularly those calling for a resuscitation of the doctrine of containment – should be discounted for their poor historical reasoning and lack of imagination. Whether Washington likes it or not, the character of the new illiberal order will be very different from what has come before, limiting the usefulness of concepts such as 'containment' and 'engagement'.

The new international order will be marked by the ascendancy of illiberal states and their value systems, and a corresponding diminishment of the political and economic influence of the United States. The character of the rising states will gradually transform both the institutions and the normative underpinnings of the liberal order through two processes. Firstly, in the new illiberal order, the institutions of the previous order (such as the UN, World Trade Organisation and others) will remain intact, but their structures and policies will be retrofitted to suit the interests of newly dominant illiberal states. To complement this process, these states will build a parallel set of institutions whose purpose will be to sideline the US and build leverage in the developing world. Secondly, the key concepts of the liberal order – such as self-determination, self-defence, democracy promotion and the 'responsibility to protect', among others – will be contested or reimagined by illiberal states with different interests. This process of institutional change and normative contestation can already be seen in the degree to which illiberal states have articulated a new, selective interpretation of the principle of non-intervention in places such as Libya, Ukraine and Syria. For the United States, adapting to the new illiberal order will require abandoning its assumption of exceptional status and rethinking what it means to be the leading liberal state in a world where that position guarantees much less than it used to.

The new order

The way in which power has diffused over the last decade away from liberal states to a wider array of players has often been characterised as an unprecedented effort by the 'rest' to undermine the political order created by the West.[21] Yet this depiction is too simple. Conceptualising the world in these terms – as the West versus the rest, or as the United States versus the rising powers – oversimplifies today's geopolitical competition and underplays the complex alliance dynamics in evidence.

There are three tiers of states that could be described as challenging the US and the system it has championed. The first tier is occupied by US *rivals* Russia and China, both of which have a substantial military capacity (including nuclear weapons) and are willing to test the US and its allies with limited military provocations. While some Americans may dismiss Russia (and, to a lesser extent, China) as rising regional powers, their governments see themselves as global competitors and seek to develop an alternative institutional architecture to weaken American power.

The second tier comprises *regional* powers, including India, Brazil, Egypt, Iran, Turkey and South Africa. These states are rising in their respective regions and looking to spread their influence as powerbrokers, though they vary in the degree to which they demand a recognised, geographically distinct sphere of influence. The third tier comprises *rentier states* whose economies are driven by the export of oil, gas and some minerals, but which have managed to translate their resource wealth into some political clout. Among these states are powerful Gulf monarchies such as Saudi Arabia, Qatar and the United Arab Emirates, as well as resource-rich, weak democracies such as Nigeria.[22] These states seek regional influence or hegemony, if possible, and tend to ally with rising regional powers to achieve this if needed.

The rise of these states has taken various forms: some, such as China, have experienced historic levels of economic growth over decades, while others, including Russia and many of the rentier states, achieved rapid gains due to high-priced commodity and oil exports. Others, like Turkey, have profited from rapid urbanisation and trade, but have struggled to convert these economic advantages into political leverage. Some of the regional players, such as Brazil and Saudi Arabia, are likely to experience problems if the recent decline in oil prices does not rebound. Indeed, most of these states have serious vulnerabilities. Even China's growth has begun to cool off due to weaknesses in its banking system, the presence of toxic, off-the-books debts and a decline in manufacturing.[23] Yet all of these states have vastly increased their power and global status relative to only a decade ago. It would be a mistake to dismiss them merely because they do not measure up to the United States, or to assume that temporary or even long-lasting economic setbacks will deter them from pressing their advantages against the US and its allies.

The emerging international system is not marked by the absence of order, as some have suggested, but rather by more of it. All three tiers of states are insisting upon restoring hierarchy in their regions and projecting their influence accordingly. Only Russia and China are overtly directing their actions against the United States and engaging in activities that could reasonably be considered balancing against the superpower.[24] The regional powers and rentier states, meanwhile, are seeking the restoration of regional orders that mostly place themselves at the centre and that require weaker states to obtain their approval and accord them due levels of respect, if not deference. As Henry Kissinger has noted, this is a return to a normal pattern in history.[25] What we are seeing today is more the restoration of a long-dormant order than the creation of a new one, as governments like Russia and Turkey seek to re-establish historical patterns of hierarchy in their regions. Democratic regional leaders, such as India, Brazil and South Africa, are more ambivalent about regional hierarchy, but have nevertheless positioned themselves as the representatives of the Global South, implying a hierarchical relationship with the vastly weaker states that they claim to represent.

To achieve this restoration, all three tiers of states are eagerly seeking alliance partners and forming ad hoc coalitions. Unlike the US-led NATO alliance or the European Union, these coalitions are neither exclusive nor static, but rather exceptionally fluid and responsive to the changing interests of their members. A rising power like China, for example, might make common cause with regional players such as Brazil and India in BRICS forums, but rely on a different array of weaker sub-Saharan African states for trading and development purposes. A Middle Eastern powerbroker such as Turkey might wish to increase its own political influence in a bid to marginalise Iran, while at the same time making common cause with Saudi Arabia over plans to restore stability to the region.[26] Equally, these alliances can rapidly shift, as the falling out between Russia and Turkey over the downing of a Russian jet in November 2015 illustrated. A world of static alliances, with relatively rare defections, is giving way to one in which states have a selection of dance partners depending on the issues they face.

From an American vantage point, these developments give the appearance of disorder because they challenge the US-underwritten post-Cold War international order in two ways. Firstly, they indicate that the division of the world into 'makers' and 'takers' of the rules of international order has ended. Although rising states are not revolutionary, and do not necessarily wish to destroy the institutional pillars of liberal order, they do reject the notion that they should abide by rules set by the United States and its allies while tolerating the exceptions to those rules that the US has carved out for itself. Many other rising powers of all types have positioned themselves as defenders of the viability of international institutions against the rule-breaking arrogance of the United States. In his speech to the UN General Assembly on 28 September 2015, Putin offered a defence of the United Nations against American exceptionalism, noting that

> we all know that after the end of the Cold War, a single centre of domination emerged in the world. And then those who found themselves at the top of the pyramid were tempted to think that if they were so strong and exceptional then we know better than anyone what to do and why at all should we reckon with the UN, which instead of automatically authorizing and legitimizing the necessary decisions, often creates obstacles or, in other words, 'stands in the way'.[27]

While some of this is hypocritical bluster, Putin is not alone in his assessment. States such as India and Brazil, for example, have emphasised the need for an international order based on the UN Charter, and called for fewer exceptions to accepted rules that favour the powerful, even if doing so limits their own options. Although they have very different material interests, all three tiers of states are populated by governments that object to notions of American exceptionalism as a matter of principle.

Secondly, the United States preferred the post-Cold War system because it had lower transaction costs and required less adaptive diplomacy to manage. A world in which existing alliances are fraying while states increasingly form flexible, issue-based coalitions is not an attractive one to US policymakers, who have long sought to avoid the ordinary combinations and collisions of great-power politics by creating vast webs of stable alliances, and by building institutions which could lock in cooperation around shared practices. Today, global competition has spilled out into the open, and there is no alliance or institution that can entirely encompass or repress it. This is neither an aberration nor a descent into disorder, but rather a return to the messy power politics that had been common prior to the consolidation of alliance blocs during the Cold War. To American eyes, however, growing ambiguity in the preferences of both allies and enemies represents an unwelcome change from Cold War predictability.

As all three tiers of states assert their influence, build regional hierarchies and form ad hoc alliances to achieve their goals, the character of the international order will change. Although there are real differences between them, states belonging to all three tiers have political and economic preferences which differ from those of the liberal states that dominated the post-Cold War era. Today, many regimes are led by economic nationalists who believe that governments have an obligation to assist private and semi-private companies to compete in global markets.[28] China, for example, has spent millions on subsidising state-backed private companies to gain a foothold in developing markets, especially the resource-rich ones.[29] Other countries, such as Brazil, extend substantial subsidies to private companies as a leading element of their diplomatic strategy. Relatively few emerging states embrace the sharp public–private distinction observed in much of the Western world; rather, most of them see the acquisition of political and economic power as the joint responsibility of governments and the private sector. Their track record, as Prime Minister Orbán noted, compares favourably to the liberal democracies that have promoted private investment with limited government subsidy or control. The idea that governments and private industry should explicitly coordinate their activities to achieve national goals – sometimes called the 'Beijing Consensus' – has become an important rival to the perspectives on development offered by the United States and its allies in the developing world.[30]

Many regimes are led by economic nationalists

Similarly, some illiberal states, including authoritarian states and democracies with weak civil societies, face fewer constraints in a world of fluid alliances because they have fewer domestic interest groups with a stake in foreign policy. This allows their governments a freer hand in striking bargains and negotiating alliances compared with liberal democracies, which are partially constrained by difficult, partisan legislatures, powerful domestic lobbies and popular opinion. It is important not to overstate this point: all three tiers of states have domestic constituencies that partially shape their foreign-policy preferences and constrain their governments in some ways.[31] Not even a strong autocracy like China is able to forge a foreign policy completely free from the influence of domestic stakeholders. Equally, liberal democracies are capable of sustaining alliances with unsavoury partners over the objections of interest groups, as America's long alliance with Saudi Arabia demonstrates. Yet on balance the constraints posed by domestic constituencies are weaker and more diffuse in authoritarian and illiberal states than they are in liberal democracies, giving the former an edge in a world of rapidly evolving alliances.[32] Indeed, this may be why some scholars have noted that the rising powers seem more adept at pursuing *raison d'état* than one might expect.[33] The adaptability benefits accruing from a repressed civil society and highly empowered executive branch have been noted by Western fans of Vladimir Putin, who laud his ability to nimbly make foreign policy in a way that the United States cannot.[34] Similarly, in Turkey, Prime Minister Recep Tayyip Erdogan has called for the elimination of the separation of powers that he believes has inhibited his efforts to restore the country to the exalted status it enjoyed during the Ottoman period.[35] To that end, he has proposed a stronger presidency and revised constitution intended to strengthen his government in dealing with a turbulent Middle East.[36]

While there are divergent interests and policies among all three tiers, what unites them is their rejection of the quintessential Western idea that a government's behaviour towards its own citizens can (or should) influence the rights that it enjoys within the international system. All three tiers include governments that are very strongly neo-Westphalian in character, emphasising government prerogatives and the right of non-interference by other states, in contrast to the pooled sovereignty and emphasis on transnational human rights seen in Europe and elsewhere. Most are jealous of their sovereignty and defensive about efforts to weaken their sovereign rights in any way. For some states, like Russia and China, this instinct derives from their fear of secession; for others, like India, Nigeria and South Africa, the experience of colonisation has made them suspicious of outside interference and anxious about relinquishing any of the sovereign prerogatives that they fought to achieve.

With some partial exceptions, the preferences of all three tiers of rising states stand in contrast to the modern Western state model in a number of ways. The traditional Western ideal – of an accountable, democratic government with an independent private sector and a commitment to human rights – differs markedly from the highly concentrated executive powers, low involvement of interest groups or civil society in foreign policy, and greater emphasis on economic nationalism seen in many neo-Westphalian states. Moreover, many of these states – authoritarian states, illiberal democracies and those in between – reject the idea of a social contract as the foundation of domestic political order. While most of them pay lip service to human rights, almost all explicitly reject the idea that their abuse can be used as justification for a humanitarian intervention in the absence of a UN Security Council mandate. Most are at least nominally committed to the reassertion of the principle of non-intervention and a defence of sovereign prerogatives under international law. These illiberal states may be located in a liberal institutional order created by the United States and supported by its allies, but they have different preferences and perspectives on the purposes of that order. The question is, whose preferences will prevail?

Why illiberal states will prevail

Given the vast power of the US and the widespread acceptance of the institutions of the existing liberal order, one might expect this order to remain liberal, or at least to favour the preferences of liberal democracies over those of rising powers. Indeed, there is some evidence that the institutional advantages enjoyed by the US and its European allies in constructing this order will endure even after any substantial shift in global power.[37] As many have pointed out, the key institutions of this order – such as the UN, IMF and World Bank – are largely accepted even by those states, such as Russia and China, that are most strident in their criticisms of it.[38] The fact that these institutions are capable of accommodating new claimants to power suggests that rising powers would have more to gain by joining them than by remaining outside. Moreover, these institutions exhibit a modest socialising effect and may induce restraint on all three classes of states, thus moderating the effect of their rise on the existing international order.[39]

Yet recent evidence suggests the future lies somewhere between the fear that Russia, China and other rising states will overturn the liberal order altogether and the hope that things will remain just as they are. Inertia, vested interests and the promise of economic advantages are likely to keep the institutional architecture of the liberal order largely intact, although there may eventually be changes to procedures for voting (affecting, for example, vetoes in the UN Security Council). Two processes will combine to produce a discernible tilt in the character of the order towards the illiberal states in the coming decades: institutional adaptation and normative contestation.

Firstly, many rising powers have made widely accepted arguments that the existing institutions of the liberal order need to adapt to accommodate their new power position. Among the clearest examples of this are the growing calls for more permanent, veto-wielding seats on the UN Security Council. At this point, most of the existing permanent members of the UN Security Council support the inclusion of new permanent members, although they disagree on which candidates should be added. In the meantime, some rising powers have sought to increase their influence within the UN in other ways. For example, China has offered to establish a $1 billion 'peace and development' fund for the United Nations and to field a permanent peacekeeping and police force of 8,000 troops.[40] Other institutions are being adapted in more subtle ways. The recent decision to 'rebalance' the IMF through quota reform has given rising states such as Brazil, Russia and India a larger share of votes, with China now possessing the second-largest share.[41] The World Trade Organisation is also facing increasing pressure to reform its lending practices to reflect greater sensitivity to the needs of rising powers.

Aside from pressing for reforms of existing institutions, rising states have also created alternative, or parallel, international institutions which will allow them to exercise leverage, and to win votes, in a variety of multilateral forums. These institutions are explicitly designed to break the hold that the US has over many global institutions. Examples include the BRICS-led New Development Bank (NDB) and the China-led Asian Infrastructure Investment Bank (AIIB). The Fortaleza Declaration, which produced the NDB in July 2014, stated explicitly that 'international governance structures designed within a different power configuration show increasingly evident signs of losing legitimacy and effectiveness, as transitional and ad hoc arrangements become increasingly prevalent, often at the expense of multilateralism'.[42] The bank will facilitate development projects with fewer legal and human-rights restrictions than traditional funders would impose, and will undercut the pressure that the US and Europe can bring to bear on authoritarian or illiberal states in the developing world. According to Vladimir Putin, this means that the NDB will allow for development without the 'harassment' involved in dealing with US-dominated institutions.[43]

While these new development institutions remain under-capitalised – the NDB began with $100bn in contingency funds and $50bn for development projects,[44] while the AIIB is expected to have an initial capitalisation of $100bn[45] – and suffer from political divisions, they have succeeded in winning support from the developing world, and even some long-standing US allies.[46] The decisions by the United Kingdom, France, Germany and Australia to join the AIIB exemplify how these parallel institutions will begin to undermine the liberal consensus which provides the foundation for much of the global order. These institutions will never replace the World Bank or the IMF, but they will stand alongside them as both peers and competitors. Their existence alone poses the risk that global economic governance will become fragmented and less effective.[47] The result may be higher transaction costs and more politicised development than occurred under Washington's preferred arrangement.

Economic governance may become fragmented

In addition to weakening the stranglehold that the US has had on global finance and development and diminishing its geopolitical influence, these institutions will also provide the BRICS governments with political leverage in the developing world, and will allow states such as China, Russia and others to engage in log-rolling to win votes in the UN and elsewhere. The potential for this can already be seen in the way that China has used trade and development incentives to deny political recognition to Taiwan in much of the developing world, thus reversing the gains that Taiwan made towards statehood during the Cold War. Similarly, China has used the votes it has won among African states to block a number of anti-China UN votes over the last decade.[48] These parallel institutions also provide a generous financial alternative and diplomatic fallback option for any government that runs afoul of Washington in traditional multilateral forums.[49]

The rising powers have also successfully offered a reinterpretation of some key political concepts that currently underlie the liberal order, such as human rights, self-determination, self-defence and, more recently, the responsibility to protect, while simultaneously offering an alternative framework that is much more sympathetic to the preferences of authoritarian and other illiberal states in the developing world. For example, China has offered a narrower interpretation of human rights – one which limits political freedoms, privileges economic development and does not circumscribe government power – which has proven attractive to dictators in the Middle East and sub-Saharan Africa.[50] Even ASEAN has adopted a version of this interpretation, noting that the exercise of human rights may be limited 'for the purpose of securing due recognition for the human rights and fundamental freedoms of others, and to meet the just requirements of national security, public order, public health, public safety, public morality, as well as the general welfare of the peoples in a democratic society'.[51] Similarly, Russia has offered an interpretation of national self-determination which grants itself the right to protect co-ethnics in other states, even at the expense of their self-interest. As William Burke-White has argued in *Survival*, this strategy allowed Putin to invoke a valid right under international law – self-determination – while redefining it in a way that enabled his invasion of Ukraine.[52]

Through this process of normative contestation, illiberal states have challenged the dominant American and European interpretations of key concepts, providing them leverage with governments in the developing world that are better served by these alternative interpretations. Whether these interpretations are more plausible or widely accepted than the dominant Western ones is irrelevant; they need only to be offered as a response to the US and European ones to produce a rhetorical stalemate which effectively blocks many US or European initiatives, or at least to undercut their leverage in the UN and elsewhere.

Ironically, one reason why these alternative conceptions are successful is that some are actually closer to the classical foundation of international law than the permissive interpretations championed by the US throughout the post-Cold War period. This foundation is fundamentally conservative: it bans aggression, protects the territorial integrity of states and upholds a sovereign right of non-interference. During the post-Cold War period, the US and some of its European allies began to carve out a series of exceptions to these principles under the banner of protecting human rights. Although it never explicitly renounced Article 2(4) of the UN Charter, which calls on UN member states to refrain from the threat or use of force against other states, all three presidential administrations since the end of the Cold War have articulated exceptions for the US. The debate over the responsibility to protect was an attempt to codify these exceptions, and has been met with considerable resistance by China, India and others. While the US has championed some aspects of international law, it has claimed a series of reservations for itself – such as refusing to accept the jurisdiction of the International Criminal Court (ICC) and other treaties – while asserting a relatively broad right for itself to use force in the territory of other states. The Obama administration's drone programme is a case in point: the US has accorded itself the right to use drone strikes against its enemies around the world while denying this option to most other states.

By contrast, all three tiers of new players behave like classical Westphalian states in rejecting these exceptions and demanding respect for the principle of non-interference in the affairs of other states. In other words, rising states have the law on their side; the basic outline of international law is more broadly consistent with their preferences than with the exception-riddled interpretations offered by the Bush or Obama administrations. This fact provides them with a powerful argument with which to stymie American or European calls for international action outside the UN – such as no-fly zones or humanitarian interventions – that are, strictly speaking, in contravention of international law.

Despite this commitment, some rising states have succumbed to hypocrisy and articulated their own selective interpretation of the right to non-interference. A clear example of this can be seen in the rationales offered by Putin for Russia's interventions in Ukraine and Syria. In the case of Ukraine, he has argued that the supposed defence of co-nationals against a predatory government in surrounding territories justifies the seizure of Crimea and the destabilisation of Ukraine. In the case of Syria, he has portrayed his military intervention as a defence of Bashar al-Assad's legitimate government against the chaos produced by dangerous Islamic militants and their Western enablers. Neither argument is particularly persuasive, but both appear sufficiently plausible to many neo-Westphalian states to effectively block the US from isolating or punishing Russia. In a way, Putin's arguments have skilfully inverted the rationale behind the responsibility to protect, effectively arguing that vast human-rights abuses are a reason to intervene to rescue a government rather than a people.

These factors – the reform of existing institutions, the creation of a parallel set of institutions and a reinterpretation of key concepts of the liberal order – have combined to give all three tiers of states greater leverage in the new global order. Together, these factors will offset some of the power advantages held by the United States and its allies and increase the level of consideration given to the preferences of illiberal states. These governments will pursue their interests inside the open, adaptive institutions of the liberal order, but they will not be constrained, or tamed, by their presence within them. The drift towards an illiberal order will be halting and incomplete, but the overall trend – towards a reassertion of geopolitical competition, inside and outside the still-standing institutions of the liberal order – has already become unmistakable.

Old rules and new constraints

The decay in the liberal order and the assertion of the prerogatives of illiberal states within that order can be seen in three successive crises faced by the Obama administration: the overthrow of the Gadhafi regime in Libya (2011), the Syrian civil war (2011–) and the dismemberment of eastern Ukraine (2014–). In each case, the US initially experienced institutional paralysis, which it was able to overcome at great cost in one case (Libya), but which produced stalemate in the others (Ukraine, Syria). In the first case, a number of illiberal states challenged the terms under which the US proposed to intervene; in the latter two cases, many of them backed Russia's selective reinterpretation of the doctrine of non-interference and supported or tolerated its military intervention over US protests. In the latter two cases, the US was frustrated by the degree to which it was asked to obey the rules of the international order even while Russia gleefully violated them. In all three cases, the degree to which rising states have drifted away from two key liberal principles – that the social contract between ruler and ruled is dispositive for the privileges that governments enjoy, and that the systematic abuse of a population by a government can be a reason to intervene – is evident.

The intervention in Libya may ultimately be seen as the last gasp of the liberal order. The events of the Arab Spring dragged Libya into a civil war in part due to Muammar Gadhafi's unwillingness to concede in the face of growing protests. As evidence of a humanitarian crisis and Gadhafi's plans to attack Benghazi mounted, the leading powers of the post-Cold War liberal concert – the United States, the United Kingdom and France – tabled and passed two UN Security Council resolutions against the Libyan government. The first, Resolution 1970, was passed with unanimous support. It not only referred Libya to the International Criminal Court, but also imposed an arms embargo and travel ban. The second resolution, Resolution 1973, authorised a no-fly zone and 'all necessary measures' to support it. It was passed with some key abstentions by rising powers, notably Brazil, China, Russia and India. With the US, the UK and France in the lead, NATO enforced Resolution 1973 by conducting thousands of airstrikes on Gadhafi's forces, which carried on until his overthrow and death in October 2011. The operation was hailed as a 'model intervention' by White House officials.[53]

After the Libya operation ended, Russia, China and a number of other states criticised NATO for going beyond the limits of its mandate to enforce a no-fly zone and for engaging in unauthorised regime change. Putin called Resolution 1973 'defective and flawed' because it 'allows everything. It resembles mediaeval calls for crusades.'[54] Similarly, India's then-prime minister Manmohan Singh attacked the West in a speech at the United Nations General Assembly for undertaking regime change in Libya, warning that the absence of democracy or the rule of law cannot be a pretext for an intervention.[55] India's permanent representative to the UN, Hardeep Singh Puri, sharply noted that the responsibility to protect 'cannot turn out to be a tool legitimizing big power intervention on the pretext of protecting populations from the violations of human rights and humanitarian law'.[56] Throughout much of the crisis, China hemmed close to its traditional approach, calling for a peaceful resolution of the conflict through dialogue, and eschewing military intervention. While Beijing did acquiesce to Resolution 1973 through its abstention, it later criticised NATO's decision to target Gadhafi's forces and provide arms to the rebels. In a subsequent discussion on protecting civilians in armed conflict, China warned that 'there must be no attempt at regime change … under the guise of protecting civilians', and insisted that the responsibility to protect lies with governments, rather than outside powers.[57] Following the Libya intervention, Brazil also voiced concerns that humanitarian interventions would be used by the powerful for regime change, offering its own reinterpretation of the responsibility to protect as a way of reducing the freedom of action enjoyed by the US and its allies.[58]

The US paid the price for its words

The US reacted angrily to these rebukes, and remarked that the behaviour of countries like India and Brazil during the Libya crisis was 'not encouraging', and was unexpected given their 'strong and proud democratic traditions'.[59] It paid the price for these words when the Syrian civil war began to have wider regional consequences. As the Assad government ramped up its attacks against civilians, the United Nations Security Council found itself deadlocked. Despite strong advocacy by the United States, Russia and China vetoed a UN resolution that was intended to put pressure on the Assad government.[60] They were not alone in their opposition: Brazil, India, Lebanon and South Africa abstained from the vote, while a second veto in July 2012 on a draft threatening sanctions against Assad received abstentions from South Africa and Pakistan.[61] Frustrated by the deadlock and enraged by a chemical-weapons attack in the Ghouta suburb of Damascus in August 2013, Obama initially threatened unilateral airstrikes against the Assad regime, but subsequently backed off, referring the matter to Congress. This earned him widespread criticism for policy incoherence and for abandoning the Syrian people.

The Syrian reversal damaged American credibility, but it also signalled a wider change in the way that the rest of the world reacts to American initiatives. After Russia negotiated a deal for the destruction of Syria's chemical weapons, Putin took to the pages of the *New York Times* to chastise the United States for making armed interventions commonplace, and to call on the Obama administration to renounce 'the language of force and return to the path of civilized diplomatic and political settlement'.[62] Putin framed his attack in terms of respect for a classical approach to international law, and positioned Russia and its allies as defenders of that system against the aggression of the powerful. For its part, China publicly defended its vetoes by offering a narrower interpretation of the responsibility to protect, effectively saying that this responsibility exists only when the government has ceased to exist. Along these lines, China insisted that no sanctions or intervention in Syria would be permissible while the Assad government remained nominally in place.[63] While many of the regional powers and rentier states called for a diplomatic solution to the conflict, none were willing to openly condemn Russia or China for their vetoes or propose any alternative to inaction.

Russia and China shielded Assad

One result of this stalemate has been a growing humanitarian crisis that has resulted in the deaths of 200,000 Syrians and caused millions more to become refugees. At each step, the United States has been thwarted by opposition from an array of illiberal states and non-interventionist democracies around the world. A non-binding UN General Assembly resolution in May 2013 condemning Assad and calling for a 'political transition' was rejected by Russia, China, Iran, Venezuela, Nicaragua and several others, while 59 states abstained, including Brazil, India and much of sub-Saharan Africa.[64] In contrast to the unanimous UN Security Council vote referring Libya to the ICC, both Russia and China again used their vetoes to shield Assad in May 2014.[65] Russia dabbled in conspiracy theories by asking whether an ICC referral was possibly a 'way to provoke an armed intervention', while China defended its veto on the grounds that ICC referrals should be 'based on the premise of respect for the judicial sovereignty of States and the principle of complementarity'.[66] Although Russia and China were willing to support UN resolutions calling for humanitarian relief or support of the Geneva process, neither was willing to step aside or tolerate any US-backed resolution with teeth for fear that it would legitimise a possible overthrow of the Assad regime.

The degree of selectivity embedded in these states' interpretations of the right to non-interference was illustrated by Russia's decision in September 2015 to send military support to the Assad regime. In a speech to the UN General Assembly, Putin blamed the chaos in Syria on US and European efforts to arm Syrian rebels, and framed the intervention as regrettable but necessary to stop the rise of ISIS. In keeping with his neo-Westphalian commitment to upholding national sovereignty, Putin later argued that Russia's goal was to stabilise 'the legitimate government and to create conditions for a political compromise'.[67] While opposing aggressive UN resolutions and US airstrikes in Syria, China supported Russia's intervention, noting that it was well within international law because it came at the request of a legitimate government.[68] Unsurprisingly, the Russian intervention also received vocal support from Iran, a long-time backer of Assad, as well as criticism from Assad's regional enemies, such as Saudi Arabia and Turkey. What is more striking was the quiet support extended to Russia and the Assad regime by other regional powers. For example, India's president publicly accepted Russia's argument that military intervention was needed to stop the rise of ISIS.[69] South Africa's government noted the similarities between its own counter-terrorism approach and Russia's, while Egypt offered its unwavering support for Russia's intervention.[70]

Similarly, the Ukraine crisis – and the ensuing inaction by the United States and others – shows how much the world has changed since the heyday of international intervention in the late 1990s. After domestic protests forced Ukrainian president Victor Yanukovich to flee Kiev in February 2014, Russia took a series of emergency steps to ensure that Ukraine remained in its geopolitical orbit. Under Putin's direct orders, Russian military forces seized Crimea in March 2014, officially annexing the territory. Over the next year, more Russian forces were deployed into eastern Ukraine to ensure that the country's Russian-speaking regions remained under Moscow's influence. Russia also delivered arms to separatist rebels and organised a sham referendum to provide cover for its annexation of Crimea. The United States and European Union imposed a series of sanctions on Russia for violating

Ukraine's territorial integrity, but these had less than full effect because so many countries refused to participate. Meanwhile, the US–EU sanctions may have had the perverse effect of pushing Russia closer to Beijing, producing a 'soft alliance' between the two powers supported by a $400bn gas deal.[71]

Russia sought to defend its actions by offering a reinterpretation of the doctrine of self-determination that echoed past claims by European governments to a right to defend co-nationals located in another territory. Seeking to exploit the tensions between national self-determination and territorial integrity, and to cover 'Russia's actions with the mantle of international law' (as William Burke-White put it[72]), Putin asserted a broad right to defend Russians in the country's 'near abroad' and adopted a loose definition of what might be considered a threat to their well-being. He also exploited the Kosovo precedent to justify his decision to send forces into Crimea, pointing out that it was a 'precedent our western colleagues created with their own hands in a very similar situation, when they agreed that the unilateral separation of Kosovo from Serbia, exactly what Crimea is doing now, was legitimate and did not require any permission from the country's central authorities'.[73] This position was hypocritical, given that Russia cited the need for governmental consent from Assad for intervention in Syria but saw no similar need in Ukraine.

What is most striking about the Ukraine crisis is that Russia's clear-cut seizure of territory – an instance of modern-day imperialism that should have triggered alarm among neo-Westphalian states everywhere as an obvious violation of a country's sovereignty – did not shift the balance of global opinion towards the United States. At the UN, the Obama administration has been unable to win the cooperation of many rising and regional powers that have trading relationships with Russia. India, for example, pointedly refused to accept sanctions or any 'unilateral measures' against Russia in response to the invasion.[74] Brazil also refused to criticise Russia for the seizure of Crimea or to join sanctions attempts.[75] The BRICS powers issued a veiled attack on the US by declaring that 'the custodianship of the G-20 belongs to all member-states equally and no one member-state can unilaterally determine its nature and character'.[76] Several regional powers, such as Iran, have also refused to criticise Russia, while Turkey initially pressed ahead with energy deals despite token objections to Russian policy in Ukraine.[77] Notably, very few South American, African or Middle Eastern governments backed sanctions against Russia. Although the Minsk agreements have produced a tense ceasefire, Ukraine remains destabilised. Meanwhile, Russia has faced no meaningful consequence for dismembering the country.

* * *

The emergence of an illiberal order is not a development to which the United States can respond with a business-as-usual approach. For the last two decades, the preponderance of power held by the United States has allowed it to construct and exploit a liberal order which has operated largely according to its interests. The gradual diffusion of power to other states means that they are increasingly able to join forces on a case-by-case basis to pursue their own interests and, if necessary, thwart the United States. This is less balancing, in its classical nineteenth-century form, than ruthless politico-economic opportunism. While the US retains many formal alliance relationships, many allied states are less beholden to the US than they once were, and are increasingly willing to join anti-US coalitions if necessary. The creation of new development institutions to stand alongside the traditional pillars of the liberal order have helped to ensure that no state can be isolated or punished by American fiat. Traditional institutions are still seen as legitimate, but are being subtly changed by illiberal states in ways that diminish American influence.

Given these trends, the United States needs to rethink its approach to preserving its power and influence. In the first instance, it needs to disabuse itself of the lazy platitudes about 'leadership' or the 'next American century' that often dominate Washington's thinking about foreign policy. For the foreseeable future, the United States will be locked in an intense geopolitical competition with China and Russia. The military component of this competition may be limited, but the other elements of power – political, economic and diplomatic – are certainly in play. Rather than assuming that US rivals will collapse due to economic weakness (Russia) or be tamed by the liberal order (China), Washington is better off preparing for a long-term economic and political knife fight with these states. To compete, Washington will have to become more agile in its diplomacy and stop assuming that the preferences of other democracies will naturally align with those of the United States. It will have to live with ambiguity. Washington should attempt to thwart the ambitions of its global rivals by making common cause with rising regional powers and rentier states. To do this, it should consider embracing new institutions such as the AIIB by encouraging its allies to sign up and by working with them to improve Washington's influence. The US may also need to offer more government-directed forms of economic investment to allow it to compete more effectively with the state-directed capitalism of its rivals.

A rethink of the US approach to humanitarian crises is also called for in light of the paralysis within the UN Security Council and the prohibitive costs of unilateral action. A world featuring paralysis in key international institutions and intense debates over the underlying concepts of global order may be a violent one. The crises today in Syria, Ukraine, Iraq and Yemen are producing suffering on a scale that exceeds what was once seen in Bosnia, Kosovo and East Timor, yet there seems to be little prospect of UN-backed intervention on the horizon. To avoid the risks of poorly conceived and internationally unpopular interventions, the United States should improve its capacity for preventive diplomacy, rapid mechanisms for humanitarian relief, and regional partnerships for peacekeeping and other forms of conflict resolution as interim measures. Such an approach may offer no easy solution to humanitarian crises, and may be ineffective in some cases, but it is likely to command more support among the rising powers in the developing world than one in which the United States acts forcefully but in violation of international law. Additionally, the US should try to capitalise on the disgust which Russian and Chinese vetoes over Syria have generated. At the September 2013 UN General Assembly meeting, 63 states called for reform of the Security Council, with many citing the over-use of vetoes on Syria as a reason for reform.[78] To increase the pressure on Russia and China, the US could back the call by outgoing French foreign minister Laurent Fabius to effectively suspend UN Security Council veto rights in cases of mass atrocities.[79] Doing so would force Russia and China to justify and win votes for their selective and often hypocritical interpretations of non-interference, which in turn might weaken their bargaining position against the US and other rising states in the system.

Finally, the United States needs to reconsider what it means to be the world's leading liberal state at a time when this matters less than it used to. At a minimum, this will entail some changes at home. The last two decades have seen the disfigurement of America's own liberal character through policies such as torture, extraordinary rendition, expanded government surveillance and drone strikes outside war zones. This has made it more difficult to convince even long-term allies, let alone rising and rentier states, to join with the United States in thwarting the ambitions of Russia and China. As its relative power wanes, Washington should eliminate those policies that make it hard for governments to say 'yes' to America. The US cannot continue to assume that it will always be the 'leader of the free world', as some might have hoped, but it may be able to position itself as the most powerful representative of the growing number of states unnerved by the hypocrisy or ruthlessness of some of the rising powers. By reclaiming its position as a defender of both a rules-based order and human rights, the US could not only consolidate the accomplishments of the liberal order, but also become a more effective geopolitical competitor in the less hospitable, more violent world to come.

Notes

1 Csaba Toth, 'Full Text of Viktor Orban's Speech at Baile Tusnad of 26 July 2014', *Budapest Beacon*, 29 July 2014, http://budapestbeacon.com/public-policy/full-text-of-viktor-orbans-speech-at-baile-tusnad-tusnad-furdo-of-26-july-2014/10592.

2 Zoltan Simon, 'Orban Says He Seeks to End Liberal Democracy in Hungary', Bloomberg, 28 July 2014, http://www.bloomberg.com/news/2014-07-28/orban-says-he-seeks-to-end-liberal-democracy-in-hungary.html.

3 Kester Eddy, 'EU Urged to Monitor Hungary as Orban Hits at Liberal Democracy', *Financial Times*, 30 July 2014, http://www.ft.com/cms/s/0/0574f7f2-17f3-11e4-b842-00144feabdc0.html#axzz40tuZhy3e.

4 David D. Kirkpatrick, 'Voter Insecurities Feed the Rise of Right-Leaning Populist Politicians', *New York Times*, 10 December 2015, http://www.nytimes.com/2015/12/11/world/europe/voter-insecurities-feed-rise-of-right-leaning-populist-politicians.html?_r=0.

5 Tony Barber, 'An Illiberal Streak Spreads Further Across Central Europe', *Financial Times*, 8 December 2015, http://www.ft.com/cms/s/0/e5f73e48-9cf4-11e5-b45d-4812f209f861.html#axzz3yHUaZBk9; 'Is Poland a Failing Democracy?', *Politico*, 13 January 2016, http://www.politico.eu/article/poland-democracy-failing-pis-law-and-justice-media-rule-of-law/.

6 See particularly the essays on Russia, Venezuela, Iran and Saudi Arabia in the *Journal of Democracy*'s special edition on the authoritarian resurgence, vol. 26, no. 2, April 2015.

7 Freedom House, 'Freedom in the World 2016', https://freedomhouse.org/report/freedom-world/freedom-world-2016.

8 Christian Caryl, 'The Age of Disillusionment', *Foreign Policy*, 11 January 2016, http://foreignpolicy.com/2016/01/11/the-age-of-disillusionment/.

9 Stanley Hoffmann, 'The Crisis of Liberal Internationalism', *Foreign Policy*, no. 98, Spring 1995, p. 160. See also G. John Ikenberry, *After Victory: Institutions, Strategic Restraint, and the Rebuilding of Order after Major Wars* (Princeton, NJ: Princeton University Press, 2001); and G. John Ikenberry, *Liberal Leviathan: The Origins, Crisis and Transformation of the American World Order* (Princeton, NJ: Princeton University Press, 2012).

10 R.H.S. Crossman, quoted in E.H. Carr, *The Twenty Years' Crisis* (London: Palgrave, 2001), p. 29.

11 See, for example, John Gerald Ruggie, 'International Regimes, Transactions and Change: Embedded Liberalism in the Postwar Economic System', *International Organization*, vol. 36, no. 2, Spring 1992, pp. 379–415.

12 Vladimir Putin, 'Speech and Following Discussion at the Munich Security Conference', Munich, 10 February 2007, http://archive.kremlin.ru/eng/speeches/2007/02/10/0138_type82912type82914type82917type84779_118123.

13 'Russia Will Not Yield to Western Pressure: FM', Xinhua, 26 January 2016, http://news.xinhuanet.com/english/2016-01/26/c_135047851.htm.

14 Susan Turner, 'Russia, China and a Multipolar World Order: The Danger of the Undefined', *Asian Perspective*, vol. 33, no. 1, 2009, pp. 159–94.

15 Fu Ying, 'The US World Order is a Suit That No Longer Fits', *Financial Times*, 6 January 2016, http://www.ft.com/cms/s/0/c09cbcb6-b3cb-11e5-b147-e5e5bba42e51.html#ixzz40QL4LOSr.

16 German Marshall Fund of the United States, 'Liberal Order in a Post-Western World', 5 May 2014, p. 7, http://www.gmfus.org/publications/liberal-order-post-western-world.

17 Barack Obama, 'Remarks by the President to the Parliament in London, United Kingdom', 25 May 2011, http://www.whitehouse.gov/the-press-office/2011/05/25/remarks-president-parliament-london-united-kingdom.

18 Will Dunham, 'Kerry Condemns Russia's "Incredible Act of Aggression" in Ukraine', Reuters, 2 May 2014, http://www.reuters.com/article/us-ukraine-crisis-usa-kerry-idUSBREA210DG20140302.

19 See 'The BRIC Economies: Is the Fastest Period of Emerging Market Growth Behind Us?', *The Economist*, 14 December 2014. See also Astrid Pange, 'BRICS Launch New Bank and Development Fund', Deutsche Welle, 16 July 2014.

20 The literature on the possible future of the international system is vast. For discussion of a unipolar future, see William Wohlforth, 'The Stability of a Unipolar World', *International Security*, vol. 24, no. 1, 1999, pp. 5–41; and Charles Krauthammer, 'The Unipolar Moment Revisited', *National Interest*, vol. 70, Winter 2002–03, pp. 5–18. For predictions of a China-dominated order, see Martin Jacques, *When China Rules the World* (New York: Penguin, 2012). For predictions of bipolarity and war, see John J. Mearsheimer, *The Tragedy of Great Power Politics* (New York: W.W. Norton, 2014). Multipolarity is discussed in Christopher Layne, 'The Unipolar Illusion: Why New Great Powers Will Rise', *International Security*, vol. 17, no. 4, Spring 1993, pp. 5–51; and Christopher Layne, 'The Unipolar Illusion Revisited: The Coming End of the United States Unipolar Moment', *International Security*, vol. 31, no. 2, 2006, pp. 7–41. For discussion of a post-American world, see Fareed Zakaria, *The Post-American World* (New York: W.W. Norton, 2011); and Joseph Nye, *The Future of Power* (New York: Public Affairs, 2011). A disordered world features in Charles Kupchan, *No One's World: The West, the Rising Rest and the Coming Global Turn* (Oxford: Oxford University Press, 2013).

21 See Zakaria, *The Post-American World*; and Niall Fergusson, *Civilization: The West and the Rest* (New York: Penguin, 2012).

22 Russia is an unusual state in this schema, as it could be seen as an example of both a BRICS member and a rentier state due to its dependence on oil and gas exports.

23 Peter Eavis, 'Toxic Loans Around the World Weigh on Global Growth', *New York Times*, 3 February 2016, http://www.nytimes.com/2016/02/04/business/dealbook/toxic-loans-in-china-weigh-on-global-growth.html.

24 On the debate over balancing, see Robert Pape, 'Soft Balancing Against the US', *International Security*, vol. 30, no. 1, Summer 2005, pp. 7–45; Keir Lieber and Gerald Alexander, 'Waiting for Balancing: Why The World Is Not Pushing Back', *International Security*, vol. 30, no. 1, Summer 2005, pp. 109–39; Stephen G. Brooks and William Wohlforth, 'Hard Times for Soft Balancing', *International Security*, Summer 2005, pp. 72–108; and T.V. Paul, 'Soft Balancing in An Age of Primacy', *International Security*, vol. 30, no. 1, Summer 2005, pp. 46–71.

25 See Henry Kissinger, *World Order* (New York: Penguin, 2014).

26 The Center for Strategic and International Studies, 'The Turkey, Russia, Iran Nexus', March 2013, http://csis.org/files/publication/130318_Flanagan_TurkeyRussiaIran_web.pdf.

27 'Statement by H.E. Mr. Vladimir Putin, President of the Russian Federation, at the 70th Session of the UN General Assembly', 28 September 2015, p. 3, http://gadebate.un.org/sites/default/files/gastatements/70/70_RU_EN.pdf.

28 Azar Gat, 'The Return of Authoritarian Great Powers', *Foreign Affairs*, vol. 86, no. 4, July–August 2007, pp. 59–69.

29 Michael T. Klare, *The Race for What's Left: The Global Scramble for the World's Last Resources* (New York: Picador, 2012).

30 See Stefan Halper, *The Beijing Consensus: Legitimizing Authoritarianism in Our Time* (New York: Basic Books, 2010).

31 On domestic constituencies in autocracies, see Jessica L. Weeks, 'Autocratic Audience Costs: Regime Type and Signaling Resolve', *International Organization*, vol. 62, Winter 2008, pp. 35–64.

32 Some believe that the absence of domestic constituencies in authoritarian states undermines their credibility in negotiations with other states. This may be the case, but it also may be less important in a world of increasingly fluid alliances, in which lasting agreements and partnerships are less valuable than swiftly struck but immediately advantageous ones. See Weeks, 'Autocratic Audience Costs'; and Jessica Chen Weiss, 'Authoritarian Signaling, Mass Audiences and Nationalist Protest in China', *International Organization*, vol. 67, no. 1, January 2013, pp. 1–35.

33 Chester Crocker, 'The Strategic Dilemma of a World Adrift', *Survival*, vol. 57, no. 1, February–March 2015, p. 11.

34 Ishaan Tharoor, 'Why U.S. Conservatives Love Russia's Vladimir Putin', *Washington Post*, 25 August 2014, https://www.washingtonpost.com/news/worldviews/wp/2014/08/25/why-u-s-conservatives-love-russias-vladimir-putin/.

35 Hillel Fradkin and Lewis Libby, 'Erdogan's Grand Vision: Rise and Decline', *World Affairs*, March–April 2013, http://www.worldaffairsjournal.org/article/erdogan%E2%80%99s-grand-vision-rise-and-decline.

36 Orhan Coksun and Ece Toksabay, 'Making Case For Stronger Presidency, Turkey's Erdogan Denies Personal Agenda', Reuters, 28 January 2016, http://www.reuters.com/article/us-turkey-politics-erdogan-idUSKCN0V613V.

37 Robert Keohane, *After Hegemony: Cooperation and Discord in the World* (Princeton, NJ: Princeton University Press, 1984).

38 G. John Ikenberry, 'The Illusion of Geopolitics: The Enduring Power of the Liberal Order', *Foreign Affairs*, May–June 2014, https://www.foreignaffairs.com/articles/china/2014-04-17/illusion-geopolitics.

39 On the mechanisms of socialisation, see Maximilian Terhalle, 'Reciprocal Socialization: Rising Powers and the West', *International Studies Perspective*, vol. 12, no. 4, 2011, pp. 341–61.

40 Jeremy Page, 'China to Create $1 Billion Fund to Support UN', *Wall Street Journal*, 28 September 2015, http://www.wsj.com/articles/china-to-create-1-billion-fund-to-support-u-n-1443463394.

41 Paola Subacchi, 'It's the End of the World as We Know It, and the

IMF Feels Fine', *Foreign Policy*, 9 October 2015, http://foreignpolicy.com/2015/10/09/end-of-the-world-as-we-know-it-imf-feels-fine-reform-developing-nations-brics-lagarde/.

42 'Sixth BRICS Summit – Fortaleza Declaration', 16 July 2014, available at http://pib.nic.in/newsite/PrintRelease.aspx?relid=106712.

43 Quoted in 'The BRICS Bank: An Acronym with Capital', *The Economist*, 19 July 2014, http://www.economist.com/news/finance-and-economics/21607851-setting-up-rivals-imf-and-world-bank-easier-running-them-acronym.

44 'BRICS Nations To Create $100bn Development Bank', BBC News, 15 July 2014, http://www.bbc.com/news/business-28317555.

45 Ben Otto, 'China-Led Bank To Focus on Big Ticket Projects, Indonesia Says', *Wall Street Journal*, 10 April 2015, http://www.wsj.com/articles/china-led-aiib-to-focus-on-big-ticket-projects-indonesia-says-1428647276; 'China: 57 Countries to Be Founding Members of AIIB', Reuters, 15 April 2015.

46 'The BRICS Bank: An Acronym with Capital'.

47 Paola Subbachi, 'The AIIB is a Threat to Global Economic Governance', *Foreign Policy*, 31 March 2015, http://foreignpolicy.com/2015/03/31/the-aiib-is-a-threat-to-global-economic-governance-china/.

48 Halper, *The Beijing Consensus*, pp. 113–15.

49 Bruce Jones and Thomas Wright, 'The BRICs Safety Net', Brookings Institution, 17 July 2014, http://www.brookings.edu/blogs/up-front/posts/2014/07/17-brics-safety-net-jones-wright.

50 See, in particular, Halper, *The Beijing Consensus*.

51 'ASEAN Human Rights Declaration', 19 November 2012, available at http://www.iglhrc.org/sites/default/files/629-1.pdf.

52 William W. Burke-White, 'Crimea and the International Legal Order', *Survival*, vol. 56, no. 4, August–September 2014, pp. 65–80.

53 For a critical account of this claim, see Alan Kuperman, 'Obama's Libya Debacle: How a Well-Meaning Intervention Ended in Failure', *Foreign Affairs*, March–April 2015, https://www.foreignaffairs.com/articles/libya/obamas-libya-debacle.

54 'Putin: West in "Medieval Crusade" Against Qaddafi', Reuters, 25 March 2011.

55 Diwakar, 'Manmohan Slams West for Using Force to Change Regimes', *Times of India*, 25 September 2011, http://timesofindia.indiatimes.com/india/Manmohan-slams-West-for-using-force-to-change-regimes/articleshow/10108923.cms?referral=PM.

56 Quoted in Herbert Wulf, 'BRICS: Realistic Alternative with a Stuttering Motor', SIPRI EPS Blog, 11 June 2015, http://www.sipri.org/media/blogs/eps-blog/brics-realistic-alternative-with-a-stuttering-motor.

57 Andrew Garwood-Gowers, 'China and the "Responsibility to Protect": The Implications of the Libyan Intervention', *Asian Journal of International Law*, vol. 2, no. 2, 2012, pp. 375–93.

58 Matias Spektor, 'The Arab Spring, Seen from Brazil', *New York Times*,

23 December 2011, http://latitude.blogs.nytimes.com/2011/12/23/the-arab-spring-seen-from-brazil/. See also Brazil's 'Responsibility While Protecting' discussion paper from November 2011, http://graphics8.nytimes.com/packages/pdf/opinion/iht-pdf/latitude-blog-20112212-UNpaper.pdf.

59 Nicole Gaouette, 'US "Not Encouraged" by India, South Africa, Brazil, at UN', Bloomberg, 13 September 2011, http://www.bloomberg.com/news/articles/2011-09-13/south-africa-brazil-india-fail-to-impress-u-s-with-their-un-performance.

60 Neil MacFarquhar, 'With Rare Double Veto on Syria, Russia and China Try to Shield Friend', *New York Times*, 5 October 2011, http://www.nytimes.com/2011/10/06/world/middleeast/with-united-nations-veto-russia-and-china-help-syria.html.

61 'Factbox: UN Security Council Action on Syrian Conflict', Reuters, 22 February 2014.

62 Vladimir V. Putin, 'A Plea for Caution from Russia', *New York Times*, 11 September 2013, http://www.nytimes.com/2013/09/12/opinion/putin-plea-for-caution-from-russia-on-syria.html.

63 Garwood-Gowers, 'China and the "Responsibility to Protect"', pp. 19–20.

64 Max Fischer, 'Map: How the World Voted on a UN Resolution for a Political Transition in Syria', *Washington Post*, 16 May 2013, https://www.washingtonpost.com/news/worldviews/wp/2013/05/16/map-how-the-world-voted-on-a-u-n-resolution-for-political-transition-in-syria/.

65 'Russia and China Veto UN Move to Refer Syria to the ICC', BBC News, 22 May 2014, http://www.bbc.co.uk/news/world-middle-east-27514256.

66 'Referral of Syria to the International Criminal Court Fails as Negative Votes Prevent the Security Council from Adopting Draft Resolution', United Nations, 22 May 2014, http://www.un.org/press/en/2014/sc11407.doc.htm.

67 Ed Adamczyk and Doug G. Ware, 'Putin Says US Should Have Given $500M to Russia Instead of Syria Rebels', UPI, 12 October 2015, http://www.upi.com/Top_News/World-News/2015/10/12/Putin-says-US-should-have-given-500M-to-Russia-instead-of-Syria-rebels/5211444650476/.

68 'China Supports Russia's Actions in Syria', TASS, 4 December 2015, http://tass.ru/en/world/841546.

69 Ankit Panda, 'Here's What India Thinks about Russian Airstrikes in Syria', *Diplomat*, 12 October 2015, http://thediplomat.com/2015/10/heres-what-india-thinks-about-russian-air-strikes-in-syria/.

70 'Russia and South Africa Have Similar Approaches to Fighting Terrorism in Syria and Iraq', TASS, 12 November 2015, http://tass.ru/en/politics/836008; Shounaz Meky, 'Why Egypt Has a Different Take on Russian Airstrikes in Syria', Al Arabiya, 6 October 2015, http://english.alarabiya.net/en/perspective/analysis/2015/10/06/Why-Egypt-has-a-different-take-on-Russian-airstrikes-in-Syria.html.

71 Alexander Gabuev, 'A "Soft Alliance"?: Russia–China Relations after the Ukraine Crisis', European Council on Foreign Relations, February 2015, http://www.ecfr.eu/page/-/ECFR126_-_A_Soft_Alliance_

Russia-China_Relations_After_the_Ukraine_Crisis.pdf.

72 Burke-White, 'Crimea and the International Legal Order', p. 70.

73 'Transcript: Putin Says Russia Will Protect the Rights of Russians Abroad', *Washington Post*, 18 March 2014, https://www.washingtonpost.com/world/transcript-putin-says-russia-will-protect-the-rights-of-russians-abroad/2014/03/18/432a1e60-ae99-11e3-a49e-76adc9210f19_story.html.

74 'India Not to Support Western Sanctions against Russia', *Indian Express*, 19 March 2014, http://indianexpress.com/article/india/india-others/india-not-to-support-western-sanctions-against-russia/.

75 Oliver Steunkel, 'Why Brazil Has Not Criticized Russia Over Crimea', Norwegian Peacebuilding Research Centre Policy Brief, May 2014, http://peacebuilding.no/var/ezflow_site/storage/original/application/65655a04cd21b64dbcc9c8a823a8e736.pdf.

76 *Ibid*.

77 Joshua Keating, 'Who's On Team Putin?', *Slate*, 20 March 2014, http://www.slate.com/blogs/the_world_/2014/03/20/the_small_group_of_countries_supporting_russia_s_position_in_ukraine_venezuela.html; Stanley Reed and Sebnem Arsu, 'Russia Presses Ahead with Gas Pipeline to Turkey', *New York Times*, 21 January 2015, http://www.nytimes.com/2015/01/22/business/international/russia-presses-ahead-with-plan-for-gas-pipeline-to-turkey.html.

78 Simon Adams, 'Failure to Protect: Syria and the UN Security Council', Global Centre for the Responsibility to Protect, 2015, p. 20, http://www.globalr2p.org/media/files/syriapaper_final.pdf.

79 Laurent Fabius, 'A Call for Self-Restraint at the UN', *New York Times*, 4 October 2013, http://www.nytimes.com/2013/10/04/opinion/a-call-for-self-restraint-at-the-un.html.

Turkey and the Changing Dynamics of the Kurdish Issue

F. Stephen Larrabee

The Kurdish issue has been a problem for the Turkish Republic since its founding in the 1920s.[1] With the onset of the Syrian conflict, that problem, from Ankara's perspective, has taken on a new dynamic and become larger and more complex, because the Syrian Kurds have emerged as an important new actor. This has sounded alarm bells in Ankara about the establishment of an independent Kurdish state on Turkey's southern border. Meanwhile, the collapse of the peace process between Turkey and the Kurdistan Workers' Party (PKK) has sparked an upsurge of violence and a resumption of attacks against Turkish security forces that pose a serious threat to Turkey's security, and to regional stability more broadly. Meanwhile, the military success of the Islamic State (also known as ISIS or ISIL) has sparked a major debate between Turkey and its Western allies, particularly the United States, over what should be given the highest priority: the defeat of ISIS, or the overthrow of Syrian President Bashar al-Assad.

The rise of the Syrian Kurds

Kurds comprise approximately 10% of the population in Syria. They are centred in the poor northeastern regions of Hasakah and Qamishli, wedged between the borders of Turkey and Iraq. When large-scale public unrest broke out in Syria in spring 2012, the Kurds initially did not join the uprising.

When Syrian government troops withdrew from the country's Kurdish-inhabited areas, Kurdish groups led by the Democratic Union Party (PYD)

F. Stephen Larrabee is a Senior Staff Member at the RAND Corporation, where he holds the Distinguished Chair in European Security.

 DOI 10.1080/00396338.2016.1161900

took over the administration of these towns. The PYD prevented any armed Kurdish presence other than its own paramilitary militias, the People's Protection Units (YPG), from emerging.

Turkey has viewed the growing strength of the PYD with concern because of the PYD's close ties with the PKK, which has carried out an armed insurgency against Turkey since 1983. Turkey has been particularly concerned about the growing cooperation between the Syrian Kurdish militias and the United States. Since the battle for Kobane in October 2014, the Syrian Kurdish militias, the only Syrian opposition group that has a reliable record of effectively fighting against ISIS, have become an increasingly important US partner. American special forces have set up communication links with the Syrian Kurds to help them call in airstrikes by the US-led coalition.[2]

The YPG, together with the Peshmerga (the military forces of the Kurdistan Regional Government in Iraq), have blunted the Islamic State's advance and begun to drive ISIS from territory which it captured last year. The YPG have also signalled in a number of ways that they do not want to threaten Turkey. Unlike Iraq's border with Turkey, for example, the Syrian border has not served as a conduit for attacks by the PKK.[3]

Ankara's fears that the current unrest and turmoil in Iraq, Syria and Turkey will lead to the establishment of an independent Kurdish state in fact are at odds with a strong political trend toward fragmentation and separatism within the Kurdish community. Kurdish politics is highly divided, and plagued by deep personal and tribal rivalries. This lack of unity has historically been an important obstacle to Kurdish national ambitions, and is likely to remain so.

The Kurdish military command provides an example: at the front, Iraqi Kurdish forces are split between the Patriotic Union of Kurdistan (PUK), the Kurdish Democratic Party (KDP) and the Kurdistan Regional Government's Ministry of Peshmerga Affairs. While the two main Kurdish parties, the KDP and PUK, have created unified brigades, these units only function jointly on paper.[4] When the fighting starts, KDP and PUK soldiers report to separate commanders. This fragmentation impedes coalition support, as well as hindering battlefield performance.

The Kurds fight well when defending or liberating their own territory, but are reluctant to carry the fight into Arab regions where their involvement is not welcome. Retaking Mosul, for instance, may prove difficult because the coalition lacks a unifying Arab force. Seizing Raqqa, the ISIS capital, may be easier, however, because the Sunni Arab tribal forces can participate in their own liberation.[5]

Relations with the PKK and the KRG

In 2012, peace negotiations with the PKK generated cautious optimism among the Turkish public that the talks could lead to an end to the fighting and the withdrawal of PKK forces from Turkey. The talks got off to a promising start, and in May 2013 the PKK withdrew a few units from Turkey as a goodwill gesture, with more expected to be withdrawn in the months to follow. However, the negotiations gradually lost political momentum, as it became clearer with time that neither side was prepared to make the type of compromises necessary to bring the talks to a successful conclusion. Turkey now confronts a growing threat from the PKK, as well as an internal threat from the Islamic State. This has resulted in a serious deterioration of Turkey's security environment and the increasing militarisation of the Kurdish issue.

The one bright spot in Ankara's relations with the Kurdish community lies in its relationship with the Kurdistan Regional Government (KRG) in northern Iraq. Once adamantly opposed to Kurdish independence, Turkey initially resisted efforts by the KRG to become more autonomous from Baghdad. In the last decade, however, Turkey has forged close economic and political ties to the region and dropped its opposition to KRG control over northern Iraq's energy resources.

In addition to the trade benefits this relationship has generated, Turkey's ruling Justice and Development Party (AKP) believes that having close ties to KRG President Masoud Barzani, who enjoys a high standing among conservative Muslim Kurds in Turkey, is a means of securing the political support of Muslims living in clan-dominated areas in southeastern Turkey. However, the AKP's ability to attract Kurdish voters has suffered a significant decline in recent years. In the 7 June 2015 general election, an overwhelming number of Kurds voted for the pro-Kurdish Peoples' Democratic Party (HDP) rather than the AKP, in large part because of Turkish President Recep Tayyip Erdogan's perceived failure to seriously address Kurdish concerns. In particular, Erdogan's reluctance to support the Syrian Kurds in their struggle against ISIS during the battle of Kobane angered many Turkish Kurds. Nevertheless, the AKP was able to regain its parliamentary majority in November 2015 by skilfully playing the nationalist card and by tarring the HDP with the terrorist brush.

The US–Turkish dimension

The emergence of the Islamic State has contributed to growing strains in relations with Turkey's Western allies, especially the United States. In Ankara's view, no settlement of the Syrian conflict is possible as long as Bashar al-Assad remains president of Syria. The United States, by contrast, regards the growing power and influence of the Islamic State as the main threat to regional peace and stability. While US President Barack Obama agrees with Erdogan that Assad must go, US officials worry that Assad's overthrow could result in a collapse of law and order and provide new opportunities for ISIS to expand its power and influence. Hence, in the US view, the ISIS threat must be dealt with first.

US and Turkish officials have worked intensively to reduce the strains caused by these differing priorities. In July 2015, Turkey announced that it would allow the United States to use Incirlik Air Base in southern Turkey to conduct airstrikes against ISIS. The two countries also announced that they were considering setting up a 'safe zone' for displaced Syrian refugees. In addition, the Turkish Air Force for the first time launched attacks on ISIS targets in Syria.[6]

The vast majority of Turkish airstrikes, however, have been directed at the PKK, not ISIS. These strikes represent a return to a military approach to the Kurdish issue – an approach that has been tried before, with no success. Indeed, this was the main reason why the AKP decided to enter into a dialogue with the PKK in 2012. Why, then, has Erdogan chosen the same approach again? The answer seems to be that he believes he needs the support of the hardline nationalists to achieve his broader political agenda.

This agenda is aimed at strengthening the powers of the president, which would allow Erdogan to remain at the centre of Turkish politics for another decade or more. Critics fear, however, that it will lead to growing authoritarianism and a hardening of Turkey's policy toward the Kurds.

* * *

Under the Turkish constitution, the country's foreign minister is responsible for executing Turkey's foreign policy on a day-to-day basis, while the president is meant to embody the interests of the Turkish state more generally. Erdogan has often ignored constitutional guidelines, however, and sought to inject himself directly into the foreign-policy decision-making process, much to the chagrin of Foreign Minister Ahmet Davutoglu and other foreign-policy officials. His frequent intrusions have even generated tensions within the upper echelons of his own party. In March 2015, for instance, Deputy Prime Minister Bulent Arinc, one of the founders of the AKP, felt compelled to publicly call on the president to stop 'interfering' in the work of government.[7]

Erdogan's intrusions into the foreign-policy realm appear to be an extension of his domestic political agenda and electoral strategy. As he has sought to gain a mandate to change the constitution and strengthen the powers of the president, he has frequently appealed to nationalist voters, often at the expense of the Kurds. This has worked to undermine the initial goodwill generated by the 2012 talks with the PKK, and has contributed to the re-militarisation of the Kurdish problem. Yet the roots of the Kurdish problem are primarily political and social in nature. They cannot be overcome by military means. Meanwhile, the security threat posed by ISIS presents a military challenge that Turkey is unlikely to be able to address without greater cooperation with the United States and certain portions of the Kurdish community as well.

Meeting this challenge will be all the more difficult because of the sharp deterioration of Turkish–Russian relations following the shooting down of a Russian military jet, which had violated Turkish airspace, in November 2015. The Turkish action infuriated President Putin. Since then, Russia has established contacts with the Syrian Kurds and there is a danger that Moscow may try to exploit the Kurdish issue as a means of exacerbating Turkey's increasing internal difficulties. This could give the Syrian crisis – and Turkish–Russian relations – a dangerous new dimension.

Notes

1 For a detailed discussion of the importance and evolution of the Kurdish issue in the early days of the Turkish Republic, see Henri J. Barkey and Graham E. Fuller, *Turkey's Kurdish Question* (New York: Carnegie Commission on Preventing Deadly Conflict, 1998). See also Quil Lawrence, *Invisible Nation* (New York: Walker and Company, 2008).

2 Tim Arango and Eric Schmidt, 'US Support For Kurds in Syria Angers Turks', *New York Times*, 29 June 2015, http://www.nytimes.com/2015/06/30/world/middleeast/turkey-uneasy-as-us-support-of-syrian-kurds-grows.html.

3 Michael Knights and Lahur Talabani, 'The Iraqi Kurdish Battle Against ISIS: Reports from the Front', *PolicyWatch*, no. 2,520, 6 November 2015.

4 Aliza Marcus and Andrew Apostolou, 'To Save Iraq, Arm the Kurds', *New York Times*, 11 October 2015, http://www.nytimes.com/2015/10/12/opinion/to-save-iraq-arm-the-kurds.html?_r=0.

5 Knights and Talabani, 'The Iraqi Kurdish Battle Against ISIS'.

6 Liz Sly, 'Turkey Strikes Islamic State in Syria for the First Time', *Washington Post*, 25 July 2015.

7 Gönül Tol, 'Erdogan: His Own Worst Enemy', Middle East Institute, 1 April 2015, http://www.mei.edu/content/article/erdogan-his-own-worst-enemy.

Noteworthy

In or out?

'There is one absolute certainty if we vote to leave ... and that is that we will be in charge of our own country, we will make our own laws, we will run our own ministerial departments.'

Nigel Farage, leader of the UK Independence Party, argues in favour of the UK leaving the EU.[1]

'If we leave the EU, that might give you a feeling of sovereignty – but is it real? Would you have power to help businesses not be discriminated against in Europe? No, you wouldn't. Would you have the power to insist European countries share with us their border information so we know what terrorists and criminals are doing in Europe? No, you wouldn't.'

Prime Minister David Cameron urges a 'remain' vote in the 23 June 2016 referendum.[2]

'I will be advocating Vote Leave – or whatever the team is called, I understand there are a lot of them.'

London Mayor Boris Johnson announces his choice. Multiple groups are currently competing for designation by the Electoral Commission as the official 'leave' campaign.[3]

850 million

Tonnes of plastic estimated to be in the sea in 2050

899 million

Tonnes of fish estimated to be in the sea in 2050[4]

Panic and proportion

'But as we focus on destroying ISIL, over-the-top claims that this is World War III just play into their hands. Masses of fighters on the back of pickup trucks, twisted souls plotting in apartments or garages – they pose an enormous danger to civilians; they have to be stopped. But they do not threaten our national existence.'

US President Barack Obama delivers his final State of the Union address on 13 January 2016.[5]

Hope for Syria?

'It is a blessing that this river of blood in this country will stop.'

Abu Samer Al-Kardoun, a resident of Homs, comments on the ceasefire that took effect in Syria on 27 February 2016.[6]

'We are very cautious about raising expectations on this. The situation on the ground is difficult.'

US President Barack Obama.[7]

'This depends entirely on the good faith of Russia, Iran and the Assad regime, none of whom have shown much good faith in the last five years.'

Frederic C. Hof, a senior fellow at the Atlantic Council.[8]

 DOI 10.1080/00396338.2016.1161901

Simple!

'Building a 2,000-mile wall across the border that Mexico's going to pay for … sounds really good, you pound your chest, but the question is: how? How are you going to do it?

New Jersey Governor Chris Christie, commenting on Donald Trump, his then-rival for the Republican nomination.[9]

'I tell everybody who goes to a Donald Trump event, if you get to ask a question, just ask him: how? I don't care which of the things he talks about, just ask him: how? How?'

Christie, at a 21 January 2016 campaign event in New Hampshire.[10]

'The answer is: he will do it.'

Christie, on being posed the same question by ABC presenter George Stephanopoulos, in an interview after he withdrew from the presidential race and endorsed Trump.[11]

22 million

Number of people living in Syria before civil war broke out there[12]

13.5 million

Number who needed humanitarian assistance as of February 2016

4.6 million

Number who had left the country altogether as of February 2016[13]

Cold worrier

'You could say even more sharply: we have fallen into a new cold war. Nearly on a daily basis, we are being blamed for the most terrible threat to NATO as a whole, to Europe, to America, to other countries. They make scary movies where Russia starts a nuclear war. I sometimes wonder: are we in 2016 or 1962?'

Russian Prime Minister Dmitry Medvedev comments on strained relations with the West.[14]

Empty bench

'The American people should have a voice in the selection of their next Supreme Court Justice. Therefore, this vacancy should not be filled until we have a new president.'

US Senate Majority Leader Mitch McConnell argues against replacing US Supreme Court justice Antonin Scalia, who died on 13 February 2016, until after the upcoming US presidential election.[15]

'Until Jan. 20, 2017 it's @POTUS' job to nominate Supreme Court justices – it's right there in the Constitution.'

US Democratic presidential candidate Hillary Clinton responds on Twitter.[16]

5,550

Number of migrants who entered Europe via the Mediterranean Sea in January 2015

73,000

Number who entered in January 2016[17]

Davos contrarian

'The key to tackling extremism is despair. Rob them of the hope that their wild fantasies will win out the day.'

Israeli Prime Minister Benjamin Netanyahu addresses the Global Economic Forum in Davos, Switzerland, on 21 February 2016.[18]

Sources

1 'Staying in the EU "Exposes UK to Terror Risk", says Iain Duncan Smith', BBC News, 21 February 2016, http://www.bbc.co.uk/news/uk-politics-eu-referendum-35624409.

2 *Ibid.*

3 Nicholas Watt, 'Boris Johnson to Campaign for Brexit in EU Referendum', *Guardian*, 21 February 2016, http://www.theguardian.com/politics/2016/feb/21/boris-johnson-eu-referendum-campaign-for-brexit-david-cameron.

4 Leo Hornak, 'Will There Be More Fish or Plastic in the Sea in 2050?', BBC News, 15 February 2016, http://www.bbc.co.uk/news/magazine-35562253.

5 President Barack Obama, 'Remarks of President Barack Obama – State of the Union Address As Delivered', White House Press Office, 13 January 2016, https://www.whitehouse.gov/the-press-office/2016/01/12/remarks-president-barack-obama-%E2%80%93-prepared-delivery-state-union-address.

6 'The Syrian Ceasefire Brought a Moment of Peace to a Country in Ruins', *Irish Examiner*, 27 February 2016, http://www.irishexaminer.com/breakingnews/world/the-syrian-ceasefire-brought-a-moment-of-peace-to-a-country-in-ruins-722799.html.

7 Patrick Wintour, 'Vladimir Putin Takes Personal Charge of Syria Ceasefire Effort', *Guardian*, 24 February 2016, http://www.theguardian.com/world/2016/feb/24/vladimir-putin-takes-charge-of-syria-ceasefire-effort-russia.

8 Mark Landler, 'U.S.–Russia Deal on a Partial Truce in Syria Raises More Doubt Than Optimism', *New York Times*, 22 February 2016, http://www.nytimes.com/2016/02/23/world/middleeast/us-russia-cease-fire-in-syria-obama-putin.html?_r=0.

9 Eric Bradner, 'Christie on Trump: "Anybody Can Do Well for a Month"', CNN, 2 August 2015, http://edition.cnn.com/2015/08/02/politics/chris-christie-donald-trump-2016-election/.

10 David Jackson, 'Christie on Trump: "I Have a Plan"', *USA Today*, 21 January 2016, http://www.usatoday.com/story/news/politics/onpolitics/2016/01/21/chris-christie-donald-trump-new-hampshire-primary/79104516/.

11 '"This Week" Transcript: Chris Christie, Ted Cruz, and Bernie Sanders', ABC News, 28 February 2016, http://abcnews.go.com/Politics/week-transcript-chris-christie-ted-cruz-bernie-sanders/story?id=37242166.

12 Uri Friedman, 'Almost Half of Syria's Population Has Been Uprooted', *The Atlantic*, 30 August 2014, http://www.theatlantic.com/international/archive/2014/08/half-of-syrias-population-is-displaced/379407/.

13 United Nations Office for the Coordination of Humanitarian Affairs, 'Syrian Arab Republic', figure as of 29 February 2016, http://www.unocha.org/syria.

14 Chris Johnson, 'Russia PM Warns of "New Cold War" Amid Syria Accusations', *Guardian*, 13 February 2016, http://www.theguardian.com/world/2016/feb/13/russia-warns-of-new-cold-war-amid-syria-accusations-munich.

15 Amber Phillips, 'Can Republicans Really Block Obama's Supreme Court Nomination for a Year? Probably', *Washington Post*, 13 February 2016, https://www.washingtonpost.com/news/the-fix/wp/2016/02/13/can-republicans-really-block-obamas-supreme-court-nomination-for-a-year-probably/.

16 Hillary Clinton, Twitter, 15 February 2016, https://twitter.com/hillaryclinton/status/699449919980072960.

17 United Nations High Commissioner for Refugees, 'Refugees/Migrants Emergency Response – Mediterranean', figure as of 1 March 2016, http://data.unhcr.org/mediterranean/regional.php#_ga=1.209209170.1961095102.1455702461.

18 José Santiago, '36 Best Quotes from Davos 2016', World Economic Forum, 23 January 2016, http://www.weforum.org/agenda/2016/01/36-best-quotes-of-davos-2016.

Modernising NATO's Defence Infrastructure with EU Funds

Daniel Fiott

A quietly important element of NATO's Readiness Action Plan (RAP), agreed at the 2014 Wales Summit, is the Alliance's need 'to reinforce its eastern Allies through preparation of national infrastructure, such as airfields and ports'.[1] Put simply, without the necessary infrastructure, including transportation networks and hubs, and energy supply lines, it will be difficult for NATO to preposition or sustain military units and ensure that the Very High Readiness Joint Task Force (or VJTF, also known as the 'spearhead force') is able to deploy within a few days. Yet the Alliance has limited collective financial means to modernise Europe's defence transportation and supply links. The European Union, with its range of financial mechanisms, might be able to help.

The need for modernisation

The RAP and spearhead force presuppose that the Alliance is able to move key military units across Europe rapidly, coherently, efficiently and sustainably. Defence infrastructure will be the lifeblood of NATO's ability to respond to any further Russian aggression in Europe. Yet the task of moving numerous troops, heavy armoured vehicles and tanks from west to east in a short space of time should not be taken lightly. The VJTF aims to deploy approximately 5,000 troops within two to three days, with up to five battalions supported by air, maritime and special forces.[2] Each C-17 *Globemaster*

Daniel Fiott is a Researcher at the Institute for European Studies, Vrije Universiteit Brussel and Fellow of the Research Foundation – Flanders (FWO). This essay won the 2015 Palliser Prize, the IISS's annual competition in honour of the late Sir Michael Palliser.

 DOI 10.1080/00396338.2016.1161905

III transporter plane can carry a total payload of around 77 tonnes. This means each flight can load either 102 paratroopers with equipment;[3] one M1 *Abrams* tank (weighing around 54–61 tonnes depending on the variant);[4] three M1126 *Stryker* infantry carrier vehicles[5] (each weighing around 16 tonnes); or five M1117 armoured security vehicles (each weighing around 13 tonnes).[6] The C-17 can land on shorter runways and is more manoeuvrable than heavier aircraft (for example the C-5), but it costs an estimated $12,000 per hour to fly. One assessment has it that US European Command 'spent almost $30 million airlifting troops and equipment for 17 war games in 2012'.[7]

Transporting, say, 5,000 VJTF troops from Ramstein Air Base in Germany to Amari Air Base in Estonia (a flight distance of approximately 1,527 kilometres) would therefore take 49 individual C-17[8] flights and cost approximately $24,000[9] per flight (a total of $1.2m). This conservative estimate does not, of course, include the transportation of armoured vehicles or tanks, nor does it represent the costs of transporting troops to and from the air bases, and it does not factor in the costs needed to protect these C-17s from attack during transportation. Nevertheless, let us now assume that NATO decides to deploy *Stryker* vehicles as part of the VJTF at a rate of eight troops per *Stryker* (the usual crew and passenger size per vehicle),[10] and that these vehicles follow the same flight path. The cost would then climb to approximately $5m, and it would take approximately 208 C-17 flights to transport all of them.

Should the full NATO Response Force (NRF) be used as a follow-on force to the VJTF, it would take 294 C-17 flights (costing approximately $7m) to transport 30,000 troops and 1,250 flights (costing approximately $30m) to transport 3,750 *Stryker*s between Germany and Estonia. Despite the fact that the US Air Force could use other airlift craft such as the C-130 *Hercules* (at least for troop transportation), and that other NATO allies would also contribute to the transportation of troops and vehicles, it is interesting to note that 187 C-17s are currently in active service[11] and there is parking space for 11 C-17s at Ramstein Air Base at any given time.[12] This is not to say that NATO is incapable of deploying a brigade-sized force such as the VJTF, but rather that such flights would be costly, and that alternative means of transportation such as rail freight and road would have to be factored in, even under these conservative calculations. As a show of strength, it might well be good enough to send *Stryker* vehicles on a 1,770km trek over land, but it would not be adequate in the case of armed aggression on NATO territory.[13]

Yet many of Europe's military installations have not been upgraded since the Cold War and railway tracks, airfields and energy pipelines need modernisation in many parts of Europe – particularly in former Warsaw Pact countries. NATO's eastern flank is especially important in this regard because, given the flexible and rotational nature of the Alliance's defensive response to Russian aggression, a number of NATO Force Integration Units (NFIUs) are located in Bulgaria, Estonia, Latvia, Lithuania, Poland and Romania and, following the 8 October 2015 meeting of NATO defence ministers, two more will be opened in Hungary and Slovakia. The NFIUs will serve as small command-and-control and reception facilities for the VJTF, and will also be responsible for identifying logistical networks, transportation nodes and supporting infrastructure that will allow spearhead-force units to deploy within two to seven days.[14] The infrastructural integrity of roads, railways, seaports, air bases and energy supply lines will be key to making the VJTF – and indeed NATO forces more generally – a credible and sustainable deterrent.

Flights would be costly

This is not to say, however, that NATO has neglected infrastructure modernisation. A number of allies are making investments. For example, since 2006, Latvia has spent $82m upgrading its Lielvarde Airfield in line with NATO standards in order to allow for both day and night operations.[15] Similarly, Bulgaria has received €62m for the modernisation of its Graf Ignatievo and Bezmer air bases.[16] NATO also plans to deliver a new aircraft hangar complex at Pápa Air Base in Hungary, in order to support C-17 heavy-lift operations.[17] Yet more needs to be done.

Until NATO allies and the US take a decision on permanent basing, flexibility will be a key element of the VJTF. NATO has opted for a rotational approach to security in Eastern Europe, instead of establishing permanent bases, because of the provisions of the 1997 NATO–Russia Founding Act, which proclaimed that the Alliance's collective defence will not be met by any 'additional permanent stationing of substantial combat forces'.[18] While the Founding Act is not a legal document in the manner of a treaty, and despite calls from eastern allies that Russia's actions in the east have violated the terms of the Act, key NATO states, including Germany, have been cautious about deploying a permanent NATO military presence in the east for fear that it might escalate a crisis or derail diplomatic efforts with Moscow.[19] To some degree, such a rotational posture also presumably suits Washington's needs, especially as it seeks to calm relations with Moscow and shift its military centre of gravity to the Asia-Pacific. A rotational force posture in the east may indeed be wise, given budget pressures and the US Army's plans to cut total troop numbers by 40,000 soldiers by 2017 – a reduction, incidentally, that is larger than the NRF.[20]

A rotational defence posture in Eastern Europe, however, raises a number of technical issues. The activation of the VJTF will imply intra-European movements of ammunition and military hardware, but such movements need to adhere to a number of NATO and EU bureaucratic procedures. The transportation of military equipment and ammunition across EU territory is governed by Articles 91(2) and 462 of the EU Customs Code (Council Regulation No. 2913/92 (1992)), which state that so long as the sending nation is in possession of NATO Form 302 (a customs-clearance form) then equipment can be circulated within the EU. Under the NATO Status of Forces Agreement (SOFA) and Allied Movement Publications, before transfers of military equipment from one NATO member to another can occur – both in peacetime and wartime – the respective national military movement agencies must issue their consent through a licence of free movement based on prearranged movement times, locations, registration of identification plates and so on. Governments may also have to give approval for the movement of forces through their territory.[21] Goods must be transported on the following basis: transfers of equipment from one method of transportation to another must occur on military-controlled ground; explosive materials must not exceed 8,000 kilograms; the load weight on any method of transportation must not exceed 90% of authorised carrying capacity; ammunition and explosives cannot be loaded together if this increases the danger of explosion; ammunition with explosive and toxic chemical agents are prohibited on all modes of transportation except by sea; all traffic regulations in the host nation must be abided by; and, in the case of rail transportation, the host station must be large enough to receive military trains.[22] NATO Form 302 is issued on the basis of adherence to such guidelines.

All of this is not to say that military equipment cannot move freely and efficiently within NATO and EU territory, but that if the VJTF's desired deployment time of two to three days is to be met in either peacetime or wartime conditions, then bureaucratic procedures may need to become more efficient. Perhaps this partly explains why the US Department of Defense is keen to preposition heavy weapons in the Baltic states, Bulgaria, Romania and Poland.[23] Indeed, the US intends initially to deploy enough military hardware to equip approximately 750 soldiers, which, while not enough to equip the entire VJTF, would presumably buy NATO enough time to transport more equipment to geographical areas where it is most needed. Such a move would also have the advantage of keeping within the letter of the Founding Act, as such equipment will remain unmanned until it is needed for exercises or operations.

NATO would stay within the letter of the Founding Act

Despite loud protests from the Baltic states and eastern allies for a permanent NATO presence, the Pentagon has been at great pains to show European NATO allies that it is able to move military units around Europe in a coordinated and relatively rapid fashion. The US military's 'Speed and Power' exercise in Bulgaria in June 2015 aimed to show European NATO allies that it could transport 70-tonne *Abram* tanks on C-17s from Germany to Bulgaria in a relatively short period of time.[24] Transporting such units to Bulgaria via air made sense, of course, given that the Alps, Tatra and Carpathian mountain ranges lie in between the Ramstein and Bezmer air bases. Yet investment in low-lying topographical areas – such as the North European Plain – need not focus only on relatively costly air-transportation solutions because rail links could lead to cost savings, albeit at the price of slower travel times.

In reality, NATO's defence infrastructure is comprised of a range of transportation links normally used in combination with each other. The idea of combining different forms of military transportation serves a critical strategic purpose. In the face of bad weather or an area protected by solid air-defence systems, it may be implausible to fly military units and equipment to a theatre of operations. Similarly, while rail transportation is efficient and relatively rapid, it can fall prey to a number of contingencies such as track sabotage (including cyber attacks),[25] and its use, obviously, is restricted to geographical areas with rail tracks. Naval transportation is, by definition, restricted to the seas, and depends on protected and capable seaports. As one military strategist puts it, 'Not only should the basic modes of transport be in place, but also within each transport mode a variety of means should be available to augment or supplement each other. Roads, canals, rail lines, and air routes should be kept open to allow movement.'[26] Finally, one should also not forget that the construction of transportation and energy-supply linkages opens up another strategic front, as infrastructure can fall prey to conventional and non-conventional attacks, such as cyber warfare.

Energy supply lines are a crucial component of NATO's overall defence infrastructure. Again, NATO has not neglected their importance, and there are programmes in place aiming to finance and maintain cross-border fuel pipelines. NATO has operated its own pipeline system since 1950 and the NATO Pipeline System (NPS) covers 12,000km through 13 NATO members. Currently, the NPS includes eight national pipeline systems, in Greece, Iceland, Italy, Norway, Portugal, Turkey and the United Kingdom. It also includes two multinational pipeline systems: the Central Europe Pipeline System (CEPS) covers Belgium, France, Germany, Luxembourg and the Netherlands, while the North European Pipeline System (NEPS) covers Denmark and Germany.[27] The RAP and the spearhead force will surely require similar energy supply systems to be established on either a national or multinational basis in NATO's eastern allies.[28]

A role for European Union funds?

A number of critical infrastructure areas therefore require modernisation, but NATO's collective financial means to do so are limited. The NATO Security Investment Programme (NSIP) is responsible for investing in critical strategic airfield, naval base and storage infrastructure, but its annual budget runs at approximately €640m.[29] The NATO Maintenance and Supply Agency (NAMSA) is also available for key infrastructure-maintenance programmes, but its yearly budget stands at €625m in common funding.[30] The EU's potential resources for infrastructure investment make NATO's pale in comparison, even though EU mechanisms need to be spread over many different policy domains. The EU Trans-European Transport Network (TEN-T) initiative was budgeted at approximately €8 billion from 2007–13,[31] and from 2014–20 the EU European Regional Development Fund (ERDF) will draw from a budget of almost €256bn.[32] The European Investment Bank (EIB), with its €242bn in available capital, also dwarfs any common resources NATO can bring to the table for infrastructure projects.[33]

While a number of existing EU projects aim to improve rail, road and waterway connections between countries such as Poland and the Baltic states,[34] greater investment – with a defence perspective in mind – is increasingly important for European states seeking to offset the threat posed by Russia in the east. Assessing the costs of modernising European defence infrastructure, including transportation, is not easy. The European Commission estimates that the EU's entire road network will require €1.5 trillion-worth of investment until 2030, and €200bn in cross-border energy links.[35] To be more specific, it is estimated that in 2011, NATO members collectively spent approximately €5.2bn on defence infrastructure.[36] These costs exceed the combined total of NSIP and NAMSA, and only relate to the maintenance of military installation – they do not include the maintenance of transport networks. NSIP and NAMSA cannot currently afford all of the costs associated with modernising transport infrastructure in Europe, and they cannot match the level of funding possible under EU programmes.

There are, however, a number of important restrictions on the use of EU funds for solely military purposes. The rule until now has been that the EU budget should only be invested in civilian projects, or that projects should at least be dual-use in nature so as to serve both civilian and military ends. Even though many transportation facilities, such as seaports, can, albeit after conversion, serve both commercial and military purposes, this is not enough to sidestep the EU's long-held embargo on using EU funds for military purposes. That being said, the embargo may well change in the future. Indeed, if EU plans to initiate a Preparatory Action on defence-relevant research and development,[37] which could see defence research being funded out of the EU budget after 2017, are any guide, then Europe may not be far off from using the EU budget for the purposes of defence.

Structural funds

Even with the embargo dropped, there would still be problems. EU funding comes with a number of restrictions, exceptions and policy-specific idiosyncrasies. A central premise of the ERDF has been to allocate funds on the basis of the level of a country's development, and whether the country suffers from geographical constraints and demographic challenges.[38] The ERDF is geared towards reducing economic-development disparities among EU member states, but any allocation of EU budget funds to defence transportation and energy infrastructure in Europe would have to meet different criteria, based on a strategic imperative. Defence-transportation infrastructure that is most in need of modernisation or replenishment could be required in countries that are considered to be 'developed' by any other measure under the ERDF. Such a situation could lead to questions about social priorities, especially in an era of economic uncertainty and reduced public spending.

This would be a particular problem for the Cohesion Fund, which finances transportation-linkage projects in EU member states whose gross national income per inhabitant is less than 90% of the EU average (including states such as Bulgaria, Czech Republic, Estonia, Hungary, Latvia, Lithuania, Poland, Romania and Slovakia). The Cohesion Fund is allocating €63.4bn to trans-European transportation networks from 2014–20. There is nothing in the Cohesion Fund's rules[39] in theory to prevent it from being used to fund defence-relevant infrastructure programmes,[40] and interestingly enough many of the development programmes currently under way already sit in countries that are playing, and will increasingly play, a central role in mobilising, hosting and supporting the RAP and spearhead force.

The restrictions outlined above should not imply that the EU's structural funds cannot be invested in defence-relevant programmes, as a number of dual-use projects have already been funded under the ERDF.[41] Indeed, the regulations governing the ERDF contain no specific provisions that hinder defence-relevant investments.[42] One of the ERDF's principal objectives is to ensure territorial cohesion in Europe, but this has so far been cast as a purely economic issue related to overcoming economic disparities between regions, even though a wider definition of 'territorial cohesion' could plausibly include defence. In this regard, the Fund could in theory finance projects relating to defence-transportation infrastructure, even though it would have to be restricted to railway linkages and seaports (as Article 3.3.E of the ERDF regulations strictly prohibits investment in airport infrastructure).

One area of EU funding that could be particularly fruitful for NATO's critical defence infrastructure relates to the €33bn-worth of funds under the Connecting Europe Facility (CEF). This is the EU's primary fund for investment into energy infrastructure and it is so far being used to invest in oil pipelines in Poland (the 'Pomeranian pipeline') and natural-gas interconnectors between Poland and Lithuania (the 'GIPL') and Estonia and Finland (the 'Balticconnector').[43] Investments under the CEF are guided by the 2014 EU Energy Security Strategy, which candidly acknowledges that a number of member states in the Baltics and Eastern Europe are bedevilled by less integrated and connected energy supplies and are dependent on Russia.[44] While one must readily acknowledge the differences between commercial energy pipelines and supply lines used for defence, it is equally true that the European Commission has a great deal of expertise in the area of energy infrastructure and it manages the funds needed to connect Europe's energy supply lines.

The European Investment Bank

One other potential funding avenue to explore could be the European Investment Bank. Indeed, the EIB is already investing in a number of transportation programmes across Europe. Poland, a strategically important NATO member, is currently receiving investment amounting to €100m for the modernisation of approximately 71km of railway in the west of the country, between Rawicz and Czempin.[45] This investment may not necessarily be of benefit to military transportation, but the EIB is – at least in theory – able to facilitate public–private partnerships, project bonds and suitable investment funds for such projects.[46] This is important in countries such as Poland that, as stipulated in its 2014 National Security Strategy, recognise that having the proper transportation infrastructure in place 'means ensuring the continuity of the functioning, resilience and strategic mobility of the national security management system'.[47]

Funds that derive from the EU budget cannot presently be used for strictly defence-related purposes, and the EIB suffers from restrictions on investing in the production of and trade in weapons and ammunition and, inter alia, to related research, development or technical applications.[48] But one interesting dimension of EIB investments is an emphasis on public–private partnerships, which could potentially play a role in investments in defence transportation infrastructure, especially if such infrastructure is dual-use in nature (as infrastructure relates to neither the production of nor trade in weapons and ammunition). A number of commercial operators could also play a role in developing, maintaining and sustaining military infrastructure through public–private partnerships. For instance, the US military currently relies on a number of commercial partners to provide sealift, airlift and rail transportation over land,[49] including inside the US with companies such as Norfolk Southern and Union Pacific.[50] During the Afghan and Iraq wars, sea-transportation companies, such as Maersk and Neptune Orient Lines Ltd, transported more than 90% of all US military cargo.[51] Commercial actors could therefore play a key role in developing ideas for defence transportation-infrastructure development in Europe.

Possible effects of EU investment

Using EU funds for the purposes of modernising NATO's critical defence infrastructure could have a number of effects on NATO–EU relations. Given that most EU member states are members of NATO, it seems reasonable to use EU funds to support NATO's Article 5 efforts in Eastern Europe. It would be naive, however, not to acknowledge that some in the EU might be aghast at the very notion that European taxpayers should pay to facilitate NATO – read: largely American – military movements across the Continent. This is especially the case for non-NATO, neutral and non-aligned members of the EU such as Ireland, Malta, Finland and Sweden, which may block any move to use EU funds for NATO purposes, especially given that they have no guarantee of military support from NATO under Article 5 of the Washington Treaty. Given its strained relations with Ankara, Cyprus might also object to the use of EU funds for NATO infrastructure programmes lest Turkey become a beneficiary. At the very least, any investment partnership between the EU and NATO would require close coordination between the European Commission, the European Parliament, the European Defence Agency (EDA) and NATO structures. As new bureaucratic competencies emerged, and each institution sought to retain or expand its respective position within the policymaking framework, such coordination might not be free from friction. Perhaps the terms of the EU–NATO relationship are changing, however, as the 2014 NATO Wales Summit declaration speaks openly about the need for the EU and NATO to commonly address issues such as energy security and defence, and related security capacity-building.[52]

Closer EU–NATO cooperation on defence transportation infrastructure could have an interesting effect on relations between the two organisations. Traditionally, the EU does crisis management and NATO takes care of territorial defence – and, if the need arises, crisis management too. Yet should the EU play a role in investing in critical defence infrastructure in Europe, the European Commission, European Parliament and EDA would arguably also be involved in territorial defence (something possibly foreseen under Article 42 of the Lisbon Treaty), especially if it means helping to connect Europe's military energy pipelines, transportation hubs, railways, seaports and airfields. As the manager of the EU budget, the European Commission would see its role in defence policy increase greatly and in different ways, and the EDA could be the obvious interface between the EU and NATO, meaning that the Agency could – barring any objections from countries such as Denmark, which sits outside the EDA but inside the EU and NATO – play a role in defence-infrastructure projects in addition to capability-development initiatives.

Using the EU budget or EIB funds to fund NATO-relevant defence transportation infrastructure could send a number of important signals of intent on behalf of the EU, particularly to Moscow. The use of the EU budget or

EIB financing could help ease the defence burden on a number of EU and NATO member states by taking up some of the costs of infrastructure-renewal programmes. In an era of a general decline in defence spending in Europe, many ministries of defence in relevant parts of Europe could benefit from EU-funded infrastructure programmes. If designed correctly, such programmes could feed into local and regional development, employment and defence.

There is an additional dynamic to using EU funds for NATO's defence infrastructure. Europe's commitment to NATO has generally been measured in two important respects: contributions to NATO operations, and defence-expenditure levels. Indeed, NATO's informal 2%-of-GDP spending rule has been a useful, if crude, way of measuring Europe's commitment to the Alliance. Investment in critical defence infrastructure under the EU budget could display to non-EU members of NATO that Europe is able to contribute to mutual defence without necessarily measuring this contribution simply in personnel costs, procurement contracts and defence research and development. This could be a way to boost Europe's standing in NATO and to allay regular accusations from Washington that Europe is simply 'free-riding' on US military power.[53]

Finally, EU–NATO relations through infrastructure development would affect Russia's own strategic calculations. One major impact could be that Moscow would find it harder to 'divide and rule' EU and NATO member states. As Ukrainian Prime Minister Arseniy Yatsenyuk recently asserted, whether through military incursions into NATO territory or the funding of extremist parties in the EU, Russia is trying to test the resilience of both organisations.[54] While closer defence-infrastructure cooperation is not a direct response to political funding, it would be a clear statement of intent that NATO and the EU recognise that their cooperation and resilience are key to deterring Russia. As François Heisbourg put it, rephrasing Lord Ismay's famous remark, Europe must find a way to 'keep NATO and the EU whole, the Europeans in Europe and the Russians satisfied'.[55] EU investment in NATO's defence infrastructure would also challenge the assumption that NATO is only as strong as US military and financial support for the Alliance. Russia would be offered evidence that the Europeans are able to do more in the name of deterrence than simply pledging to spend 2% of their GDP on defence.

If Moscow believes the United States' rotational force posture in Eastern Europe is a sign of weakness, and if this force posture is unlikely to change in the near future, then improving the efficiency and speed at which NATO can deploy military forces in case of aggression is a critical component of NATO's ability to deter. EU–NATO defence-infrastructure cooperation would send a signal, albeit limited, that despite America's increasingly austere military footprint and indirect defence strategy in Europe, European NATO members are able to take up some of the slack.[56] Improving defence infrastructure is, admittedly, not the most effective imaginable response to Moscow's hybrid tactics. Nevertheless, it is a serious, non-escalatory way for NATO to ensure it is militarily ready, without exacerbating the already damaging split within the Alliance over the letter and spirit of the NATO–Russia Founding Act.

Acknowledgements

The author wishes to thank Alexander Mattelaer, Tomas Wyns, and a number of EU and NATO officials who wish to remain anonymous, for commenting on earlier drafts of this article.

Notes

1 NATO, 'NATO's Readiness Action Plan – Fact Sheet', May 2015, http://www.aco.nato.int/readiness-action-plan.aspx.

2 NATO, 'Very High Readiness Joint Task Force – Fact Sheet', 9 March 2015, http://www.aco.nato.int/page349011837.aspx.

3 US Air Force, 'C-17 Globemaster III – Fact Sheet', May 2014, http://www.af.mil/AboutUs/FactSheets/Display/tabid/224/Article/104523/c-17-globemaster-iii.aspx.

4 US Air Force, 'Air Force C-17s Deliver Abrams Tanks to Afghanistan', 12 August 2010, http://www.amc.af.mil/news/story.asp?id=123233903.

5 'AF Tapped to Fly 300 Strykers to Afghanistan', *Air Force Times*, 25 February 2009, http://archive.airforcetimes.com/article/20090225/NEWS/902250332/AF-tapped-fly-300-Strykers-Afghanistan.

6 Christopher Bolkcom, 'Military Airlift: C-17 Aircraft Program', CRS Report for Congress, 5 June 2007, https://www.fas.org/sgp/crs/weapons/RL30685.pdf.

7 Joseph Trevithick, 'How Do You Get All Those Army Tanks

to Europe? Unique Units and Private Companies Help American Forces Haul Heavy Gear', *War is Boring*, 10 September 2014, https://medium.com/war-is-boring/how-do-you-get-all-those-army-tanks-to-europe-cdfeed713bfa.

8 Estimates show that a C-17 costs $12,000 per hour to fly. A C-17 travels at 450 knots (or 830km per hour) at 28,000 feet, meaning that it would take approximately two hours to get from Ramstein Air Base to Amari Air Base. See http://www.af.mil/AboutUs/FactSheets/Display/tabid/224/Article/104523/c-17-globemaster-iii.aspx.

9 'U.S. Air Force Should Buy New C-17s, Not Fixed-Up C-5s', *Defense News*, 22 November 2010, http://archive.defensenews.com/article/20101122/DEFEAT05/11220302/U-S-Air-Force-Should-Buy-New-C-17s-Not-Fixed-Up-C-5s.

10 This estimate is taken from the US Army. Indeed, from January to March 2015, the US Army deployed 550 soldiers and 75 *Stryker* vehicles from the 2nd Cavalry Regiment to the Baltic states and Poland as part of *Operation Atlantic Resolve*. See: http://www.eur.army.mil/atlanticresolve/.

11 US Air Force, 'C-17 Globemaster III – Fact Sheet'.

12 Michael J. Lostumbo et al., *Overseas Basing of U.S. Military Forces: An Assessment of Relative Costs and Strategic Benefits* (Santa Monica, CA: RAND Corporation, 2013), p. 50, table 2.1.

13 John Vandiver, 'Dragoon Ride will Send US Troops Through Eastern Europe in Show of Support', *Stars and Stripes*, 12 March 2015, http://www.stripes.com/news/dragoon-ride-will-send-us-troops-through-eastern-europe-in-show-of-support-1.334021.

14 NATO, 'Very High Readiness Joint Task Force – Fact Sheet'.

15 'Latvia Increases Defence Spending; Priorities Home Guard, Anti-Aircraft Systems and Personnel Morale', *Baltic Times*, 26 December 2014, http://www.baltictimes.com/latvia_increases_defence_spending__priorities_home_guard__anti-aircraft_systems_and_personnel_morale/.

16 'Bulgaria Receives Funds for Military Bases Modernisation', *Sofia Echo*, 10 April 2006, http://sofiaecho.com/2006/04/10/644802_bulgaria-receives-funds-for-military-bases-modernisation.

17 NATO, 'NATO Airlift Management Programme', 2015, http://www.nspa.nato.int/en/organization/NAMP/home.htm.

18 NATO, 'Founding Act on Mutual Relations, Cooperation Security between NATO and the Russian Federation Signed in Paris, France', 27 May 1997, http://www.nato.int/cps/en/natohq/official_texts_25468.htm.

19 Henry Foy, 'Eastern Members Pressure NATO for Permanent Bases', *Financial Times*, 17 August 2015, http://www.ft.com/intl/cms/s/0/8595ae2a-44ea-11e5-b3b2-1672f710807b.html#axzz30MJJDjHe.

20 Joe Gould and Jen Judson, 'House Bill Would Halt US Army, Marine Drawdowns', Defense News, 11 February 2016, http://www.defensenews.com/story/defense-news/2016/02/10/us-house-bill-would-halt-army-marine-drawdowns/80206898/.

21 For example, in March 2015 the Czech Cabinet had to approve the passage of NATO forces through Czech territory. See http://www.vlada.cz/en/media-centrum/aktualne/cabinet-adopts-resolution-approving-the-passage-of-nato-forces-through-the-czech-territory-at-the-end-of-march-2015-127707/.

22 NATO, 'Manual of NATO Safety Principles for the Transport of Military Ammunition and Explosives', September 2005, https://www.unog.ch/80256EDD006B8954/(httpAssets)/A80AD5A6BEBCAC05C12579FE00489A2A/$file/ManualofNATOSafetyPrinciplesfortheTransportofMilitaryAmmunition-andExplosives.pdf.

23 Eric Schmitt and Steven Lee Myers, 'U.S. Is Poised to Put Heavy Weaponry in Eastern Europe', *New York Times*, 13 June 2015, http://www.nytimes.com/2015/06/14/world/europe/us-poised-to-put-heavy-weaponry-in-east-europe.html.

24 Matt Millham, 'Air Force, Army Team Up to Move Tanks for Bulgaria Exercise', *Stars and Stripes*, 20 June 2015, http://www.stripes.com/news/europe/air-force-army-team-up-to-move-tanks-for-bulgaria-exercise-1.353470.

25 See, for example, Richard Westcott, 'Rail Signal Upgrade "Could Be Hacked to Cause Crashes"', BBC News, 24 April 2015, http://www.bbc.co.uk/news/technology-32402481.

26 Milan N. Vigo, *Joint Operational Warfare: Theory and Practice* (Newport, RI: Naval War College, 2007), p. 88.

27 NATO, 'NATO Pipeline System', 7 June 2012, http://www.nato.int/cps/en/natohq/topics_56600.htm.

28 I owe this observation to the ever-astute Alexander Mattelaer.

29 NATO, 'A Layman's Guide to NATO (Common) Funding', http://www.nato.int/docu/briefing/nato_funding_final.pdf.

30 NATO, 'What is the NATO Support and Procurement Agency', http://www.nspa.nato.int/en/organization/nspa/nspa.htm.

31 European Commission, 'TENtec Public Portal', http://ec.europa.eu/transport/infrastructure/tentec/tentec-portal/site/en/abouttent.htm.

32 European Parliament, 'European Regional Development Fund – Fact Sheet', http://www.europarl.europa.eu/atyourservice/en/displayFtu.html?ftuId=FTU_5.1.2.html.

33 Daniel Fiott, 'Financing European Defence: Time to Call the European Investment Bank?', Institute for European Studies–VUB, *Policy Brief* 5, 2014, http://www.ies.be/node/2522.

34 European Commission, 'Infrastructure – TEN-T – Connecting Europe', http://ec.europa.eu/transport/themes/infrastructure/index_en.htm.

35 European Commission, 'Infrastructure in the EU: Developments and Impact on Growth', *Occasional Papers* 203, December 2014, p. 17, http://ec.europa.eu/economy_finance/publications/occasional_paper/2014/pdf/ocp203_en.pdf.

36 Joachim Hofbauer, Priscilla Hermann and Sneha Raghavan, *European Defense Trends 2012: Budgets, Regulatory Frameworks, and the Industrial Base* (Washington DC: Center for Strategic and International Studies, 2012), p. 17.

37 European Defence Agency, 'Preparatory Action for CSDP-Related

Research', 18 June 2015, http://www.eda.europa.eu/our-work/projects-search/preparatory-action-for-csdp-related-research.

38 European Union, 'Regulation No. 1301/2013 Concerning the European Regional Development Fund', http://eur-lex.europa.eu/legal-content/EN/TXT/?uri=CELEX:32013R1301.

39 European Union, 'Regulation on the Cohesion Fund', Regulation No. 1300/2013', http://eur-lex.europa.eu/legal-content/EN/TXT/PDF/?uri=CELEX:32013R1300&from=EN.

40 European Union, 'Council Regulation No. 1084/2006 establishing a Cohesion Fund', http://eur-lex.europa.eu/legal-content/EN/ALL/?uri=CELEX:32006R1084.

41 European Defence Agency, 'Your Guide to European Structural Funds for Dual-Use Technology Projects', https://www.eda.europa.eu/docs/default-source/brochures/esf-brochure.

42 European Union, 'Regulation No. 1301/2013 concerning the European Regional Development Fund', http://eur-lex.europa.eu/legal-content/EN/TXT/?uri=CELEX:32013R1301.

43 European Commission, 'Energy: Projects of Common Interest – Interactive Map', http://ec.europa.eu/energy/infrastructure/transparency_platform/map-viewer/.

44 European Union, 'European Energy Security Strategy', COM/2014/0330 final, http://eur-lex.europa.eu/legal-content/EN/ALL/?uri=CELEX:52014DC0330&qid=1407855611566.

45 European Investment Bank, 'EIB Supports Modernisation of Polish Railways, Development of the City of Łódź and Eco-Friendly Investments', http://www.eib.org/infocentre/press/releases/all/2015/2015-048-ebi-wspiera-modernizacje-polskiej-kolei-rozwoj-lodzi-i-inwestycje-proekologiczne.htm.

46 Georg Inderst, 'Private Infrastructure Finance and Investment in Europe', *European Investment Bank Working Papers* 2013/02, p. 3.

47 Government of Poland, *National Security Strategy of the Republic of Poland 2014*, Warsaw, p. 44.

48 European Commission, 'EU Funding for Dual Use: A Practical Guide to Accessing EU Funds for European Regional Authorities and SMEs', http://ec.europa.eu/growth/sectors/defence/industrial-policy/smes/index_en.htm.

49 US Joint Chiefs of Staff, 'The Defense Transportation System', *Joint Publication 4-01*, 2013, http://www.dtic.mil/doctrine/new_pubs/jp4_01.pdf.

50 'Rail Issue: U.S. Military Needs New Way to Ship Heavy Vehicles', Defense News, 3 April 2013, http://archive.defensenews.com/article/20130403/DEFREG02/304030004/Rail-Issue-U-S-Military-Needs-New-Way-Ship-Heavy-Vehicles.

51 Brendan McGarry, 'Maersk Gains from U.S. Military's $11.5 Billion War Shipments', Bloomberg Business, 26 April 2012, http://www.bloomberg.com/news/articles/2012-04-26/maersk-gains-from-u-s-military-s-11-5-billion-war-shipments.

52 NATO, 'Wales Summit Declaration 2014', point 104, http://www.nato.int/cps/en/natohq/official_texts_112964.htm.

53 For a critique of the free-riding charge, see Alexander Lanoszka, 'Do Allies

Really Free Ride?', *Survival*, vol. 57, no. 3, June–July 2015, pp. 133–52.

54 Alex Barker and Peter Spiegel, 'Ukraine PM Warns EU Against Putin's Divide-and-Conquer Tactics', *Financial Times*, 19 March 2015, http://www.ft.com/intl/cms/s/0/413b977a-ce5d-11e4-86fc-00144feab7de.html#axzz30WfeYyZu.

55 François Heisbourg, 'Preserving Post-Cold War Europe', *Survival*, vol. 57, no. 1, February–March 2015, p. 35.

56 Luis Simón, 'Understanding US Retrenchment in Europe', *Survival*, vol. 57, no. 2, April–May 2015, p. 168.

NATO, A2/AD and the Kaliningrad Challenge

Stephan Frühling and Guillaume Lasconjarias

In NATO's 2014 Wales Summit declaration, the members of the North Atlantic Alliance acknowledged that 'Russia's aggressive actions against Ukraine have fundamentally challenged our vision of a Europe whole, free, and at peace'.[1] Signalling a renewed focus on Euro-Atlantic security, NATO decided to beef up its readiness and give collective defence greater emphasis in its longer-term strategy and defence posture. After a decade of out-of-area and crisis-response operations, demonstrating to allies and adversaries alike that NATO is willing and able to defend its members has become crucial for the credibility of the Alliance.

The Ukrainian crisis has highlighted new aspects of Russian warfare, usually described as 'hybrid', 'non-linear' or 'ambiguous', of which the invasion of Crimea was a successful example.[2] NATO's eastern members, in particular the Baltic states (which only gained independence from the Soviet Union a generation ago), feared they would be next. Encompassing a mixture of covert and overt military operations, large-scale disinformation and propaganda, and the use of proxy actors such as 'nationalist' militias and terrorist groups, Russia's hybrid warfare increases the political difficulty of achieving a coherent and timely military response by the Alliance. Seeking to reassure its allies, NATO therefore agreed a Readiness Action Plan in Wales that includes increased exercises and a small rotational presence of 'reassurance forces' in the eastern member states, as well as

Stephan Frühling is an Associate Professor in the Strategic and Defence Studies Centre, Australian National University. **Guillaume Lasconjarias** is a Research Advisor in the Research Division of the NATO Defense College. This essay was shortlisted for the 2015 Palliser Prize.

Survival | vol. 58 no. 2 | April–May 2016 | pp. 95–116 DOI 10.1080/ 00396338.2016.1161906

adaptation of the NATO Response Force to create a brigade-sized Very High Readiness Joint Task Force (VJTF), and new NATO Force Integration Units (NFIUs) headquarters elements that are to prepare for the reinforcement of the Alliance's eastern members.

Nevertheless, despite the commitment made by US President Barack Obama that none of NATO's eastern members would 'stand alone',[3] defending these countries remains a challenging proposition. NATO's strategy continues to be based on strategic warning and reinforcing allies under threat, and therefore requires assured access throughout the territory of member countries. In recent months, however – especially in the context of Russia's intervention in Syria – it has become increasingly obvious that Russia's military modernisation has given it significant new capabilities for high-intensity conventional operations. By emplacing highly capable and long-range anti-air, anti-shipping and surface-to-surface missiles in 'bastions' on the Kola Peninsula in Russia's arctic, in the Kaliningrad enclave, in Crimea and, to some extent, in Syria, Russia can deny NATO forces the use of large areas of the sea and air surrounding, and even within, the Alliance's territory. This emerging military threat in the Euro-Atlantic area has been called 'anti-access and area denial', or 'A2/AD', by, among others, NATO's Supreme Allied Commander Europe, General Philip Breedlove,[4] the Commander of the US Air Forces in Europe, General Frank Gorenc,[5] and Deputy NATO Secretary-General Alexander Vershbow.[6]

Yet it is worth asking whether the A2/AD concept, which has risen to prominence as a way of describing China's military modernisation and the resulting threat to the United States and its allies in the Western Pacific, is a useful lens through which to view the challenges that a belligerent Russia poses to NATO. Of the Russian A2/AD bastions, only Kaliningrad threatens NATO's ability to reinforce its Baltic allies by air and sea, and via the adjacent, thin land corridor at Suwalki that connects Poland to Lithuania.[7] Certainly, the fact that reinforcements by land, air and sea must pass by Kaliningrad represents a major predicament for NATO's defence posture on the eastern flank, to which neither the Readiness Action Plan agreed in Wales, nor the increased reassurance forces that are currently being debated among the allies,[8] are a sufficient answer. At the same time, however, making use of A2/AD capabilities in the Kaliningrad enclave, which is isolated from the Russian mainland itself and hence liable to be besieged by NATO, also represents a strategic gamble for Russia.

Therefore, while it is true that NATO forces must learn to operate despite Russian A2/AD capabilities, technical adaptations alone will be insufficient to maintain the credibility of NATO's collective defence. Russia's A2/AD capabilities are a threat to NATO first and foremost because of the geostrategic position of Kaliningrad. What NATO needs is a strategy that mitigates its own geostrategic vulnerabilities from Kaliningrad's position as a Russian outpost, while exploiting the geostrategic advantage that makes Kaliningrad a hostage to the Alliance.

What is A2/AD?

The basic idea of anti-access and area denial is very simple: the best way of prevailing over a distant adversary, especially if it is superior in overall military power, is to prevent it from deploying its forces into the theatre of conflict in the first place.[9] The history of the concept dates back to the construction of fortresses, long walls and coastal defences to keep threats at bay. More recently, the recognition by Air Chief Marshal Hugh Dowding of the importance of radar, and its integration into an overall air strategy to defend the British Isles, enabled the Royal Air Force to win the Battle of Britain in 1940. During that same conflict, Germany's *Festung Europa* coastal-defence system, stretching over 2,000 kilometres from Norway to the Spanish–French border, was intended to prevent an allied invasion. Meanwhile, in the Pacific theatre, Japan first tried to hold back US forces by occupying potential bases on the islands of the Western Pacific. It then used kamikaze bombers to wear down US forces in the hope of deterring an invasion. Later, during the Cold War, the Soviet Union prepared to stop the reinforcement of Europe via the Atlantic through submarines and air- and surface-launched anti-ship cruise missiles, as well as through air and missile attacks on major sea- and airports in NATO Europe.

The term 'A2/AD' itself was coined after the 1991 Gulf War, in which the United States and its allies had demonstrated the stunning effects of their 'Revolution in Military Affairs' (RMA), based on superior training, communications, intelligence and precision-attack capabilities. Potential adversaries realised that they would not be able to beat US expeditionary forces in a force-on-force conflict, and that it was therefore essential to prevent them from establishing themselves in the theatre in the first place as part of a broader 'asymmetric' response. Developing a nuclear deterrent of their own was one way of doing so; another was to threaten air bases and seaports that US forces rely upon for tactical airpower and movement into the theatre. Ballistic and cruise missiles, which were relatively easy to acquire and operate, but difficult to defend against, provided the backbone of these A2/AD capabilities,[10] together with conventional diesel submarines and long-range anti-air defence systems then exported by Russia. A2/AD thus entails a strong technological component.

The US is dependent on sea control

All of these capabilities have featured prominently in China's military modernisation, which was spurred by the country's inability to stop the transit of US carrier battle groups through the Taiwan Strait during the crisis of 1995–96. The technologies that underpinned the US RMA – in particular, precision guidance, stand-off strike and targeting based on real-time intelligence, reconnaissance and surveillance (ISR) – are no longer the sole preserve of the West.[11] The Chinese development of an anti-ship ballistic missile demonstrates that China is now creating dedicated systems for A2/AD, which it combines with long-range ISR systems, including over-the-horizon radar, drones and satellites, into a comprehensive A2/AD system. Having drawn lessons from the 1991 Gulf War and 1999 war in Kosovo, China is increasingly giving itself the means to push US and allied air and naval forces in wartime beyond the 'first island chain' that runs off the Asian mainland from Japan in the north, to the Philippines in the south.[12] Indeed, the country has become the pacing threat driving Western concern about denial of access, and is the principal cause of the prominence the concept has gained in recent years.[13]

The A2/AD concept thus also has a strategic, and even a grand strategic, aspect. Strategically, it highlights the fact that, as a maritime power, the United States is more dependent on sea control than a continental adversary would be. An A2/AD system allows a defender to diminish the superiority of US forces by keeping them beyond effective operating range from their main objective, threatening such a high rate of attrition – or even decisive defeat – that the United States might lose the political will to support its allies.[14] As such, A2/AD in Asia is the military component of a broader geostrategic contest between China and the United States (and its allies) to shape the future regional order in the military, diplomatic and economic spheres.

The A2/AD concept therefore figures prominently in the current debate about the direction and priorities of US defence policy. Overcoming the A2/AD challenge has emerged as one of the main US defence priorities of the post-Afghanistan era, as seen most clearly in the Obama administration's 2012 Strategic Guidance.[15] This goal is inseparably connected to broader arguments supporting the US 'pivot' or 'rebalance' to Asia, which led to a significant reduction of US military capabilities in Europe.[16] Moreover, the maritime nature of the Western Pacific theatre has made A2/AD a major argument for increased spending on the US Air Force and US Navy, after a decade during which prolonged conflicts in Iraq and Afghanistan led to significant increases in the manpower and budgets of the US Army and Marine Corps. To a large extent, then, the US debate about A2/AD is also a debate about where US defence dollars should flow.

The first articulation of how the US military might overcome the A2/AD challenge focused on new technology for, and increased cooperation between, the US Navy and US Air Force under the rubric of the 'Air–Sea Battle' concept, which was intended to help the United States overcome the vastness of the Pacific Ocean.[17] In 2012, the concept was subsumed under a broader US Joint Operational Access Concept, which also highlights the role of the US Army and Marine Corps, especially for amphibious operations, for air and missile defence, and for supporting relations with regional partners that can help the United States gain a legal and political foundation for access in wartime.[18] Overall, however, the concept of A2/AD in the US defence debate continues to focus on defence technologies, operating conditions and even geopolitical priorities that have served to draw US attention away from NATO, Russia and the Euro-Atlantic area.

Old strengths: Russia's A2/AD capabilities

Russia's A2/AD capabilities, however, underscore the point that high-level, conventional threats to US and allied forces are not only to be found in the Pacific, but also have made a resurgence in Europe.[19] Although the Soviet military–industrial complex fell into a political, economic and administrative hole during the Yeltsin years, it has made considerable progress since then. The poor performance of the Russian Army in the Chechen wars led to radical changes in terms of budget, organisation, leadership and hardware, which were further accelerated by the lessons drawn from the Georgian conflict in 2008. Despite some ongoing difficulties and challenges, Russian forces continue to benefit from the significant resources that have been allocated to them by President Vladimir Putin, and are better prepared, better trained and better equipped than only a few years ago.[20]

> *Air defence was a Soviet priority*

Notwithstanding this progress, however, a large-scale, conventional force-on-force conflict with NATO would almost certainly prove disastrous for Russia. Not only are NATO forces as a whole still more effective, numerous and better trained than their Russian counterparts, they also benefit from access to the territory of the NATO allies in what Russia considers its backyard. In other words, the strategic depth on which Russia and the Soviet Union traditionally based their security is no more. In its search for alternatives, Russia has moved in two different directions. By pursuing hybrid warfare, it hopes to avoid a full-scale, conventional Western reaction to Russian advances in its immediate neighbourhood. At the same time, it has focused on developing significant conventional capabilities to deny Western forces access to contested areas, based on strengths in air defence and guided missiles that Russia inherited from the Soviet Union.

Air defence based on integrated and overlapping layers of radar systems and missiles was a particular priority of the Soviet armed forces during the Cold War. Soviet doctrine dictated the use of mutually supporting air-defence weapons throughout the entire altitude envelope. From the mid-1960s onwards, the Soviets expanded their air-defence coverage through the S-75 (SA-2 in NATO terminology) and S-200 (SA-5) long-range missile systems, followed by the S-300 series (the land-based SA-10 and the SA-N-6 naval version) which entered service in 1979 and could engage several targets simultaneously. The S-300PM (SA-20) was able to engage ballistic missiles, and saw the missiles' range extended to 150km, while the export versions (S-300PMU-2, unveiled in 1997) were equipped with larger warheads and better guidance, reaching a 200km range.[21] The next-generation S-400 (SA-21) was expected to replace both the S-200 and S-300 series, but its development was hampered by financial constraints. While the first test was conducted as early as 1993, the system entered service only in 2007. Russia claims that the S-400 can 'engage all types of aerial targets – up to 36 simultaneously – including aircraft, unmanned aerial vehicles (UAV), and ballistic and cruise missiles within the range of 400km, at an altitude of up to 30km'.[22] Networked with other systems, the S-300 and S-400 present a genuine challenge,[23] which explains General Gorenc's warning about Russia's 'ability to create anti-access/area denied [zones] that are very well defended'.[24]

Russia has also applied its significant guided-missile expertise to the defence of its sea approaches. According to some reports, when an American frigate entered the Black Sea as part of the NATO reassurance measures in March 2014, it faced the presence of K300P *Bastion*-P anti-ship missiles (SSC-5),[25] a land-based version of the supersonic 3M-55 missile with a range of up to 300km that can also be launched from the air, as well as from surface combatants and submarines.[26] For export markets, Russia also advertises the *Club-K* (initially code-named *Pandora's Box*), an anti-ship cruise-missile system that can be concealed in civilian shipping containers. A missile hidden in a container and fired from the deck of a cargo ship, a train cart or a container truck would severely complicate an attacker's defence challenge.[27]

Russian ballistic and cruise missiles also pose threats to the air and naval bases from or through which an adversary might deploy forces against the country. In 2015, Russia fired several land-attack cruise missiles at targets in Syria from ships in the Caspian Sea, more than 1,600km away.[28] Its Kh-101/102 cruise missiles reportedly have a range of 4,000km.[29] In 2010, Russia began fielding the highly precise *Iskander*-M surface-to-surface ballistic missiles with a range of 400km. Russia's A2/AD capabilities also comprise capable delivery platforms. At sea, the development of the *Lada*-class conventional submarine has encountered difficulties in recent years, but all four of Russia's fleets are to receive a number of new *Kilo*-class submarines, optimised for anti-surface warfare.[30] Russia is also modernising 12 of its nuclear attack submarines.[31] In the air, long-range Tu-22M (*Backfire*) bombers are being modernised as delivery platforms for anti-ship cruise missiles, in addition to the acquisition of new versions of the Sukhoi Su-35 (*Flanker*-E) fighter–bombers.

Showcasing these capabilities is essential not only for Russia's national defence, but also for sustaining the export income that has underpinned funding for research and development in Russia's defence industry in recent years, especially during the reforms launched by Anatoly Serdyukov during his tenure as defence minister in 2007–12.[32] This has included a number of partnerships by Russian companies with international customers, such as the Indo-Russian *Brahmos* supersonic anti-ship missile, which is based on the Russian *Yakhont* missile. At the same time, Russia, which has always used its weapons exports as a diplomatic tool, has exported (or committed to export) advanced air-defence systems to China, Iran and even NATO member Greece. Most of China's A2/AD capabilities are based on Russian exports, licenced productions or domestic improvement of Russian-sourced systems. Vietnam has bought a suite of A2/AD capabilities, including coastal-defence systems and *Kilo*-class submarines.[33] A recent communiqué from Russia's defence exporter, Rosoboronexport, highlights how 'Russian-made helicopters and aircraft [have] proved their effectiveness in large-scale antiterrorist operations all over the world', continuing, '[our] partners are cognizant of their air-superiority and ground precision strike capabilities'.[34] This description of the complementary strengths of aircraft, helicopters and various air-defence systems is reinforced by high-profile deployments to Syria[35] and the newly occupied Crimean Peninsula.

Geostrategy and Russia's A2/AD bastions

Although Russia's A2/AD capabilities are based on technologies and doctrinal concepts drawn from Soviet times, its geostrategic position has changed dramatically since then. The dissolution of the Warsaw Pact and of the

Soviet Union itself have, as noted above, deprived Russia of its traditional strategic depth. Whereas the Soviet Union used to be protected by extensive air-defence rings along its borders, the independence of Ukraine, Belarus and the Baltic states have denied Russia access to these states' infrastructure and territory. With the exception of Belarus, Russia's attempts to gain strategic influence over former Soviet states in Europe have met with little success, and Moscow notably failed to prevent the integration of Eastern European countries and the Baltic states into NATO and the EU.[36] Instead, Russia has had to implement alternative strategies – notably, hybrid warfare and the extension of A2/AD capabilities – as part of a larger manoeuvre to exercise influence in what it considers to be its backyard.

That said, the way in which Russia has established 'bastions' to protect key assets and areas is not a new approach: the notion of developing a strategic bastion on the Kola Peninsula was already prominent during the Cold War. Since most Soviet nuclear ballistic-missile submarines (SSBNs) were in its Arctic Fleet, protecting these 'boomers' from NATO's anti-submarine forces was a major concern for the Soviet Navy. Whereas the US, French and British navies sought protection for their SSBNs through covert patrols in the depths of the North Atlantic, the Soviet Navy used significant surface, submarine and land-based air forces to create a heavily protected area both on and surrounding the Kola Peninsula: the Kola bastion. It addition to protecting Russia's SSBNs, the Kola bastion was the source of submarine, air and surface threats to NATO sea lines in the Atlantic. Today, Russia's defence build-up in the High North again comprises ships and submarines for the Arctic Fleet, as well as new air bases, air defences and ground troops, under a newly established Joint Forces Command.[37]

Whereas the Kola bastion is located at NATO's northern flank, Russian-occupied Crimea is fast becoming the southern anchor of Russia's bastion system. By asserting its control over Crimea, Moscow has gained some 1,000km of additional shoreline, and ports such as Feodosia and Kerch. This complements the strategic harbour of Sevastopol, home to the Russian Black Sea Fleet, and other harbours for naval use on sovereign Russian territory that Russia started developing as far back as 2005.[38] The deployment of land-based anti-air and anti-ship missiles, which are to be permanently based in silos in the future,[39] allows Russia to constrain the ability of NATO's air and naval forces to operate in the area. Already, Russian forces based in Crimea are shadowing NATO ships entering the Black Sea.[40] In addition, Moscow announced the permanent deployment of additional fighter and bomber aircraft and attack helicopters for maritime patrols and anti-submarine warfare in 2014.[41] Some analysts see the deployment of *Iskander* missiles in Crimea as a response to the emplacement of US missile-defence interceptors in Romania,[42] and Crimea itself has become a stepping stone for Russia's operations in the Middle East.[43]

Between Crimea in the south and the Kola Peninsula in the north lie Russia's Baltic territories. Of the Soviet Union's former defence system in the area, only the Kaliningrad oblast, home to the Russian Baltic Fleet and an upgraded strategic early-warning radar system,[44] and the air-defence system around St Petersburg remain. Both areas became heavily militarised after the Cold War, as Russian units from the Baltic states, Poland and East Germany relocated to bases in the Kaliningrad Special Defence District and the Leningrad Military District.[45] Over time, military personnel in Kaliningrad were reduced by around three-quarters; the number of tanks was slashed by half; the airborne brigade was disbanded; and combat aircraft were reduced from 155 to 28 (in 2004), submarines from 42 to 2, and surface ships from 450 to 190.[46] This decline has now been halted, however. In recent years, Russia has refurbished airfields in the enclave,[47] increased the capability of the Baltic Fleet (including with new corvettes), fully manned the resident marine and rifle brigades, deployed batteries of S-400 air-defence missiles, and conducted prominent exercises to prepare for the rapid reinforcement of the territory.[48] Russia has repeatedly used prominent A2/AD capabilities for geostrategic signalling, as when it threatened to deploy *Iskander* missiles to Kaliningrad in 2008 in response to American missile-defence plans for Europe.[49] While it remains unclear whether the missiles are indeed permanently based there,[50] they have been included in exercises,[51] and are likely to replace the currently deployed SS-21 missiles in coming years.

Unlike the other two bastions, Kaliningrad also threatens NATO communications on land: only two main roads connect NATO allies Poland and Lithuania, running through a corridor between Kaliningrad and Belarus that is, at its narrowest, only 65km wide. All NATO reinforcements by land must pass through this 'Suwalki gap' on their way to the Baltic states.[52] Even if Russian and Belarusian forces did not physically cross the border at this point, the corridor is well within the range of Russian artillery. The *Smerch* multiple-rocket-launch system has a range of 90km, and there are reports that Russia has developed a 120km version, as well as a successor with a range of up to 200km.[53]

Kaliningrad: threat to NATO, hostage to NATO

A2/AD capabilities are clearly a prominent element of Russia's military modernisation, and the A2/AD bastions the country has established must now be seen as a significant element in NATO's security environment. However, the geostrategic location of each bastion, and hence its strategic effect on NATO, are very different.

The Kola bastion is of importance to Norway, which is once again growing concerned about the defence of its Finnmark region and Russia's forward air and naval operations (which now often extend to the UK–Iceland gap), in defence of its northern bastion.[54] During the Cold War, these concerns gave rise to the creation of the 'Allied Mobile Force' (a conceptual forebear of today's VJTF), extensive prepositioning of equipment (in particular for the US Marine Corps, which still uses facilities in Norway) and increased NATO exercises in the High North during the 1980s. While all of these also figure prominently in NATO's reassurance of the Baltic countries today, the Alliance's increased attention to the High North has so far been largely limited to some additional exercises.[55] Ultimately, the area remains a theatre of secondary importance, whose strategic significance to NATO as a whole derives from the presence of Russian SSBNs, and the potential threat to Atlantic sea lines of communication. During the 1980s, the maritime strategy of the US Navy included a forward battle by nuclear attack submarines and multiple carrier groups to break into the Kola bastion. In the absence of such a strategy today, there is no need to make the targeting of the Kola bastion a priority for the Alliance.

In the Black Sea, too, Russia's ability to deny NATO air and maritime forces use of the area is no different than during the Cold War. Of course,

Romania and Bulgaria are today NATO members, so that NATO territory now stretches to the southern as well as to the western shore of the Black Sea. Both allies can, however, be reinforced by air and land from the west, across NATO territory via Hungary or Greece. In that sense, Russia's denial of the Black Sea does not directly undercut NATO's ability to defend the territorial integrity of its allies, even if it challenges the Alliance's ability to access Russian territory from the southern flank.

Kaliningrad, however, is different. Located on the southeastern corner of the Baltic Sea, it separates NATO members Denmark, Germany and Poland to its west from Lithuania, Latvia and Estonia to its north. After the admission of Poland and the Baltic countries to the Alliance, NATO relied on the reinforcement of its new members in case of a threat, rather than forward-basing significant allied forces on their territory, which had been its approach on the Central Front during the Cold War.[56] Even now, the Readiness Action Plan adopted at the Wales Summit continues to rely on the reinforcement of the new allies in a crisis. All of these reinforcements, however, must either pass through the Suwalki gap on land, or travel by air or sea across the Baltic Sea, which only measures 260km between Kaliningrad and the Swedish shore – well within the range of Russian anti-air and anti-ship missiles based in the enclave.

Prepositioning and the VJTF both rely on access

The ability of Russia's A2/AD forces in Kaliningrad to block access to the northern Baltic Sea area thus challenges the very basis of NATO's post-Cold War defence strategy. To defend Estonia, Latvia and Lithuania, NATO must have the ability to break through a possible blockade, based on Kaliningrad, of regional air, land and sea communications. This challenge differs substantially from those NATO faced during the Cold War, or that faced by the United States in Asia today.[57] No other Russian bastion presents a comparable problem – Kaliningrad is the only place where NATO needs to be able to neutralise Russia's A2/AD capabilities if its collective-defence guarantee is to remain credible.[58] However, this is a task that cannot be accomplished either by the largely symbolic reassurance forces created in 2014, which are far too small to defend the Baltic states against an attack unaided, or by increased prepositioning or the VJTF, which both rely on access in a crisis.

Luckily for NATO, Kaliningrad's geography offers advantages not just to Russia, but also to the Alliance. Kaliningrad itself is an enclave, surrounded by NATO territory on land and by the Baltic Sea, measuring about 200km from east to west, and 100km from north to south. NATO members have so far been understandably reluctant to highlight the obvious difficulties that the defence of the enclave would present to Russia. Today, however, this reluctance means that NATO might neglect what would be the best way of neutralising Russia's A2/AD capabilities in Kaliningrad, which would be by deterring their use in the first place. To do so, the Alliance must acknowledge that the Kaliningrad enclave is a threat to NATO, but that it could become a hostage to NATO at the same time.

Existing Russian land forces around Kaliningrad City are largely defensive, comprising the 336th Naval Infantry Brigade, 7th Motor Rifle Regiment, 244th Artillery Brigade and 3rd Aerospace Defence Brigade. The 79th Motor Rifle Brigade and 152nd Missile Brigade (with SS-21 surface-to-surface missiles) are the only permanent units in the eastern part of the enclave.[59] Arrayed opposite these forces is the Polish 16th Mechanised Division comprising four armoured and mechanised brigades, three of which are based along the southern border of the enclave. Poland alone could concentrate significant additional forces in the area, especially if Belarus was not participating in Russian operations against NATO.[60] There are significant quantities of military materiel in Kaliningrad that would enable Russia to rapidly reinforce the enclave, but in wartime, NATO could isolate the area by fighter aircraft and air-defence batteries, and by mining the sea and deploying submarines.

The geographic isolation of Kaliningrad thus creates a strategic dilemma for Russia. Kaliningrad may threaten to isolate the Baltic states at the beginning of a conflict, but for Russia to actually attack NATO's air, naval or land forces from the enclave would mean tearing up any tacit agreement with the Alliance on limiting the geographic scope of a conflict, and risk the loss of the territory once NATO mobilised sufficient forces in the area. For NATO, this means that the best way of dealing with the Russian A2/AD threat in the Baltic would be to isolate Kaliningrad as soon as possible in wartime, and to threaten an invasion of the territory to deter Russia from conducting military operations from the enclave in the first place.

How might Russia react to such a strategy? A favourable outcome for NATO would be if Russia decided to avoid testing the Alliance's resolve, and refrained from using Kaliningrad to interfere with NATO lines of communication. Instead, Moscow could still seek to adopt a 'hybrid' approach to A2/AD itself. Mining of the Baltic Sea could be done covertly and with (more or less) plausible deniability. This reinforces the importance for NATO of mine countermeasures in general, and of the regular presence of Standing NATO Mine Countermeasures Group 1 in Baltic waters in particular. In the Suwalki gap, Russia might use a proxy force based in Belarus as a front for Russian attacks.[61] Given the sorry state of Belarus's armed forces today,[62] such a threat would probably have to rest on Russian regular forces operating, without attribution, from Belarusian territory. If NATO decided against an occupation of Belarusian territory to secure the roads into Lithuania from this threat, Russia could potentially reduce the flow of NATO reinforcements by land. Alternative air and sea routes across the Baltic Sea would remain open, however, unless Russia made open use of the anti-air and anti-ship missiles in Kaliningrad.

Alternatively, Russia might seek to prevent NATO from implementing its deterrent threat. It could drop any pretext of a limited conflict and invade Lithuania or Poland (or both), with the aim of breaking the NATO siege and establishing reliable land communications to Kaliningrad via Belarus. Alternatively, it could seek to deter NATO with threats to use tactical nuclear weapons. Both of these options would therefore require it to significantly escalate any conflict into a major attack on the Alliance, unless it were willing to sacrifice control of Kaliningrad for the short-term gain of interdicting NATO lines of communication by air, sea and land. In other words, if NATO could present a credible threat of invasion to Kaliningrad, it is likely either that Russia's A2/AD systems in the enclave itself would not come into play in a limited conventional conflict involving the Baltic states at all, so that NATO could reinforce its Baltic allies unhindered; or that Russia would have to escalate the conflict to such a point that NATO security and strategy would come to rest on the credibility of its nuclear capabilities. Either way, it is the geographic location of Kaliningrad – rather than Russia's A2/AD capabilities as such – that holds the key to understanding the strategic challenge to NATO presented by Russia's conventional modernisation, in the spectrum between hybrid warfare on the one hand, and its nuclear deterrence on the other.

Towards a NATO strategy for access to the Baltic states

It is clear that NATO requires a credible response to fears about the security of its allies in the Baltic region. Terms such as 'hybrid warfare' and 'little green men' have been useful in highlighting the immediate challenges to NATO demonstrated by the Ukraine crisis, and catalysed the response at the Wales Summit centred on the Readiness Action Plan and the creation of the VJTF. Member states can no longer close their eyes to the risk of open, state-on-state confrontation with a revanchist Russia. Bellicose pronouncements by Vladimir Putin, who putatively said that he could, if he wanted, have Russian troops not only in Kiev, but also 'in Riga, Vilnius, Tallinn, Warsaw and Bucharest' within two days,[63] are not just provocative but create a sensation of insecurity that NATO needs to address.

Conceptualising the conventional threat from Russia in terms of A2/AD has many advantages. It aligns with the direction of Russia's military modernisation; links the issues of deterrence and territorial defence; relates to prominent themes in the current US defence debate; shows the importance of air and naval capabilities at a time when land forces are the most prominent instrument of reassurance; and demonstrates that any NATO–Russia conflict would likely make large parts of NATO Europe into an active theatre of operations.

NATO needs access to all of its member states, including the Baltic allies that are geographically separated from the rest of NATO by the Kaliningrad enclave. Because of this, some have argued for a substantial increase of NATO combat forces in the region.[64] Yet it would be politically, operationally and financially impossible for the Alliance to build up these forces to such an extent that they would not depend on secure lines of communication to Western Europe and beyond. Even during the Cold War, NATO strategy relied on reinforcing its front-line allies before and after the outbreak of conflict. To bolster deterrence and collective defence, NATO therefore needs a strategy to ensure access to the Baltic states despite the presence of Russian A2/AD capabilities in Kaliningrad.

The best way of overcoming Russia's A2/AD threat from Kaliningrad, as discussed above, would be to deter it from being used in the first place. The range of Russia's A2/AD systems that are or could be deployed to Kaliningrad, including the S-400, the *Iskander* missile and the *Bastion* anti-ship cruise missile, represent a severe threat to NATO's ability to defend its allies, even if no Russian soldier crossed the border into NATO territory. In its public and private communication with Russia, NATO should make clear that, whatever restrictions might be put on NATO ground operations into Russia's mainland, it would consider an invasion of Kaliningrad a legitimate and non-escalatory response to Russian use of the territory to interfere with NATO's lines of communication. Deploying reassurance forces in Poland close to the enclave in a crisis, practising the reinforcement of Poland's 16th Division, and directing the Headquarters of Multinational Corps Northeast in Szczecin to focus on the safeguarding of NATO communication lines would all help to bolster this deterrent posture.[65]

Deterrence must be complemented by mitigation, which would make Russian use of Kaliningrad for A2/AD less attractive to Moscow, and less damaging to NATO. War stocks of ammunition and fuels for allied and local forces in the Baltic states need to reflect the risk of a temporary disruption in supply. NATO's Joint Logistic Support Group, which is so far based on the same process as the NATO Response Force and insufficiently manned, needs to be equipped, manned and trained to deal with adversary use of A2/AD capabilities in the Baltic area. Live exercises should be conducted in the specific geographic and meteorological conditions of the Baltic Sea, with naval convoys and (low-flying) strategic air transport, missile-defence drills, electronic warfare, mine countermeasures and anti-submarine warfare to gain a better understanding of the threat, of NATO forces' vulnerabilities, and of the extent to which NATO plans must make provision for the disruption of movement of forces and supplies. On land, engineering capabilities to repair roads and lay mine barriers, as well as counter-battery radars and long-range artillery (including possibly prepositioning US ATACMS surface-to-surface missile units) would make it harder to interdict land communications through the Suwalki gap.

The best way of mitigating the threat to NATO lines of communication from Kaliningrad, however, would be to open new and less vulnerable lines through Swedish (and, to some extent, Finnish) territory and airspace. These two countries are of crucial importance to NATO's collective-defence task in a way that cannot be said of any other NATO partner. Somewhat paradoxically, the increased prominence of the mutual-assistance clause in the EU treaty, particularly its invocation by France after the terrorist attacks in Paris in November 2015, might provide scope for exploring the political feasibility of greater cooperation on collective defence between Sweden, Finland and the countries' other NATO and EU partners. Joint studies forming part of the Nordic Defence Cooperation (NORDEFCO) framework, which combines regional NATO members as well as Sweden and Finland, could explore the political and practical aspects of various levels of cooperation, such as NATO transit through Swedish and Finnish airspace, provision of refuelling, NATO use of air bases, or the passage of naval convoys through Swedish territorial waters with or without active support from the Swedish Navy and Air Force. In addition, NATO would significantly benefit if it could gain both countries as new members.

A2/AD is a useful lens through which to view the challenges NATO faces in the defence of its members, but the concept must not be confined to exercises in 'capability-based planning' that focus on technology and operational concepts. Instead, it should be placed into the geostrategic context of the Baltic Sea region. A2/AD systems are certainly a tool with which Russia can threaten the integrity of NATO and its members, but NATO likewise has strengths rooted in its existing military capabilities, geography and relations with neutral countries that it can bring to bear. For NATO, coming to terms with A2/AD means, first and foremost, coming to terms with the strategic geography of Kaliningrad.

Notes

1 NATO, 'Wales Summit Declaration', 5 September 2014.

2 For a definition of hybrid warfare and analysis of discussions on this topic within the NATO community, see Guillaume Lasconjarias and Andreas Jacobs, 'NATO's Hybrid Flanks: Handling Unconventional Warfare in the South and the East', Research Paper no. 112 (Rome: NATO Defense College, 2015), p. 3. See also Élie Tenenbaum, 'Le piège de la guerre hybride', *Focus stratégique* no. 63 (Paris: IFRI, 2015), pp. 23–5.

3 'Remarks by President Obama at 25th Anniversary of Freedom Day', Warsaw, 4 June 2014, www.whitehouse.gov/the-press-office/2014/06/04/remarks-president-obama-25th-anniversary-freedom-day-warsaw-poland.

4 Remarks by General Philip Breedlove at Joint Press Conference, Trapani, 19 October 2015, http://www.nato.int/cps/en/natohq/opinions_124035.htm.

5 Sydney J. Freedberg, 'Russians "Closed The Gap" for A2/AD: Air Force Gen. Gorenc', Breaking Defense, 14 September 2015, http://breakingdefense.com/2015/09/russians-closed-the-gap-for-a2ad-air-force-gen-gorenc/.

6 Ion M. Ioniță and Octavian Manea, 'Vershbow: NATO Needs Strategy to Address Threats from the South and the East', Defence Matters, 5 November 2015, http://defencematters.org/news/vershbow-nato-needs-strategy-to-address-threats-from-the-south-and-the-east/410/.

7 Russia could also interfere with the flow of reinforcements to northern Norway.

8 Julian E. Barnes, 'NATO Looks at Stationing More Troops Along Eastern Flank', *Wall Street Journal*, 28 October 2015, http://www.wsj.com/articles/nato-looks-at-stationing-more-troops-along-eastern-flank-1446050987.

9 Sam J. Tangredi, *Anti-Access Warfare: Countering A2/AD Strategies* (Annapolis, MD: Naval Institute Press, 2013), p. 1.

10 See, for example, John Stillion and David T. Orletski, *Airbase Vulnerability to Conventional Cruise-Missile and Ballistic-Missile Attacks* (Santa Monica, CA: RAND, 1999).

11 Barry Watts, *The Evolution of Precision Strike* (Washington DC: CSBA, 2013).

12 For a net assessment supporting this evaluation, see Eric Heginbotham et al., *The U.S.–China Military Scorecard* (Santa Monica, CA: RAND, 2015).

13 Post-Cold War concern about denial of access first arose in the Persian Gulf in the 1990s. Iran's acquisition of advanced anti-air, anti-surface and surface-to-surface missiles and submarines is also sometimes discussed as a local A2/AD challenge.

14 Andrew F. Krepinevich, *Why AirSea Battle?* (Washington DC: CSBA, 2010).

15 US Department of Defense, 'Sustaining U.S. Global Leadership: Priorities for 21st Century Defense', January 2012, http://archive.defense.gov/news/Defense_Strategic_Guidance.pdf.

16 Luis Simón, 'Understanding US Retrenchment in Europe', *Survival*, vol. 57, no. 2, April–May 2015, pp. 157–72.

17 Jan van Tol et al., *AirSea Battle: A Point-of-Departure Operational Concept* (Washington DC: CSBA, 2010).

18 US Joint Chiefs of Staff, 'Joint Operational Access Concept (JOAC)', 17 January 2012, http://www.defense.gov/Portals/1/Documents/pubs/JOAC_Jan%202012_Signed.pdf.

19 Richard Fontaine and Julianne C. Smith, 'Anti-Access/Area Denial Isn't Just for Asia Anymore', Defense One, 2 April 2015, http://www.defenseone.com/ideas/2015/04/anti-accessarea-denial-isnt-just-asia-anymore/109108/.

20 Jonathan Masters, 'The Russian Military', Council on Foreign Relations, 17 November 2014, http://www.cfr.org/russian-federation/russian-military/p33758; Jakob Hedenskog and Carolina Vendil Pallin (eds), *Russian Military Capability in a Ten-Year Perspective – 2013* (Stockholm: FOI, 2013).

21 'Intruder Alert: Russia's Long-Range Air-Defence Missiles', *Jane's International Defense Review*, vol. 47, no. 11, November 2014.

22 'S-400 Triumph Air Defence Missile System, Russia', Army-technology.com, http://www.army-technology.com/projects/s-400-triumph-air-defence-missile-system/.

23 Dave Majumdar, 'American F-22s and B-2 Bombers vs. Russia's S-300 in Syria: Who Wins?', *National Interest*, 22 September 2015, http://nationalinterest.org/blog/the-buzz/american-f-22s-b-2-bombers-vs-russias-s-300-syria-who-wins-13905.

24 Freedberg, Jr, 'Russians "Closed the Gap" For A2/AD: Air Force Gen. Gorenc'.

25 'Fortress Mentality: Focus on Anti-Access Coastal Defences', *Jane's International Defense Review*, vol. 48, no. 4, November 2015. The missiles were later displayed during the 'Victory Day' parade in Crimea in May 2014.

26 '3M55 Oniks / P-800 Yakhont / P-800 Bolid / SS-N-26', GlobalSecurity.org, http://www.globalsecurity.org/military/world/russia/ss-n-26.htm.

27 See Lajos F. Szaszdi, 'The Club-K: A Deadly "Pandora's Box" of Cruise Missiles', *Daily Signal*, 2 August 2011, http://dailysignal.com/2011/08/22/the-club-k-a-deadly-%E2%80%9Cpandora%E2%80%99s-box%E2%80%9D-of-cruise-missiles/; and Robert Clarke, 'The Club-K Anti-Ship Missile System: A Case Study in Perfidy and its Repression', *Human Rights Brief*, vol. 20, no. 1, 2012, pp. 22–8.

28 Richard Johnson, 'How Russia Fired Missiles at Syria From 1,000 Miles Away', *Washington Post*, 23 October 2015, https://www.washingtonpost.com/graphics/world/russian-cruise-missile/.

29 'All Missiles Great and Small: Russia Seeks Out Every Niche', *Jane's International Defense Review*, vol. 47, no. 9, 2014.

30 K. Soper, 'All Four Russian Fleets to Receive Improved Kilos', *Jane's Navy International*, vol. 119, no. 3, 2014.

31 K. Soper, 'Russia Details Ambitious Effort to Modernize Nuclear-Powered Submarines to Bolster Order of Battle', *Jane's Navy International*, vol. 120, no. 9, 2015.

32 Katri Pynnöniemi, 'Russia's Defence Reform: Assessing the Real "Serdyukov Heritage"', Briefing Paper 126 (Helsinki: Finnish Institute of International Affairs, 2013), p. 7.

33 Carl Thayer, 'With Russia's Help, Vietnam Adopts A2/AD Strategy',

Diplomat, 8 October 2013, http://thediplomat.com/2013/10/with-russias-help-vietnam-adopts-a2ad-strategy/.

34 'Russia's Aerial and AD Systems Gaining Popularity in the Middle East', Rosoboron Export official communiqué, 6 November 2015, http://www.roe.ru/eng_pr/eng_pr_15_11_06.html.

35 Darren Boyle, 'Putin Rolls Out the Big Guns', *Daily Mail*, 12 November 2015, http://www.dailymail.co.uk/news/article-3316195/Vladimir-Putin-deploys-advanced-Growler-anti-aircraft-missile-Syria-able-hit-jets-altitude-90-000-feet-far-away-Tel-Aviv.html.

36 While the growing Euro-Atlantic community around the Baltic Sea was successful in reducing geo-political 'grey zones', it did not achieve enduring stability and security. See Andris Spruds and Karlis Bukovskis (eds), *Security of the Broader Baltic Sea Region: Afterthoughts from the Riga Seminar* (Riga: Latvian Institute of International Affairs, 2014), pp. 4–5.

37 Vincent R. Stewart, Director, Defense Intelligence Agency, 'Worldwide Threat Assessment', testimony before the US House Armed Services Committee, 3 February 2015, www.dia.mil/News/SpeechesandTestimonies/ArticleView/tabid/11449/Article/567087/worldwide-threat-assessment.aspx.

38 Igor Delanoë, 'La Crimée, un bastion stratégique sur le flanc méridional de la Russie', note no. 14 (Paris: FPRS, 2014), p. 4.

39 'Russia Will Deploy First Bastion Surface-To-Surface Missile System in Crimea by 2020', *International Business Times*, 2 July 2015, http://www.ibtimes.com/russia-will-deploy-first-bastion-surface-surface-missile-system-crimea-2020-1993679.

40 Stephen Blank, 'The Militarization of the Black Sea', CEPA, 20 July 2015, http://www.cepa.org/content/militarization-black-sea.

41 'Russian Airbase in Crimea Reinforced by New Fighter Jets', Sputnik News, 26 November 2014, http://sputniknews.com/military/20141126/1015194983.html.

42 Delanoë, 'La Crimée', p. 5.

43 'Professor Stephen Blank on Eastern Flank in A2/AD Age', Romania Energy Centre, 7 June 2015, http://www.roec.biz/bsad/portfolio-item/professor-stephen-blank-on-eastern-flank-in-a2ad-age/.

44 'Russia Launches New Missile Defense to Cover Atlantic', RT News, 29 November 2011, https://www.rt.com/politics/opens-kaliningrad-radar-station-459/.

45 Adrian Hyde-Price, 'NATO and the Baltic Sea Region: Towards Regional Security Governance', NATO Research Fellowship Scheme 1998–2000 Final Report, http://www.nato.int/acad/fellow/98-00/hyde.pdf.

46 Poul Wolffsen and Alexander Sergounin, *Kaliningrad: A Russian Exclave or a Pilot Region?* (Nizhny Novgorod: Nizhny Novgorod State Linguistic University Press, 2004), pp. 13–14.

47 B. Jones, 'Russia Rejuvenates Kaliningrad Naval Base', *Jane's Navy International*, vol. 117, no. 3, 2012.

48 'Russian Military Completes Rapid-Deployment Drills in Kaliningrad',

RT News, 16 December 2014, https://www.rt.com/news/214667-russia-drills-kaliningrad-region/.

49 D. Richardson, 'Russia Plans More Iskander-M systems', *Jane's Missiles & Rockets*, vol. 15, no. 9, 2011.

50 Andrzej Wilk, 'Iskander Ballistic Missiles on NATO's Borders', OSW, 18 December 2013, http://www.osw.waw.pl/en/publikacje/analyses/2013-12-18/iskander-ballistic-missiles-natos-borders.

51 'Russian Military Completes Rapid-Deployment Drills in Kaliningrad'.

52 See 'U.S. Army Commander Warns of Russian Blocking of Baltic Defence', *Baltic Times*, 9 November 2015, http://www.baltictimes.com/u_s__army_commander_warns_of_russian_blocking_of_baltic_defence/; and Paul McLeary, 'Meet the New Fulda Gap', *Foreign Policy*, 29 September 2015, http://foreignpolicy.com/2015/09/29/fulda-gap-nato-russia-putin-us-army/.

53 D. Richardson, 'Russia Plans a 200 km-range MRL', *Jane's Missiles & Rockets*, vol. 17, no. 1, 2013.

54 Expert Commission on Norwegian Security and Defence Policy, *Unified Effort* (Oslo: Norwegian Ministry of Defence, 2015), pp. 16–24.

55 See, for example, Norwegian Armed Forces, 'Cold Response', 13 June 2015, https://forsvaret.no/en/exercise-and-operations/exercises/cold-response.

56 Ronald Asmus et al., 'NATO, New Allies and Reassurance', policy brief (London: Centre for European Reform, 2010).

57 For a comparable situation, one must go back to Britain and France's failed Gallipoli campaign of 1915, which sought to force the opening of the Dardanelles so the Allies could support Russia against Germany.

58 This does not mean that Russian anti-air and surface-to-surface missiles elsewhere, in its bastions or other parts of Russia and Belarus, could not also threaten NATO forces operating close to Russia's borders. They would not, however, be positioned to block NATO from reinforcing the whole territory of one of its members.

59 IISS, *The Military Balance 2015*, 'The 2015 Military Balance Chart: Russia's Armed Forces' (Abingdon: Routledge for the IISS, 2015).

60 Jacek Bartosiak and Tomasz Szatkowski, 'Geography of the Baltic Sea: Military Perspective', Recommendation Report (Warsaw: NCSS, 2013).

61 We are grateful to an anonymous reviewer for pointing out this possibility.

62 See Siarhei Bohdan, *Belarusian Army: Its Capacities and Role in the Region*, Analytical Paper no. 4, Ostrogorski Centre, London, 2014.

63 Douglas Ernst, 'Putin Says He Could Have Troops Inside Poland "In Two Days": Report', *Washington Times*, 18 September 2014, http://www.washingtontimes.com/news/2014/sep/18/putin-says-he-could-have-troops-inside-poland-in-t/.

64 See, for example, Elbridge Colby and Jonathan Solomon, 'Facing Russia: Conventional Defence and Deterrence in Europe', *Survival*, vol. 57, no. 6, December 2015–January 2016, pp. 21–50.

65 In this context, it would also be useful for NATO and Poland to review the location of the new NATO

Force Integration Unit in Bydgoszcz, which is close to the NATO Joint Forces Training Centre but not to Headquarters Multinational Corps Northeast, nor to the Polish national command in Warsaw. Interviews with senior Polish officers, Bydgoszcz, November 2015.

Can Poland Defend Itself?

Tomasz Paszewski

Because of its steady insistence on the importance of NATO's Article 5 and the credibility of security guarantees, Poland has long been perceived by its Western partners as a country whose focus on collective defence amounts to something of an obsession. One could argue that that obsession has now been vindicated by the Russian threat. Poland finds itself in the spotlight, and is expected to play a pivotal role on NATO's threatened northeastern periphery.

Yet Poland's strong stance at NATO headquarters in favour of collective defence has never been matched at home by consistent, long-term efforts at the development of strong territorial defence. Notwithstanding some progress in organisational transformation and technical modernisation, and valuable field experience gained during operations in Iraq and Afghanistan, the Polish Armed Forces (PAF) are currently ill-prepared to wage a conventional war against a powerful and technologically advanced adversary. Paradoxically, even though Poland is one of very few NATO members exposed to the threat of a classic air–land invasion, the PAF's air-defence systems and armoured forces are among the most neglected and technically obsolete of Poland's capabilities. Given Russia's growing regional military power, and Poland's position as the only NATO member contiguous to the exposed Baltic states, this is a disturbing state of affairs.

Tomasz Paszewski is a Research Fellow at the Institute of Political Studies, Polish Academy of Sciences.

Survival | vol. 58 no. 2 | April–May 2016 | pp. 117–134 DOI 10.1080/00396338.2016.1161907

The Russian challenge

Even after Russian aggression against Ukraine began, most Western observers tended to exclude the possibility of open aggression against a NATO member, or even a member of the EU. Over the last year, this mood has significantly changed. Today the potential military threat to North–Central Europe is taken seriously by NATO, the United States and a number of other NATO members. The military nature of this threat comprises three dimensions, all of which have been the subject of intensive discussion: the so-called 'hybrid' or 'ambiguous' warfare of the kind employed in Crimea and eastern Ukraine; the decisive use of superior conventional forces (as was used in Donbas and before that in Georgia); and nuclear brinkmanship, made credible by Russia's vast and diverse arsenal of tactical nuclear weapons.

More important than the modes of warfare, however, are the possible scenarios in which Russia might employ them. Here it is possible to distinguish two essentially different types of aggression that correspond to different political objectives. The first is an ambiguous, low-intensity operation, employing hybrid, largely non-military tactics and deliberately kept under the threshold of war to avoid triggering NATO's collective-defence mechanism. The other is a sudden and decisive strike on another country or countries. Conceivable variants include action aimed at seizing a territory populated predominantly by ethnic Russians; occupation of a swathe of NATO territory in order to use it as a bargaining chip in confrontation with the West;[1] and a lightning invasion of Norway to seize oil and gas fields, which would have a good chance of causing an increase in oil prices similar to that which occurred after Iraq's invasion of Kuwait. Western thinking about the Russian challenge has focused excessively on the first scenario and wrongly dismissed the possibility of the second.[2]

It has been all too readily assumed that hybrid warfare is a new and preferred tool of Russian expansionism in its backyard, and that Moscow would again be prepared to launch such a low-intensity, ambiguous attack in order to undermine one of its neighbours, setting the scene for yet another protracted conflict. Even in the much-discussed case of the Baltic states, this threat is probably much exaggerated. While large Russian minorities make the Baltic states likely targets, these countries are nonetheless far more stable, viable and well governed than Ukraine, and could not be so easily undermined from within.[3] If the so-called 'little green men' were ever to appear in a Baltic state, they would most likely be propped up by a large conventional force, which in fact would constitute the main threat.

The importance of ambiguity and deniability, as well as the role of Russia's intensive information campaign, has generally been exaggerated. These factors should not be discounted, but in the event of Russian armed aggression, the main problem will not be establishing facts on the ground, but rather the availability of adequate military assets and the political readiness to use them. It is entirely imaginable that in the event of Russian aggression some European countries would be ready to go to great lengths to pretend that the peace between NATO and Russia had not essentially been violated, and hybrid-warfare techniques could make such a position easier to adopt. But this would be less a matter of military innovation than of the Alliance's political coherence. And ultimately, as the strategist Colin Gray has aptly put it, 'war is about the peace that follows'.[4] Even if it is started largely for domestic motives, war has geopolitical ends. Military harassment combined with information, cyber and economic warfare might inflict some damage, but alone it would not bring any important political gains for Moscow.

In order to change facts on the ground and establish a new political reality, more direct employment of force would be needed. In such a scenario Russia could still prevent a military response from NATO in accordance with Article 5 by replacing ambiguity with rapidity. Given Russia's conventional advantage over all its European neighbours, the actual hostilities might well cease by the time NATO leaders were able to come to any decisions. According to General Sir Adrian Bradshaw, Deputy Supreme Allied Commander Europe, there is a danger that Russia could use a large-scale conventional force, which it could generate at very short notice, 'not only for intimidation or coercion but to seize NATO territory and then use the threat of escalation to prevent reestablishment of territorial integrity'.[5] The odds that NATO allies would be willing to initiate hostilities in order to recapture lost territory seem low, especially given Moscow's thinly veiled threat of resorting to nuclear warfare.[6]

Such a scenario is a realistic prospect, and should be taken seriously by policymakers and defence planners. From 2009 onwards, Russia has conducted a number of snap, or very lately announced, large exercises that included mock attacks on northeastern members of NATO and on Finland.[7] While assessments of Russian military modernisation vary, there is little doubt that Russia possesses meaningful conventional offensive capabilities which, despite its ailing economy, might even grow in the coming years.[8] In fact, Russia's conventional-arms modernisation programme is largely focused on the development of well-equipped, combat-ready and easily deployable forces that could be used for short but intensive interventions on Russia's periphery.[9] Another important priority is the development of anti-access/area-denial (A2/AD) capabilities, intended to prevent Western powers from intervening in Russia's local conflicts. Some of these capabilities have already been deployed to the Baltic region.[10]

All these considerations indicate that a traditional conventional aggression is by far the most important threat, in terms of both likelihood and consequences, that Russia can pose to NATO. And this threat would involve not just NATO's northeastern flank, but the Alliance as a whole. A failure to defend or regain the territory of a NATO member would be a devastating blow to the Alliance.[11]

Poland's role

The best way for NATO to address this threat, as a number of experts have already argued, is a preclusive forward presence that would be aimed at deterring potential Russian aggression. If deterrence failed, it would engage enemy forces as early as possible, in order to prevent them from taking effective control of a part of NATO territory.[12] The question is: where in the east should forces be deployed?

The prospects for more robust and enduring western military presence in northeastern Europe, especially in the form of permanent bases, remain slim, because of still-limited resources,[13] proliferating threats in the Middle East and North Africa, internal NATO disagreement, including NATO's 1997 pledge not to permanently quarter large forces on the new members' territory, and, in the case of the United States, China's growing challenge in

Asia. The 2014 NATO Wales Summit decisions will improve NATO's rapid-response capability, but they lack any strictly forward-presence elements.[14] Planned deployment of US forces and armoured equipment will partly fill the gap, but given the relatively small numbers of troops and hardware, these steps are hardly sufficient to affect the balance of power in the east. The bulk of the defence of the frontier states is most likely to fall mainly on their own shoulders.

In this context, Poland, given its geographic location, population, economy and Atlanticist strategic culture, is seemingly well placed to be a NATO stronghold on its eastern flank, or, more precisely, on the boundary between the Gulf of Finland and the Carpathian Mountains. Unfortunately, at least for now, it is ill-prepared to play this role.

Over the last quarter-century, Poland has been both unwilling and unable to build a credible, autonomous deterrence posture that could also serve as the country's contribution to NATO's collective-defence system. This is, of course, hardly a unique situation in Europe. If the Polish experience is by some measure surprising and peculiar, it is because of Poland's bloody history and vulnerable location, and the fact that it is a large enough country to think seriously about its own defence.

A flawed premise

Since the collapse of communism, an enduring axiom of Polish defence policy, albeit one rarely expressed explicitly, has been a deeply rooted conviction that Poland would never be able to repel large-scale military aggression on its own, at least with its regular armed forces.[15] This assumption has not been based on an in-depth assessment of the regional balance of power and its possible evolution, but stems from vivid memories of Poland's turbulent history in the twentieth century. Given Poland's exposed location, it might seem to make sense. In fact, as a key premise of defence policy, it has been deeply detrimental, effectively precluding some options well within the range of possibility.[16]

This mistaken premise has contributed to the failure of Poland's armed forces either to adopt a long-term territorial-defence strategy or specify its most important defensive capabilities. For some 20 years, the attachment to territorial defence manifested itself mostly in the insistence on the viability of Article 5 guarantees in NATO corridors, some resistance to downsizing the armed forces (and abandoning conscription), and the recurring idea of popular resistance. A former Polish deputy defence minister even went so far as to state that in the 1990s Poland did not have an independent defence policy.[17] More specifically, as one observer aptly pointed out, 'the greatest failing is the lack of clear thinking about the role Poland is to play within NATO and the military's new equipment needs and the future of the country's defence industry'.[18] And this problem especially affected territorial defence. In contrast to many other middle powers, such as Israel, Turkey, South Korea, South Africa and Sweden, until recently Poland had not made any steady efforts to determine the country's most critical military needs, nor to try to meet these needs in cooperation with the national defence industry.

For Polish leaders, full integration with the West and forging close security ties with the US have been seen over the last quarter-century as far more important to Poland's security than investing in the country's own national capabilities. This reliance on the transatlantic security umbrella was at times so overwhelming that it put Poland's own defensive preparations on the back burner. Moreover, as a sense of security arose over time, a large number of Polish leaders seemed to agree with their Western counterparts that the era of hard security threats in Europe was over, and as a consequence they de-emphasised the question of territorial defence, in both the national and the transatlantic framework.

According to Poland's first post-Cold War strategic documents on national security, adopted in November 1992, in case of a large-scale invasion, the country was to resist the enemy by all available means (including guerrilla warfare) for as long as possible, while simultaneously seeking international assistance.[19] At that time this kind of threat was thankfully absent; Polish defence policy focused instead on internal challenges, including managing a radical downsizing of the armed forces, putting the army under civilian oversight and reallocating some military units from the west to the east of the country.

After joining NATO in 1999, Allied assistance was taken virtually for granted, and Polish leaders had even less reason to plan for a defensive war against a powerful aggressor. The May 2000 defence strategy stated that the probability of a large-scale war was small, and that the biggest military threat that Polish armed forces would conceivably have to tackle by themselves would be a 'surprise military aggression', which by definition would be 'limited in scope, time and space'.[20] In the event of a larger conflict, the Polish armed forces would operate from the very beginning as part of a NATO multinational contingent, together with Allied forces that would be deployed in advance on Polish soil. The document completely disregarded any scenarios in which NATO would not come to Poland's aid with full military support in a contingency. This way of thinking was increasingly reflected in the government's approach to the development and composition of Poland's armed forces. The clearest and most striking demonstration of this attitude is to be found in 'Vision of the Armed Forces of the Republic of Poland – 2030', released by the Ministry of Defence in May 2008.[21] The question of defending national territory, and of the preparedness of the armed forces to do so, was completely ignored. Instead, according to the Vision, the PAF's principal mission would be participation in international operations, even thousands of kilometres from Poland or Europe.[22]

Kaczynski strongly disagreed

The gradual shift from territorial defence towards expeditionary capability did not take place without resistance. It was excoriated not only by large numbers of senior military commanders but also by the late president Lech Kaczynski, who strongly disagreed with the decision to abolish the draft and reduce the PAF's numerical strength to 100,000 active-duty soldiers, arguing simply that Poland needed a bigger army to defend itself.[23] The government's policy was also contested by the advocates of popular resistance. According to this vision, voiced repeatedly since at least the mid-1990s, the Polish armed forces should consist of two components: professional, well-equipped and highly manoeuvrable regular forces, capable of conducting a wide spectrum of operations at home and abroad; and a territorial army based on a country-wide network of local defence units that would be dormant during peacetime but could be made operational quickly in the event of a looming external invasion or natural disaster.[24] This territorial-army model clearly draws on the experiences of the Home Army, the Polish resistance movement during the Second World War, which was one of the largest and most effective in Nazi-occupied Europe. The concept of a two-component army gained a certain degree of support both in the military, where for many years it was under development by the General Staff, and amongst the public, where it was endorsed by such distinguished figures as the Polish-American former US national security advisor Zbigniew Brzezinski, and the late Jan Nowak-Jezioranski, legendary war hero and long-time director of the Polish section of Radio Free Europe.[25]

While membership in NATO has been undeniably beneficial for the PAF, the Alliance's goals, requirements and less formally stated political expectations have tended to prioritise expeditionary capabilities, and thus led to a preference for smaller, lighter and more deployable forces. In Poland's early years as a member, the country's strong attachment to territorial defence was perceived by NATO and specifically by some of the most important allies as misplaced, and even caused some irritation.[26] Politically, Poland was hardly in a position to ignore these concerns. Moreover, at the beginning of the twenty-first century, only around 10% of Poland's defence budget was allocated to equipment, so it was extremely hard to reconcile Polish decision-makers' preference for territorial defence with NATO requirements for capability development.[27] The four major procurement programmes launched in the 2000s – F16 fighters, *Rosomak* wheeled armoured vehicles, CASA M-295 utility aircraft and *Spike* anti-tank guided missiles (ATGMs) – clearly demonstrate the necessity of striking a balance between territorial defence on the one hand, and capabilities dedicated mostly to overseas operations on the other.

Development of the PAF was also significantly affected, for the most part positively, by involvement in the US- and NATO-led operations in Iraq and Afghanistan, in which Poland punched far above its weight, deploying some 30,000 troops in total.[28] Military engagement in Iraq and Afghanistan brought valuable field experience and strengthened Poland's credentials as a committed ally, but also sapped resources that could have been spent on new equipment instead. Here, external expectations and political pressure did not play a major role. Heavy involvement in these operations had many motivations, but probably the most important was a widely held belief that in order to ensure its own security, Poland has to be ready to show commitment to the viability of NATO and that it should foster close security and military ties with the United States. Polish support for the US operation in Iraq, as Marcin Zaborowski put it, appeared to be 'aimed at developing a sense of obligation and responsibility for Poland's security in America'.[29]

Lastly, as has been the case almost everywhere in Europe, the pace of technological modernisation of the PAF has been hampered by financial constraints. After recovering from deep recession at the beginning of the 1990s, by the end of the decade Poland's public finances were again in a deplorable condition. Even though Poland navigated the 2008 economic crisis relatively well, the government was forced temporarily to reduce defence spending. Periods of remarkably high economic growth in the mid-1990s and 2000s were too short to support sustainable financing for ambitious long-term military-modernisation programmes. Nevertheless, thanks largely to a 2001 legal commitment ensuring that at least 1.95% of GDP (raised to 2% in 2015) would be spent on defence, and also to savings obtained through continuous downsizing of the armed forces, starting from the early 2000s, Poland has been able gradually to increase the procurement share of the defence budget and to purchase certain new platforms, weapons, communications systems and other equipment.[30]

The Komorowski doctrine

Since 2012, Poland's defence policy has been undergoing a remarkable change. Under defence minister Tomasz Siemoniak, the Polish Armed Forces have shifted their focus from international operations to improving territorial-defence capabilities against traditional military threats. This change of direction was strongly promoted by former president Bronislaw Komorowski, who in accordance with the constitution also served as the supreme commander of the armed forces, thus lending it the name 'the Komorowski Doctrine'. When it came to specifics, however, there were some remarkable differences between the government and the president's office.

The approach championed by the presidential National Security Bureau (NSB) was extensively elaborated in the April 2013 *White Book on National*

Security,[31] containing unclassified conclusions of the National Strategic Security Review, and it also visibly influenced the new November 2014 National Security Strategy.[32] The concept is based on a key assumption that a large-scale aggression is highly unlikely, and if it were to take place, Poland could rely on NATO assistance, as had been widely assumed until then.[33] Thus, the Polish Armed Forces should be ready to counter surprise military threats, such as 'military pressure, air and missile strikes, special operations, border incidents or subversive incursions', that would be 'limited in scope and not intended to seize territory', and might be classed below the level of a NATO Article 5 contingency.[34] To address this type of threat, the technical modernisation of the Polish armed forces should focus on three priorities: air and missile defence, communication and command systems, and tactical mobility of ground forces, ensured mainly through deployment of helicopters.[35]

The Ministry of Defence assumed a somewhat different approach, based on different strategic assessment. As deputy defence minister Robert Kupiecki argued, NATO and Poland should avoid being seduced into seeing 'hybrid warfare' as the only possible type of military threat in Europe.[36] In his view, 'much worse scenarios' cannot be excluded. While a multilayered air-defence system and utility helicopters occupied a central place in the government's ambitious ten-year technical-modernisation programme (2013–22),[37] with planned expenditure amounting to almost 140 billion zloty (at that time over $43bn),[38] the programme also put strong emphasis on traditional conventional platforms and weapons, including self-propelled howitzers, automatic mortars, wheeled armoured vehicles, land-based anti-ship missiles (ASMs), anti-tank guided missiles, new tracked infantry fighting vehicles, advanced individual soldier gear, reconnaissance and armed drones, and new small warships dedicated mostly to coastal defence.[39] The subsequent changes made after the outbreak of war in Ukraine strengthened this high-intensity warfare profile. The government purchased an additional 114 *Leopard* 2 tanks from the German Bundeswehr (of which 105 were the A5 variant) and acquired 40 US joint air-to-surface stand-off missiles for Polish F-16s.[40] It also decided to bring forward the procurement of a new multiple-launch rocket system (MLRS), capable of launching tactical ballistic missiles with a range of 300km, and attack helicopters, and announced plans to arm new submarines with long-range cruise missiles.[41]

By the end of 2015, however, after three years of implementation of the government's procurement programme, few contracts had been signed and the vast majority of specific programmes, including the most important ones, were proceeding at a much slower pace than planned, remaining mostly in their early stages.[42] It has become clear that the programme was not financially affordable in its original version. The costs of some major foreign systems, such as utility helicopters and missile defence, were remarkably underestimated; meanwhile, the zloty has depreciated against the dollar by around 25%. The final fate of the programme will be decided by the new government, which will most likely decide to change course.

The defence policy of the new Law and Justice government, which came to power after the October 2015 parliamentary elections, has not yet been fully elaborated. Decisions on equipment issues in particular are expected to be announced after the end of the current audit of procurement policy, which should be finished in early 2016. The statements of the new minister of defence and his deputy, however, suggest that the two biggest programmes launched by the previous government – the procurement of 50 Airbus H225M *Caracal* helicopters and eight batteries of the US *Patriot* missile and air-defence system – will be discontinued.[43] The new government intends to steadily increase defence spending to more than 2% of GDP, which scarcely seems possible in light of an already tight budgetary situation. Other plans include the relocation of some military bases to northeastern Poland, the preferential treatment of national defence industry in military acquisition policy, and a gradual increase of military manpower from 100,000 to 150,000.[44] Part of this increase is to be made up by the establishment of local defence as an integral part of the armed forces. The new leaders would also like to see NATO or US military bases on Polish soil.[45]

* * *

Poland's efforts to enhance its national-defence capabilities are a natural complement to the strengthening of NATO's defences. If the Alliance fails to ensure credible deterrence on its northeastern flank, it will live in the shadow of a Russian surprise attack that would not only destroy the Alliance's credibility but could also seriously undermine Europe's post-Cold War order. Leaving the region militarily vulnerable is an unacceptable, and unnecessary, gamble.

An ideal solution would be a two-track strategy: a short- to medium-term increase of Western military presence in the region, combined with significant enhancement of frontier countries' national-defence capabilities.

In the short term, there is no viable alternative to increased US and possibly Western European presence in the threatened region. The frontier countries are not able to deploy sufficient effective capabilities within the next two years. The cost of deployment of US assets, according to RAND's estimates, would not exceed a few hundred million dollars annually,[46] a sum that does not seem prohibitively high, especially if it would be partly covered by host countries. Given the threat of possible Russian nuclear blackmail, the Alliance could also consider redeployment to Europe of tactical nuclear weapons, which have been almost completely withdrawn over previous decades.[47] These steps would not only raise the bar for a possible Russian invasion in strictly military terms, but would also send a clear signal of NATO's determination. In the longer term, however, such heightened interest and military involvement of the US and major European powers in the region does not seem sustainable, given their other international security commitments and priorities, not to mention serious fiscal challenges at home. The main burden of defending NATO's northeastern periphery will inevitably fall on the shoulders of the countries of the region themselves.

Poland, with its relatively large demographic, economic and military potential, could play an important role in this effort. But this is contingent upon the country's ability to modernise at least selected elements of its armed forces. Realistically, most of its major equipment programmes will not be accomplished before the mid- to late 2020s, but some capabilities in the key areas of armour, anti-tank weapons, drones, artillery, advanced ammunition, C4ISR and, to some extent, air defence might be upgraded within a couple of years. Poland's defence preparedness can also be enhanced by improving the command system, and intensifying training and retraining of reserve forces.

A policy shaped simply by urgency, however, will be inadequate. In order for modernisation efforts to be effective, sustainable and tailored to Polish needs, they must be based on a long-term vision. Poland's leaders, in close cooperation with its defence industry, should work to develop one.

Acknowledgements

The research on which this article is based was funded by the Polish–Norwegian Research Programme, operated by the National Centre for Research and Development, under the Norwegian Financial Mechanism 2009–14 (project contract number Pol-Nor/202499/39/2013).

Notes

1 It is worth citing in full a long-time Russia observer, Dmitri K. Simes: 'The Russian government is denying that they have any interest in any aggression in Baltic states. But if you talk to Russian officials, some of them do believe that Russia is being encircled and threatened with domestic destabilization. And they say that the only way they can protect themselves is to demonstrate their strength and determination in the most dramatic way possible. Furthermore, while many in the Russian political establishment think that President Obama has been quite aggressive and insensitive to their legitimate concerns, they don't believe he would dare use nuclear force against Russia to protect Riga or Tallinn.' See interview with Dimitri K. Simes, 'The Perils of a New Cold War', Council on Foreign Relations, 21 October 2015, http://www.cfr.org/russian-federation/perils-new-cold-war/p37132. Graham Allison, assistant secretary of defence during the Clinton administration, thinks that 'Russia may believe that the use of threats and military force will produce the best outcomes in a serious confrontation with the West'. See John Allen Gay, 'Countdown to War: The Coming U.S.–Russia Conflict', *National Interest*, 22 April 2015, http://nationalinterest.org/feature/countdown-war-the-coming-us-russia-conflict-12698. See also Graham Allison and Dimitri K. Simes, 'Russia and America: Stumbling to War', *National Interest*, 20 April 2015, http://nationalinterest.org/feature/russia-america-stumbling-war-12662.

2 As Keir Giles aptly pointed out: 'If you focus on irregular elements and all aspects of hybrid warfare, as some people are now doing, then you neglect the high-end warfighting capability which is actually still a very important component of deal-

ing with Russia.' See Jon Harper, 'NATO Funding Shortfalls Likely to Continue', *National Defense*, September 2015, p. 26.

3 See Samuel Charap, 'The Ghost of Hybrid War', *Survival*, vol. 57, no. 6, December 2015–January 2016, pp. 51–8.

4 Colin S. Gray, *Transformation and Strategic Surprise* (Carlisle, PA: Strategic Studies Institute, April 2005), p. 15.

5 General Sir Adrian Bradshaw, speech to the Royal United Services Institute (RUSI), London, February 2015, https://rusi.org/multimedia/latest-security-challenges-facing-nato.

6 Matthew Kroenig, 'Facing Reality: Getting NATO Ready for a New Cold War', *Survival*, vol. 57, no. 1, February–March 2015, p. 61.

7 See Ian Brzezinski and Nicholas Varangis, 'The NATO–Russia Exercise Gap', Atlantic Council, 23 February 2015, http://www.atlanticcouncil.org/en/blogs/natosource/the-nato-russia-exercise-gap; Thomas Frear, Ian Kearns and Lukasz Kulesa, 'Preparing for the Worst: Are Russian and NATO Military Exercises Making War in Europe More Likely?', European Leadership Network Policy Brief, August 2015; and Damien Sharkov, 'Russian Snap Military Drill "Could Turn Into Assault on Baltic Capital"', *Newsweek*, 23 February 2015, http://www.newsweek.com/russian-snap-military-drill-could-turn-quick-assault-baltic-capital-308752.

8 See Adrian Croft, 'Russia Could Soon Run Multiple Ukraine-Sized Operations: U.S. General', Reuters, 16 January 2015; and Igor Sutyagin, 'Russian Forces in Ukraine', RUSI, March 2015, https://rusi.org/publication/briefing-papers/russian-forces-ukraine.

9 See Jakob Hedenskog and Carolina Vendil Pallin (eds), *Russian Military Capability in a Ten-Year Perspective – 2013*, Swedish Defence Research Agency, December 2013, http://www.foi.se/ReportFiles/foir_3734.pdf; Mikhail Barabanov (ed.), *Russia's New Army*, Center for Analysis of Strategies and Technologies, 2011, http://www.cast.ru/files/book/NewArmy_sm.pdf; and Rod Thorton, *Military Modernization and the Russian Ground Forces* (Carlisle, PA: Strategic Studies Institute, June 2011).

10 Marcus Weisgerber, 'Russia Could Block Access to Baltic Sea, US General Says', Defense One, 9 December 2015, http://www.defenseone.com/threats/2015/12/russia-could-block-access-baltic-sea-us-general-says/124361.

11 As Terrence Kelly of the RAND Corporation put it: 'If a Russian invasion of the Baltic states could not be deterred or defeated, the North Atlantic Council and the US president would be faced with a very unpleasant choice: conduct a costly counteroffensive and risk nuclear escalation, or abandon the Baltics to renewed subservience to Moscow. Such a catastrophic failure to uphold the mutual defence responsibilities of NATO could cripple or even destroy the North Atlantic alliance.' See Terrence Kelly, 'Stop Putin's Next Invasion Before It Starts', *US News and World Report*, 20 March 2015, http://www.rand.org/blog/2015/03/stop-putins-next-invasion-before-it-starts.

html. The same view is also expressed in Jonathan Eyal, 'Ukraine and Russia: The Thorny Questions That Will Not Go Away', RUSI, 27 February 2015, https://rusi.org/publication/newsbrief/ukraine-and-russia-thorny-questions-will-not-go-away.

12 See Elbridge Colby and Jonathan Solomon, 'Facing Russia: Conventional Defence and Deterrence in Europe', *Survival*, vol. 57, no. 6, December 2015–January 2016, pp. 21–50; and Jakub J. Grygiel and A. Wess Mitchell, 'A Preclusive Strategy to Defend the NATO Frontier', *American Interest*, 2 December 2014, http://www.the-american-interest.com/2014/12/02/a-preclusive-strategy-to-defend-the-nato-frontier/.

13 The Wales Summit pledge on defence spending will most likely not be honoured by many member states, including some of the most important. See Denitsa Raynova and Ian Kearns, 'The Wales Pledge Revisited: a Preliminary Analysis of 2015 Budget Decisions in NATO Member States', European Leadership Network, February 2015

14 Jeffrey A. Larsen, 'The Wales Summit and NATO Deterrence Capabilities', NATO Defence College, November 2014, pp. 3–5, http://www.ndc.nato.int/download/downloads.php?icode=427.

15 The problem of Polish scepticism concerning the country's ability to defend itself has been raised in Kerry Longhurst, 'Where From, Where To? New and Old Configurations in Poland's Foreign and Security Policy Priorities', *Communist and Post-Communist Studies*, no. 46, 2013, p. 364.

16 There is little reason to insist that it will always be beyond Poland's means to defend itself with regular armed forces against Russia, a country with approximately twice Poland's GDP but gloomy economic prospects.

17 Andrzej Karkoszka, 'Reflections on the Defence of Poland at the Threshold of the Twenty-First Century', in Roman Kuźniar (ed.), *Poland Security Policy, 1989–2000* (Warsaw: Scholar Publishing House, 2001), p. 529.

18 David H. Dunn, 'Poland: America's New Model Ally', in Marcin Zaborowski and David H. Dunn (eds), *Poland: A New Power in Transatlantic Security* (London: Frank Cass, 2003), p. 79.

19 See Council of Ministers, 'Założenia polskiej polityki bezpieczeństwa' [Polish Security Policy Guidelines], 2 November 1992; and 'Polityka bezpieczeństwa i strategia obronna Rzeczypospolitej Polskiej' [Security Policy and Defence Strategy of the Republic of Poland], 2 November 1992.

20 Ministry of National Defence, 'Defence Strategy of the Republic of Poland', 23 May 2000, p. 6.

21 Ministry of National Defence, 'Vision of the Armed Forces of the Republic of Poland – 2030', May 2008, http://en.mon.gov.pl/z/pliki/dokumenty/rozne/2014/02/vision_of_paf_2030.pdf.

22 *Ibid.*, pp. 14–15.

23 'Prezydent apeluje o umiar w odchudzaniu armii' [President Calls for Moderation in Cutting the Army], TVP INFO, 24 October 2008, http://www.tvp.info/345682/informacje/polska/prezydent-apeluje-o-umiar-w-odchudzaniu-armii/.

24 Many versions of this concept have been voiced and published over the last 20 years. One of the most elaborate studies was presented by two military experts from the National Defence University in Warsaw. See Ryszard Jakubczak and Józef Marczak, *Obrona terytorialna – nowy element system obronnego RP* [Territorial Defence – A New Component of Poland's Defence System], Biuro Prasy i Informacji Mionisterstwa Obrony Narodowej, Warsaw, 1996.

25 Jan Nowak-Jeziorański, 'Sojusze to nie wszystko' [Alliances Are Not Enough], *Gazeta Wyborcza*, 30 August 2002; Zbigniew Brzeziński, 'Myśli o obronności Polski' [Thougths on Defending Poland], in Zbigniew Brzeziński, *O Polsce, Europie i świecie, 1988–2001* [On Poland, Europe, and the World, 1988–2001] (Warsaw: Bellona, 2002), p. 466.

26 See Kerry Longhurst, 'From Security Consumer to Security Provider – Poland and Transatlantic Security in the Twenty-First Century', *Defence Studies*, vol. 2, no. 2, 2002, pp. 57–9; Dunn, *Poland: America's new model ally*, pp. 72 and 82; Vanda Knowles, 'Security and Defence in the New Europe: Franco–Polish Relations - Victim of Neglect?', *Defence Studies*, vol. 2, no. 2, 2002, pp. 92 and 100; Silke Pottebohm, 'Poland and Britain, the Future of an Atlanticist Partnership in Europe', in Zaborowski and Dunn (eds), *Poland: A New Power in Transatlantic Security*, pp. 137 and 141.

27 Janusz Onyszkiwicz, 'Polskie wojsko i potrzeby paktu' [The Polish Military and NATO's Needs], *Rzeczpospolita*, 14 February 2002.

28 Tomasz Szatkowski, 'Polish Defence Modernization in the Era of U.S. Strategic Rebalancing', Center for European Policy Analyses, 1 March 2013, http://www.cepa.org/content/polish-defense-modernization-era-us-strategic-rebalancing.

29 Marcin Zaborowski, 'From America's Protegé to Constructive European: Polish Security Policy in the Twenty-First Century', European Union Institute for Security Studies Occasional Paper, no. 56, December 2004, p. 12, http://www.iss.europa.eu/uploads/media/occ56.pdf.

30 Andrew Michta, 'Polish Hard Power: Investing in the Military as Europe Cuts Back', American Enterprise Institute, December 2013, p. 2, https://www.aei.org/wp-content/uploads/2013/12/-polish-hard-power-investing-in-the-military-as-europe-cuts-back_170557821177.pdf.

31 National Security Bureau, 'White Book on National Security of the Republic of Poland', 2013, http://en.mon.gov.pl/z/pliki/dokumenty/rozne/2014/02/White Book_NationalSecurity_PL_2013.pdf.

32 National Security Bureau, 'National Security Strategy of the Republic of Poland', 5 November 2014, pp. 29–32, 45–6, http://www.bbn.gov.pl/ftp/dok/NSS_RP.pdf.

33 Interview with Staniław Koziej, the chief of National Security Bureau, *Rzeczpospolita*, 23 May 2013.

34 National Security Bureau, 'White Book', pp. 128, 167.

35 *Ibid.*, p. 205.

36 Robert Kupiecki, 'NATO w czasach triumfalizmu Kremla' [NATO at the Time of the Kremlin's Triumphalism], *Rzeczpospolita*, 6 October 2014.

37 Ministry of National Defence, 'Plan modernizacji technicznej Sił Zbrojnych Rzeczpospolitej Polskiej w latach 2013–2022' [Plan of Technical Modernisation of the Armed Forces of the Republic of Poland, 2013–2022], Warsaw, 12 December 2012, pp. 1–5.

38 Michta, 'Polish Hard Power', p. 2.

39 *Ibid.*

40 'Stan realizacji Planu Modernizacji Technicznej' [Technical Modernisation Plan Update], *Dziennik Zbrojny*, 18 December 2015, http://dziennikzbrojny.pl/artykuly/art,2,4,9380, armie-swiata,wojsko-polskie,stan-realizacji-planu-modernizacji-technicznej-systematyczna-aktualizacja.

41 *Ibid.*

42 *Ibid.*

43 Maciej Milosz, 'Nowa armia PiS' [New PIS Army], *Dziennik Zbjojny*, 28 September 2015, http://wiadomosci.dziennik.pl/polityka/artykuly/501539,na-zakup-caracali-na-pewno-sie-nie-zgodzimy-to-szkodliwa-transakcja.html.

44 'Polska zwiększy liczebność armii do 150 tysięcy?' [Poland to Increase Armed Forces to 150,000?], Defence24.pl, 20 November 2015, http://www.defence24.pl/273739,polska-zwiekszy-liczebnosc-armii-do-150-tysiecy.

45 Henry Foy, 'NATO Treats Poland Like a Buffer State, Says New President', *Financial Times*, 13 August 2015, http://www.ft.com/cms/s/0/d6749156-410e-11e5-b98b-87c7270955cf.html.

46 See Kelly, 'Stop Putin's Next Invasion Before It Starts'; and Olga Oliker, Michael J. McNerney and Lynn E. Davis, 'NATO Needs a Comprehensive Strategy for Russia', RAND, 2015, p. 8, http://www.rand.org/content/dam/rand/pubs/perspectives/PE100/PE143/RAND_PE143.pdf.

47 See Kroenig, 'Facing Reality'; and the responses in Steven Pifer, Lukasz Kulesa, Egon Bahr, Götz Neuneck, Mikhail Troitskiy and Matthew Kroenig, 'Forum: NATO and Russia', *Survival*, vol. 57, no. 2, April–May 2015, pp. 119–44.

The Three Faces of German Leadership

Matthias Matthijs

For Angela Merkel, 2015 was a year full of anniversaries. Europe's longest-serving incumbent head of government celebrated a decade in power as Germany's chancellor, and 15 years at the helm of her party, the Christian Democratic Union (CDU). Together with her fellow Germans, she also celebrated the quarter-century commemoration of her country's peaceful reunification of East and West. And as Europe's most influential leader, she observed how the Old Continent marked the 70th anniversary of Germany's defeat on Victory in Europe (VE) Day, 8 May 1945, and remembered the end of the Second World War.

On the one hand, the festivities were a welcome reminder of how far both Germany and Europe as a whole have come. They underscored the truly transformative effects of the process of European integration. From that point of view, Merkel was the justly admired leader of a newly confident Germany, at the heart of a Europe reborn – whole, free and at peace. Through her emblematic 'politics of small steps', Merkel had deftly managed to steer the Continent through stormy waters.

On the other hand, the celebrations masked a darker reality: of a Europe adrift and unable to come to grips with a deep, triple crisis involving shaky eurozone debt, Russian aggression in the east and a sudden surge in migrants and refugees. Seen from this angle, Merkel's reputation for caution, and her preference to delay and obfuscate so as to avoid big decisions, epitomised

Matthias Matthijs is Assistant Professor of International Political Economy at Johns Hopkins University's School of Advanced International Studies (SAIS) in Washington DC. This essay was shortlisted for the 2015 Palliser Prize.

Survival | vol. 58 no. 2 | April–May 2016 | pp. 135–154 DOI 10.1080/00396338.2016.1161908

Germany as a reluctant leader, and thus as a central part of Europe's problems, rather than their solution.

How the European Union eventually makes it through its threefold crisis, and whether it is able to emerge stronger and more united, will largely depend on how Berlin uses its new-found power. Europe's future ultimately depends on whether Germany's destiny to lead will be met by its desire to do so.

Europe's indispensable nation

Since 2010, the calls for German leadership in Europe have been insistent. The most striking appeal came from Radoslaw Sikorski in a November 2011 speech in Berlin:

> I will probably be the first Polish foreign minister in history to say this, but here it is. I fear German power less than I am beginning to fear its inactivity. You have become Europe's indispensable nation. You may not fail to lead.[1]

Especially during the most intense moments of the euro crisis – in spring 2010, autumn 2011, spring 2012 and summer 2015 – there was no shortage of prominent policymakers calling on Germany to 'do something'. These included the president of the United States, the president of the European Central Bank (ECB), the Italian prime minister, the US treasury secretary, the Greek finance minister and the European commissioner for financial affairs.[2] Even rock band U2's lead singer, Bono, in November 2014 wanted 'the German people to lead us in demolishing ... the scourge of extreme poverty and preventable disease'.[3]

Why this sudden gusto for German leadership? After all, it was not too long ago that many observers of the European Union dismissed Germany as the sick man of Europe.[4] In the early 2000s, more than a few graduate students were writing thoughtful dissertations on the question of what it was about Germany that made it patently incapable of reforming its economy. What were the institutional constraints that prevented it from growing faster, and why was its rate of unemployment chronically stuck above 10%?

By 2005, after Merkel had taken over at the chancellery from Social Democrat Gerhard Schröder, Germany's economy started to outperform both that of the United States and the eurozone in terms of industrial production. Merkel had arrived just in time to pick the economic fruits of the long adjustment process of German reunification, as well as of the structural reforms initiated by the 2002 Hartz Commission, whose deep unpopularity had cost Schröder his re-election. Germany's export-driven economy thrived during the international economic boom of 2003–07. Its GDP also saw a robust recovery in 2010 and 2011 after the Great Recession of 2008–09, largely fuelled by exports to emerging markets. In less than a decade, Germany had transformed itself from sick man of Europe to economic miracle and export *Weltmeister*.

In autumn 2009, Merkel's CDU received a ringing endorsement from the German electorate. The chancellor was able to ditch her centre-left coalition partners from the Social Democratic Party (SPD) and switch to her preferred centre-right Free Democratic Liberals (FDP). This made Merkel the first Western leader to be re-elected after the global financial crisis. It was therefore no surprise that Europe looked to Germany when it became apparent, in spring 2010, that a Greek fiscal calamity threatened the overall integrity of the eurozone. Not only was Germany the eurozone's largest economy, with close to 28% of its overall GDP, it was also Europe's main creditor nation, and had often played the role of European paymaster in previous crises.[5]

The other large countries in the European Union, furthermore, were relatively weak. France, Germany's traditional ally and reliable co-engine of European integration, suffered from persistently high unemployment and chronically low growth – under both Nicolas Sarkozy and François Hollande – and therefore found its diplomatic clout much reduced. The United Kingdom under David Cameron was in thrall to 'Brexit' – a potential exit from the EU – as a result of Cameron's foolish promise to his Conservative Party's eurosceptic wing to renegotiate the basic terms of British membership in the club. Italy and Spain soon found themselves swept up in the contagion that ensued from the fears of a potential Greek default, and were quickly relegated to the peripheral-debtor camp by the international bond markets. Both Rome and Madrid came to rely heavily on Berlin for financial support to prop up the ailing eurozone. And Poland, despite being one of the fastest-growing EU economies, could not play a leading role as long as it remained out of the eurozone.

By 2010, a combination of German strength and the weakness of others had put Germany, almost by default, into the driver's seat in Europe. By late 2014, the rest of the world looked to Germany as an example to follow, and aspired towards its own version of a German success story. Its appealing multi-ethnic football team had just won the World Cup in Brazil in style, and Germany would also top the Anholt-GfK Roper Nation Brands Index for the first time, beating the United States, the United Kingdom and France to the title of the world's best-regarded country.[6] Berlin had become a favourite destination for Europe's young, either in search of work or attracted by its cultural scene. Henry Kissinger's rhetorical question – 'Who do I call when I want to call Europe?' – finally had an answer: Angela Merkel, in Berlin. (The United States' National Security Agency, of course, had long since understood this, having tapped the phones of Merkel and her senior ministers.[7])

Given the steady beat of success in all things economic, political and even cultural, Germany's sudden rise happened before most observers had even noticed it, and thereby held the tint of inevitability. But Germany's peculiar and twisted history pointed in a very different direction.

The German question

For students of nineteenth- and twentieth-century German history, the loud calls from the rest of Europe and the world for *more* German leadership must have seemed rather outlandish. After all, it was not so long ago that German historians debated whether Germany could ever be considered a 'normal' country, and thereby ever take on a mantle of regional or global leadership.[8] The *Historikerstreit*, or historians' dispute, of the late 1980s pitted left- and right-wing intellectuals against each other in a fierce debate about Germany's past. The former argued that Germany had followed a *Sonderweg* (or 'unique path') in Western Europe, as the country had singularly failed to embrace a liberal-democratic system, which they held to be the natural complement of capitalist industrial development in the late nineteenth century. The latter argued that Germany's atrocities, as wicked as they were, were not as exceptional as their opponents made them out to be.[9]

For left-wing intellectuals such as Jürgen Habermas, the Nazi crimes of the 1930s and 1940s were uniquely evil, and comparing the Holocaust to other crimes against humanity equated to a malicious attempt to whitewash Germany's past. On the right, the historian Ernst Nolte, who had triggered the great historians' dispute, advanced the thesis that the German people had turned to fascism and race murder in response to the existential threat and class murder of Soviet communism. He had no qualms about comparing Germany's atrocities under Hitler with those of Stalin's Soviet Union or Mao's China. Also on the right, prominent historian Michael Stürmer openly lamented the gaping void of an alternative 'positive' history, in which the German people could rightfully take pride.[10]

A solution to the 'German problem' – a large country at the very heart of Europe that was simply too strong and too dynamic for its neighbours to accommodate and contain – was, after all, a central tenet of Europe's post-war political system. A Germany split in two during the Cold War between capitalist West and communist East to a large extent assuaged its neighbours' fears of renewed dominance. François Mauriac, the French Nobel laureate in literature, once wrote that he loved Germany so much that he was glad there were two of them.[11] Hastings Ismay, NATO's first secretary-general, has been credited with the quip that the purpose of the transatlantic security alliance was 'to keep the Russians out, the Americans in, and the Germans down'.[12] For most of the Cold War, it seemed unlikely that Germany would ever be considered a 'normal' state, let alone a leader of Europe.

Peter Katzenstein, the Cornell University political scientist, captured this idea of West Germany as a 'semi-sovereign state' in 1987.[13] Katzenstein looked beyond Germany's international-security situation to examine the domestic structures that tamed power from within, acting as a check against too strong a central government. West Germany's strict proportional-representation electoral system all but guaranteed coalition governments in Bonn, while powerful independent institutions such as the Deutsche Bundesbank in Frankfurt and the Federal Constitutional Court in Karlsruhe significantly constrained executive power. Furthermore, a federal division of labour between a weak central government and powerful *Länder* (states), as well as a strong state bureaucracy, significantly limited the chancellor's policy discretion. This led British political scientists Simon Bulmer and William Paterson to describe West Germany as a 'semi-Gulliver' or a 'shackled, gentle giant'.[14]

In 1990, after the 'two plus four' talks that eventually resulted in German reunification, the United States was ready to offer Germany a 'partnership in leadership'.[15] But Helmut Kohl politely declined, and instead chose to forge a closer alliance with François Mitterrand's France, culminating in the signing of the Maastricht Treaty in 1992. While Germany during the 1990s was preoccupied with the economic consequences of reunification, and in the early 2000s with the painful Hartz reforms, it was more than happy to leave Europe's leadership in the hands of the French. The British enjoyed the heyday of their 'special relationship' with the Americans, especially during the run-up to the Iraq War of 2003, which was bitterly opposed by both Jacques Chirac's France and Schröder's Germany. This caused a significant transatlantic crisis, even a 'parting of ways' between Washington and Berlin, as Stephen Szabo put it at the time.[16]

By 2010, however, it was clear that Germany had emerged as the leader of Europe. Suddenly and distressingly, Angela Merkel found herself compared with Otto von Bismarck, and even Hitler, in the European media. Scholars were no longer describing Germany in 'semi-sovereign' terms, nor asking the question of whether it could ever be considered a normal state. Instead, they started referring to Germany as a 'geo-economic' power or a 'reluctant hegemon'.[17] Did this rejuvenation of German power imply the return of the German problem? *The Economist* in October 2010 responded in characteristic fashion: 'The German question never dies. Instead, like a flu virus, it mutates.'[18]

Three dimensions of German power

Power is a matter of getting someone to do what he or she would otherwise not do. Writing in the pluralist tradition of American democratic theory, the Yale political theorist Robert Dahl defined power from an interactive point of view, where one individual can modify the behaviour of another individual within a given decision-making process.[19] Power belongs to the person who prevails within that process. Dahl saw power largely in structural terms, broadly along the lines of the realist tradition in international relations, where states are the central actors in the international system, and a state's national interest is materially given. A country's power depends on factors such as its economy, trade relations, total land mass, natural resources, population and military prowess.[20]

Translated to the context of the European Union, Germany's structural power is substantial. But while it has grown considerably since 1990, it remains uneven. Germany's structural power is largely limited to the realm of trade and economics, where it enjoys the financial firepower and prestige of being Europe's largest economy, main export dynamo and chief creditor nation. It has enjoyed the trust of financial markets, and can borrow at permanently lower rates than its neighbours, giving it its own unique kind of 'exorbitant privilege'.[21] Ever since the creation of the European Economic Community in the 1950s, Germany has served as Europe's paymaster.

In the key fields of international security and diplomacy, however, Germany remains a second-rank power at best. It lacks a strong navy, army and air force of its own, and possesses few natural resources apart from coal and steel. When it comes to foreign policy, it more often than not yields to nations with much stronger militaries, such as France and Great Britain.

But power is complex and multidimensional. As the neo-Marxist social scientists Peter Bachrach and Morton Baratz have argued, power can also lie in the ability to shape the agenda or set the boundaries of a decision-making process: 'To the extent that a person or a group – consciously or unconsciously – creates or reinforces barriers to the public airing of policy conflicts, that person or group has power.'[22] Put differently, power can be institutional, giving one state significant decision-making powers within a regional group of states, either in the field of economics or foreign affairs. This dimension of power corresponds to the liberal-institutionalist tradition in international relations, in which international treaties are the outcome of the grand bargains struck by powerful states based on their material preferences and interests.[23]

Germany's institutional and agenda-setting power within the European Union comes from its significant voting powers within the European Parliament and European Council. Germany is by far the largest net contributor to the EU budget. It was pivotal in agreeing to the creation of an Economic and Monetary Union in the early 1990s, and therefore managed to set the terms of the euro's governance. The European Central Bank was set up as the mirror image of the German Bundesbank, and has its seat in Frankfurt, while a 'no bailout' clause and a Stability and Growth Pact largely reflected German preferences. Even in foreign and security policy, where decisions are taken unanimously, Germany's voice carries significant weight, given that it holds the purse strings. The size of its domestic economy also gives Germany significant leverage, especially when the EU wants to implement economic sanctions against third parties.

Beyond the structural and institutional dimensions, power can also lie in ideas. As the sociologist Steven Lukes has observed, a dominant actor can shape the preferences of other actors in such a way that they end up reinforcing its position of dominance: 'A may exercise power over B by getting him to do what he does not want to do, but he also exercises power over him by influencing, shaping or determining his very wants.'[24] This dimension of power matches the constructivist tradition in international relations, which gives causal explanatory power to ideas, and explains certain puzzling outcomes – like the design of international institutions – by looking into the ideas rather than the pure material interests of the most powerful actors.[25]

German ideas, both in the areas of economics and foreign policy, have been very influential in the process of European integration, shaping the nature and design of European institutions. Germany's strict adherence to ordoliberalism – emphasising competition, price stability, fiscal restraint and the importance of rules over discretion – has been central in drawing up a blueprint for economic and monetary union.[26] Given its economic dynamism, its ideas carry considerable weight with other eurozone members, manifested by the importance of fiscal austerity and structural reform in EU economic policymaking. The legacy of the Second World War and the Holocaust have turned Germany into a 'civilian' power,[27] a concept largely taken over by the EU's vision of soft-power projection in the world, emphasising universal values of peace, democracy, human rights and the rule of law. Ian Manners, politics professor at the University of Copenhagen, has argued that the European Union today could best be conceived of as a 'normative power'.[28]

Germany's power to act, however, faces significant constraints on all three dimensions. Germany's membership of NATO and of the European Union enables as well as limits its room for manoeuvre. To reverse the famous dictum of nineteenth-century British prime minister Lord Palmerston, it means that Germany has permanent friends (and values), rather than just permanent interests. Its military remains weak for largely self-imposed reasons, and Germany remains dangerously dependent on oil and natural gas from Russia. Germany's reliance on exports also makes it vulnerable to growth slowdowns abroad.

Furthermore, all of the West German domestic institutional checks and balances Peter Katzenstein pointed out in the 1980s have largely endured in today's reunified Germany. Federalism, coalition governments, strong *Länder* and a weak chancellery, as well as a powerful Bundesbank and constitutional court, all continue to limit the potential for German leadership and discretionary decision-making within Europe. And, finally, ordoliberalism as an economic philosophy can also serve to act as a significant constraint on Germany's imagination when it comes to finding comprehensive solutions to fix the design flaws of the eurozone.

Whether Germany will be able to shrug off or loosen some of these constraints will define its leadership potential in the future. Three contemporary crises highlight the dynamics behind Germany's leadership conundrum.

German leadership during Europe's triple crisis

The survival of the euro, the security threat of a revanchist Russia and a dramatic surge in migration from the Middle East and North Africa have dominated the political agenda in Brussels since 2010. All three challenges have required some form of collective action by the Union's now-28 member states. And in all three crises, Germany has used its new-found power and influence to take the lead and shape Europe's collective response. But all three crises underscored a different face of German leadership, as the three dimensions of its power – structural, institutional and ideational – played out in different ways depending on whether the issue area was mainly concerned with economic and financial affairs, foreign policy or domestic politics.

Euro crisis: enforcer-in-chief

While the euro crisis started as a Greek budgetary debacle in autumn 2009, it swiftly escalated into a full-scale sovereign-debt crisis in spring 2010, not least because of Germany's initial procrastination and inaction.[29] By insisting that the onus of the Greek crisis lay with a bankrupt political elite in Athens, whose profligacy had violated the EU's Stability and Growth Pact in the most egregious way, Germany's policy statements not only frightened the bond markets but also quickly reframed the euro crisis into a morality tale of southern fiscal sinners and northern budgetary saints. This made the crisis worse, and meant that large bailouts of the countries in trouble would become inevitable, and go hand in hand with strict conditionality mandating budgetary austerity, wage cuts and labour-market reforms to regain competitiveness.[30]

Rather than focusing on the systemic flaws of the euro's design, Berlin's crisis narrative was one of national redemption on the part of the eurozone's periphery, which could solve the crisis only through budgetary austerity and structural reform. Systemic solutions like a eurobond, common deposit insurance or an economic government to correct for the ECB's 'one size fits none' monetary policy were largely dismissed due to fears of moral hazard.[31] Both Chancellor Merkel and her finance minister, Wolfgang Schäuble, saw Germany's role as being the main underwriter of the fiscal rules that were agreed at Maastricht, and making sure those rules would be strictly enforced in the future. That, it was argued, would guarantee the viability and the strength of the euro in the long term.

Interestingly, in a speech in Paris in November 2010, Schäuble invoked the teachings of Charles Kindleberger on the importance of leadership in times of crisis to apply to both Germany and France.[32] However, his interpretation of Kindleberger's theory of public-goods provision during crises was the exact opposite of what the MIT economist had originally intended.

For Kindleberger, the Great Depression had been so severe because of the failure of Britain and the reluctance of the US to play the role of hegemon, by declining to serve as a market for 'distress goods', act as a lender of last resort or provide counter-cyclical lending.[33] The United States seemed to have learnt from its past mistakes eight decades later, during the 2008 financial crisis, when it did exactly that, providing global public goods by acting as consumer, investor and lender of last resort.

Germany during the euro crisis, however, rejected calls to play the role of regional hegemon. Instead, Berlin continued to act as though Germany was a small, open economy with an export-led growth model. It refused to inflate its own economy, while insisting that the countries of the periphery deflate theirs. It dramatically reversed its private lending during the downturn, and refused for a long time to let the ECB operate as a real lender of last resort.[34] It was only when the more pragmatic and less 'German' Mario Draghi took over from the very 'German' Jean-Claude Trichet in November 2011 that market panic gradually started to ease, and the crisis slowly started to fade. Draghi chose to interpret the ECB's institutional mandate in a much more flexible manner, contrary to the German view, and managed to restore confidence in the markets by promising to do 'whatever it takes' within the ECB's mandate to safeguard the euro.[35]

In the euro crisis, Germany acted as the enforcer-in-chief of European rules. Berlin combined its significant structural power as a major creditor nation and the Continent's biggest economy, as well as its institutional power in the European Council, to all but guarantee that the main burden of adjustment was pushed onto the periphery. It did this by insisting on draconian austerity and reform measures in the countries receiving a bailout, while at the same time giving its own vulnerable banks enough time to rebuild their balance sheets. A much weaker euro further benefited Germany's export industry, and lower sovereign-bond yields have been a boon for its own budgetary situation during the crisis. Finally, its close obedience to ordoliberalism ruled out any systemic solutions.

Today, the crisis lingers on, with the eurozone stuck in a catastrophic equilibrium of low growth and high unemployment, its economy teetering on the brink of outright deflation. Politicians so far have relied on ever greater doses of Draghi magic at the ECB to keep the show on the road. As Mark Blyth and I have argued, however, for the euro to become a stable global reserve currency in the longer term it will need to be much more firmly embedded into supranational social and political institutions, which include a common debt instrument, a genuine financial union and some sort of solidarity mechanism of intra-eurozone fiscal transfers.[36] Germany's policy elite has so far rejected any of those mechanisms out of fear of domestic political opposition and going against prevailing economic wisdom. As long as Berlin interprets its leadership role as following rules, and continues to pander to its electorate's fears of a 'transfer union', the euro's future will remain fragile at best.[37]

Ukraine crisis: facilitator-in-chief

In recent years, Germany has started to play a much more active role in foreign policy. Berlin played a key part in the nuclear deal with Iran, alongside Britain and France, and took the lead in negotiating a ceasefire between Russia and Ukraine. It also initiated and implemented a multilateral sanctions regime to punish Russia for its unilateral annexation of Crimea and its continued support for pro-Russian rebels in Ukraine's breakaway eastern provinces. This foreign-policy activism is a far cry from Germany's decision to abstain from UN Security Council Resolution 1973 in 2011, which authorised NATO's military intervention in Libya. As France and Britain led the military operation that would eventually result in the overthrow of Muammar Gadhafi, Germany largely stood on the sidelines.

Over the past 15 years, Germany has slowly morphed from a 'civilian power' into a 'geo-economic power'.[38] In the 1990s, Germany defined its interests broadly in civilian or normative terms, within a liberal-internationalist framework of multilateral cooperation. Human rights, international peace, democracy promotion and a willingness to take on an uneven share of the burden in order to develop supranational institutions used to be the hallmarks of German policy. But since the early 2000s, Berlin has increasingly acted in a geo-economic fashion, by elevating its narrow economic interests over other political interests.[39] It has been less shy about imposing its national preferences onto others, and has shifted to a more selective multilateralism with a more realist approach to international affairs. Since the end of the Cold War, Germany has gradually transformed itself into a more 'normal' middle power, and leveraged its ample economic strength to increase its diplomatic clout and international prestige.

In dealing with Russia over the conflict in Crimea and eastern Ukraine, Germany has led Europe's response, but wrestled to reconcile its values with its interests, acting as facilitator-in-chief. On the one hand, Berlin strongly opposes Russia's annexation of part of another sovereign country's territory as a clear violation of international law. Just like in economic policy, Berlin believes rules exist to be respected. On the other hand, Berlin quickly ruled out any military response, given its structural weakness, and was well aware that any economic- and financial-sanctions regime against Russia would hurt Germany's economy and business interests more than most other EU members'.

Germany's desire to 'lead from the middle', in the words of its defence minister Ursula von der Leyen, summed up that dilemma. It wants to play what Foreign Minister Frank-Walter Steinmeier has called the role of Europe's 'chief facilitating officer'.[40] But unlike its clout in matters that deal with the euro, where Germany is an economic giant and can influence another country into radically changing its behaviour, Berlin suffers from a large military deficit and remains a dwarf in foreign and security policy. It has largely relied on NATO to provide its security since the end of the Second World War. In 2014, it still spent only 1.1% ($43 billion) of its GDP on defence, a figure well below the NATO target of 2%, and a different order of magnitude from Russia's spending, at 3.7% ($70bn) of GDP.[41] Unlike Britain and France, it also lacks nuclear weapons, which would add significant weight and leverage in a confrontation with another nuclear power.

Furthermore, in dealing with Russian President Vladimir Putin, military vulnerability is exacerbated by large German business interests in Russia and a significant domestic dependence on Russian oil and gas.[42] This has left Germany in the unattractive position of pushing for NATO sanctions against Russia, of which it bears the main financial brunt, while at the same time brokering a ceasefire between the warring parties at Minsk that it has no way of enforcing militarily. At the same time, Germany's insistence on fiscal austerity at home and in the rest of Europe has created the risk that the EU has bitten off much more than it can chew in the case of Ukraine, a large country mired in corruption and deep financial troubles. The task of stabilising Ukraine's economy makes Greece's problems look like a walk in the park. After five years of euro crisis, there is substantial bailout fatigue all over Europe, and it is undeniable that the future of Ukraine remains much more important to Moscow than it will ever be to Brussels or Berlin.

While Germany's foreign-policy balancing act has managed to bring about a brittle ceasefire in Ukraine, and the Western sanctions against Russia have held up remarkably well so far, Crimea seems irrevocably lost. This has set a dangerous precedent in Europe's near abroad, where a stronger country that is willing to use force has permanently violated a weaker country's sovereignty. Putin plays by different rules.

Moreover, Europe and the US need Russia's support in ending the civil war in Syria, and in the fight against the Islamic State (also known as ISIS or ISIL), which together are the main reasons for the massive outflows of refugees into Europe via the Mediterranean. While Germany's foreign-policy leadership has been largely successful in keeping the West united and the sanctions in place, it has not been able to rein in Russia's territorial ambitions. Europe's borders are more vulnerable today than they have been since the end of the Cold War.

Refugee crisis: benefactor-in-chief

The most recent crisis facing the European Union is one of large migration flows from the Middle East and North Africa. The crisis is the direct consequence of the ongoing conflicts in Europe's near abroad and the inability or unwillingness of both the EU and the US to do anything about them. Large flows of people across Europe's borders have proven to be just as much a source of political tension as were large and sudden flows of capital during the euro crisis. With more than 1.8 million people reported to have crossed Europe's borders in 2015, according to Frontex, the EU's external-border force, the migratory flow into Europe is roughly four times that in 2014 and eight times that in 2013.[43] At the time of writing in February 2016, there were no signs of the volume of refugees lessening any time soon. Most of these migrants – asylum seekers and economic immigrants – are headed towards Germany in the hope of a better future.[44]

In dealing with this sudden upsurge in refugees and migrants, Germany has unambiguously taken the lead by accepting a hugely disproportionate share of all asylum seekers. It received around a million in 2015 alone, and is expected to welcome even more in 2016. Rather than insisting that EU rules be followed to the letter, as it did during the euro crisis, Germany proved much more pragmatic in dealing with refugees. The EU's Dublin Regulations stipulate that the first point of entry into the EU determines which member state is responsible for processing the applications of asylum seekers, before transferring them on to other countries. Merkel soon realised that it would be impossible for Italy, Greece and Hungary – the main EU points of entry for new refugees – to process all of them on their own before sending them onwards. Merkel's promotion of a German *Willkommenskultur* (culture of welcoming) and open-door policy gained her worldwide admiration, and stood in stark contrast with her dithering in dealing with the euro crisis and initial caution in handling Russia over Crimea.

Merkel herself promised refugees a warm welcome in Germany, and committed an extra €18bn to state and local governments to accommodate arrivals and help pay for additional expenses, such as state benefits. Here, Germany acted as Europe's benefactor-in-chief, and images of refugees holding up posters of Merkel as their saviour have been a welcome break from the ones in Athens that portrayed her as a Nazi occupier. Merkel's decision to lead by example on refugees was made possible by German economic strength, with more budgetary room than any other European country, but was also motivated by humanitarian concerns. Merkel was conscious of Germany's historic duty, keeping in mind, too, the many Germans displaced in Central Europe in the mid- to late 1940s. She acted decisively, despite facing a serious potential backlash at home.

Berlin's policy establishment would quickly realise, however, that Merkel's promise did not match Germany's absorptive capacity. Merkel's critics soon called her decision naive and foolish rather than bold and brave, as thousands more refugees crossed the Austrian border into Bavaria every day. The migration problem would need a collective response at the European level, rather than unilateral action, no matter how well intentioned. But while the euro crisis revealed a schism between North and South, the refugee crisis laid bare a fault line between West and East. The EU commission led by Jean-Claude Juncker, and supported by Germany and France, tried to impose a mandatory quota system to resettle 160,000 refugees across the EU. Eastern member states led by Hungary, however, and supported by Slovakia, Romania, and the Czech Republic, openly opposed and voted against such a system. Their leaders saw migration as a threat to their culture and a huge burden to their public services. The crisis hence continued unabated, and a comprehensive EU solution looked elusive.

Hungary and Bulgaria were building walls and wired fences

All over Europe, internal borders were being re-erected. While Hungary and Bulgaria were building walls and wired fences on their external EU borders, many other members reinstated internal EU border controls to deal with the refugee flows. This temporary violation of Europe's Schengen agreement, which guarantees the free flow of people across the borders of 26 European countries, was made more permanent after the terrorist attacks in Paris on 13 November 2015 were linked to ISIS. The sheer size of the refugee flows from the Middle East, combined with renewed threats of fundamentalist Islamic terrorism on European soil, pushed European countries to rely on nationalist responses when a European-level response would have been more effective. By February 2016, the Schengen system of open borders had all but collapsed.

Unlike in the euro crisis, Germany decided to lead the rest of Europe on the refugee crisis by taking on the main humanitarian burden and by breaking the EU rules set out in the Dublin Convention. But despite its economic size and moral leadership on refugees, Berlin was not able to get the rest of Europe to follow its lead. Leadership, in the end, requires others willing to follow, and the rest of Europe seemed all too happy for Berlin to take on the bulk of the asylum seekers. Berlin forced the Greeks to radically reform their economy during the euro crisis, but it was not able to get the Slovaks or the Czechs to accept even a handful of refugees.

* * *

Since 2010, Germany has proven to be the only EU member state capable of taking on Europe's leadership mantle. But it has been hugely frustrated in this role. In all three crises – over the euro, Ukraine and migration – Germany has led, but not effectively. A stubborn devotion to ordoliberalism, fear of a restless domestic electorate, the pressure of powerful commercial interests and the burden of history in military affairs have stood in the way. The euro remains an unfinished and fragile currency; the conflict between Ukraine and Russia is frozen at best; Europe's near abroad is more volatile than before; and the refugee crisis is unlikely to go away any time soon.

All three crises have served to underscore both the promise and the pitfalls of German leadership while at the same time reopening old wounds and revealing fault lines within Europe, both between North and South, and between East and West. This has left policymakers and electorates in both Germany and the rest of the EU deeply frustrated with the status quo. In order to make German leadership in Europe more effective, and more palatable to the rest of Europe, two things will need to happen.

Firstly, in economic policy, Germany needs to allow for more discretion. Rules that make sense only during good times are an ineffective guide in hard times. Rules can only work if they allow for enough flexibility in dealing with crises, and need to be counter-cyclical rather than pro-cyclical. Ordoliberalism might work for a small, export-driven economy, but not for a large, relatively self-sufficient one. At the same time, Berlin needs to start preparing its electorate for the next steps in building a true economic and monetary union, including permanent mechanisms of social solidarity and financial stability. In foreign policy, Germany should lead the EU military effort by stepping up its own defence spending, as well as pushing for a European energy union so as to decrease the EU's dependence on Russian oil and gas.[45] This is the only way to coerce Putin's Russia to start playing by the rules of the post-war international system.

In a speech in Hamburg in 1953, German novelist Thomas Mann told an audience of German students:

> It is the task of the new German generation, of the German youth, to disperse [Europe's] doubts [and] fears by denying the politics of the past

> and by clearly proclaiming their own vote: not for a German Europe, but rather for a European Germany.[46]

For that to become reality, Germany needs to become a 'normal' Western power, and other EU members need to shed their historic fears of a Germany that dominates the rest of Europe. We are a long way away from 1945, and Germany has behaved as a model citizen in the world system ever since. The only way for Europe to remain prosperous and influential in world affairs is for it to complete its economic and monetary union and to act in unity abroad. Europe will not get there through the dreams of EU technocrats in Brussels. It needs a political push, and one country strong enough to lead the effort, though that in itself is simply a necessary, and not a sufficient, condition. For that first and necessary step to be taken, German desire for leadership needs to match its destiny to lead. Europe and the world will be better for it.

Notes

1 Radoslaw Sikorski, 'I Fear Germany's Power Less Than her Inactivity', *Financial Times*, 28 November 2011.

2 Wade Jacoby, 'Europe's New German Problem: The Timing of Politics and the Politics of Timing', in Matthias Matthijs and Mark Blyth (eds), *The Future of the Euro* (New York: Oxford University Press, 2015), pp. 189–90.

3 'Bono Calls for German Leadership to End the Scourge of Extreme Poverty and Preventable Disease', press release, One, 13 November 2014.

4 See, for example, *The Economist*, 3 June 1999 and 24 July 2003.

5 Author's calculations. European Commission, Ameco Database, 2016, http://ec.europa.eu/economy_finance/ameco/user/serie/SelectSerie.cfm.

6 GfK, 'Germany Knocks USA Off Best Nation Top Spot after 5 Years', press release, 12 November 2014.

7 'WikiLeaks: US Spied on Angela Merkel's Ministers Too, Says German Newspaper', *Guardian*, 1 July 2015.

8 Mary N. Hampton, '"The Past, Present, and the Perhaps": Is Germany a "Normal" Power?' *Security Studies*, vol. 10, no. 2, Winter 2000–01, p. 182.

9 Peter Pulzer, 'Unified Germany: A Normal State?' *German Politics*, vol. 3, no. 1, April 1994, p. 7.

10 Michael Stürmer, 'Geschichte im geschichtslosen Land', *Frankfurter Allgemeine Zeitung*, 25 April 1986.

11 The quote is often misattributed to French president Charles de Gaulle. Walter Isaacson, 'Is One Germany Better than Two?', *Time*, 20 November 1989.

12 Quoted in Michael Lind, *The American Way of Strategy: U.S. Foreign Policy and*

the American Way of Life (New York: Oxford University Press, 2008), p. 134.

13 Peter Katzenstein, *Policy and Politics in West Germany: The Growth of a Semisovereign State* (Philadelphia, PA: Temple University Press, 1987).

14 Simon Bulmer and William Paterson, 'West Germany's Role in Europe: "Man-Mountain" or "Semi-Gulliver"?' *Journal of Common Market Studies*, vol. 28, no. 2, 1997, pp. 95–117.

15 George H.W. Bush, 'A Europe Whole and Free: Remarks to the Citizens in Mainz', 31 May 1989, http://www.usembassy.de/usa/etexts/ga6-890531.htm.

16 Stephen F. Szabo, *Parting Ways: The Crisis in German–American Relations* (Washington DC: Brookings University Press, 2004). See also Philip Gordon and Jeremy Shapiro, *Allies at War: America, Europe, and the Crisis over Iraq* (New York: McGraw Hill, 2004).

17 See Hans Kundnani, *The Paradox of German Power* (New York: Oxford University Press, 2014); Stephen F. Szabo, *Germany, Russia, and the Rise of Geo-Economics* (New York: Bloomsbury, 2014); Simon Bulmer and William E. Paterson, 'Germany as the EU's Reluctant Hegemon? Of Economic Strength and Political Constraints', *Journal of European Public Policy*, vol. 20, no. 10, 2013, pp. 1,387–405; Matthias Matthijs and Mark Blyth, 'Why Only Germany Can Fix the Euro', *Foreign Affairs*, 17 November 2011; Abraham Newman, 'The Reluctant Leader: Germany's Euro Experience and the Long Shadow of German Reunification', in Matthijs and Blyth (eds), *The Future of the Euro*, pp. 117–35.

18 'Will Germany Now Take Centre Stage?', *The Economist*, 21 October 2010.

19 Robert Dahl, 'The Concept of Power', *Behavioral Science*, vol. 2, no. 3, 1957, pp. 201–15

20 See Kenneth Waltz, *Theory of International Politics* (Long Grove, IL: Waveland Press, 1979); and Robert Gilpin, *Global Political Economy: Understanding the International Economic Order* (Princeton, NJ: Princeton University Press, 2002).

21 Jacoby, 'Europe's New German Problem', p. 189. Like the US, Germany is perceived by international investors as a financial 'safe haven', and therefore enjoys permanently lower interest rates on its sovereign debt compared to its EU neighbours. This has become painfully clear again in the euro crisis, with Germany enjoying negative interest rates on its short- and medium-term bonds, making it much easier for the German government to balance its budget.

22 Peter Bachrach and Morton S. Baratz, 'Two Faces of Power', *American Political Science Review*, vol. 56, no. 4, 1962, p. 949.

23 See Robert O. Keohane, *After Hegemony: Cooperation and Discord in the World Political Economy* (Princeton, NJ: Princeton University Press, 1984); and Andrew Moravcsik, 'Taking Preferences Seriously: A Liberal Theory of International Politics', *International Organization*, vol. 51, no. 4, Autumn 1997, pp. 513–53.

24 Stephen Lukes, *Power: A Radical View* (London: Macmillan, 1974), p. 23.

25 Alexander Wendt, 'Anarchy is what States Make of it: The Social Construction of Power Politics',

International Organization, vol. 46, no. 2, Spring 1992, pp. 391–425; Mark Blyth, *Great Transformations: Economic Ideas and Institutional Change in the Twentieth Century* (Cambridge: Cambridge University Press, 2002).

26 Matthias Matthijs, 'Powerful Rules Governing the Euro: The Perverse Logic of German Ideas', *Journal of European Public Policy*, vol. 23, no. 3, 2016, pp. 375–91.

27 Hans W. Maull, 'Germany and Japan: The New Civilian Powers', *Foreign Affairs*, vol. 96, no. 5, September/October 1990, pp. 91–106.

28 Ian Manners, 'Normative Power Europe: A Contradiction in Terms?', *Journal of Common Market Studies*, vol. 40, no. 2, 2002, pp. 235–58.

29 Erik Jones, 'Merkel's Folly', *Survival*, vol. 52, no. 3, June–July 2010, pp. 21–38.

30 Matthias Matthijs and Kathleen McNamara, 'The Euro Crisis Theory Effect: Northern Saints, Southern Sinners, and the Demise of the Eurobond', *Journal of European Integration*, vol. 37, no. 2, 2015, pp. 229–46.

31 *Ibid.*, pp. 230–1.

32 Wolfgang Schäuble, 'Rede des Bundesministers der Finanzen Dr. Wolfgang Schäuble an der Université Paris-Sorbonne', Bundesministerium der Finanzen, 2 November 2010, http://www.bundesfinanzministerium.de/Content/DE/Reden/2010/2010-11-02-sorbonne.html.

33 Charles Kindleberger, *The World in Depression, 1929–1939* (Berkeley, CA: University of California Press, 1973).

34 Matthijs and Blyth, 'Why Only Germany Can Fix the Euro'.

35 Mario Draghi, speech at the Global Investment Conference, London, 26 July 2012, https://www.ecb.europa.eu/press/key/date/2012/html/sp120726.en.html.

36 Matthijs and Blyth (eds), *The Future of the Euro*, p. 8.

37 *Ibid.*, p. 268.

38 Maull, 'Germany and Japan', p. 91.

39 See Szabo, *Germany, Russia, and the Rise of Geo-Economics*; and Kundnani, *The Paradox of German Power*.

40 Jackson Janes, 'Germany's Policy Preoccupations', *AICGS Commentary*, 24 February 2015, http://www.aicgs.org/issue/germanys-policy-preoccupations/.

41 IISS, *The Military Balance 2015* (Abingdon: Routledge for the IISS, 2015), p. 484.

42 Kundnani, *The Paradox of German Power*, p. 80.

43 'Migrant Crisis: Migration to Europe Explained in Seven Charts', BBC News, 18 February 2016.

44 Sebastian Mallaby, 'Borderline Chaos: The EU's New Challenge', Council on Foreign Relations, 10 September 2015, http://www.cfr.org/europe/borderline-chaos-eus-new-challenge/p36981.

45 Matthias Matthijs and R. Daniel Kelemen, 'Europe Reborn: How to Save the European Union from Irrelevance', *Foreign Affairs*, vol. 94, no. 1, January/February 2015, pp. 96–107.

46 Thomas Mann, *Gesammelte Werke in XIII Bänden*, Band XIII (FrankFurt-am-Mainz: S. Fischer Verlag, 1974). With thanks to Professor Dr Ulrike C. Nikutta-Wasmuht at the Free University of Berlin for the translation.

The Munich Consensus and the Purpose of German Power

Bastian Giegerich and Maximilian Terhalle

In December 2015, *Time* chose German Chancellor Angela Merkel as its person of the year, calling her 'Chancellor of the Free World'.[1] A month earlier, *The Economist* had named her 'the indispensable European'.[2] The tendency to project outsized expectations onto the individual reflects a wider phenomenon: German economic and political power in Europe has grown, partly because Germany weathered the 2008 economic crisis relatively well, and partly because of the lethargy of other European powers, including France and the United Kingdom.

With power came responsibility: firstly, for financial and economic stability, goals pursued with vigour by Germany's minister of finance, Wolfgang Schäuble, whose medicine of fiscal discipline for all left a bitter aftertaste; secondly, for crisis diplomacy, when Russia's illegal annexation of Crimea and its continued support for separatists in eastern Ukraine shook the foundations of Europe's security order; and thirdly, for a wave of international refugees fleeing savage violence and collapsing states, when the humanitarian impulse led Merkel to welcome migrants in numbers that now threaten to overwhelm capacity in Germany and beyond, putting the stability of her own government in doubt. Nevertheless, Germany watchers see the 'sleep-walking giant' finally awakening.[3] There is thus a 'new German question' to answer: will Germany be able to provide the leadership Europe needs?[4]

Bastian Giegerich is the Director of Defence and Military Analysis at the IISS. **Maximilian Terhalle** is Senior Lecturer of Politics and Global Studies at the University of Winchester.

Survival | vol. 58 no. 2 | April–May 2016 | pp. 155–166 DOI 10.1080/X00396338.2016.1161909

Germany is indeed trying to do its share to close the gap between supply and demand in foreign-policy leadership, both within and beyond the European Union. A new White Paper on security policy and the future of the German armed forces, expected in the summer of 2016, is an opportunity to provide further strategic direction. To put German security policy on a sustainable footing, policymakers should try to answer a question they traditionally have tried to avoid: what is German power for?

The Munich consensus

Just five years ago, in March 2011, Germany's foreign-policy leadership had drifted off the transatlantic reservation. Berlin's decision to abstain from UN Security Resolution 1973, which authorised intervention in Libya to protect civilians, raised questions about its willingness and ability to join key allies and partners in their pursuit of international-security goals. Former Polish foreign minister Radoslaw Sikorski famously said in Berlin in November 2011 'I fear German power less than I am beginning to fear German inactivity', signalling that the times when other European governments welcomed German restraint had passed.[5] Retrospective unease and a sense of isolation, paired with appeals by important partners for a more active German role, simmered for a good three years before a new narrative, aptly summarised by a think-tank report under the heading 'New Power, New Responsibility', was constructed.[6]

The 2014 Munich Security Conference provided the venue for the official articulation of this narrative. Speeches by Federal President Joachim Gauck, Foreign Minister Frank-Walter Steinmeier and Minister of Defence Ursula von der Leyen expressed a growing realisation that some adjustment to close the gap between expectations and output in security policy had become necessary. The themes of the Munich speeches were mutually reinforcing. Gauck argued, in a powerful address:

> Germany is globalised more than most countries and thus benefits more than most from an open world order – a world order which allows Germany to reconcile interests with fundamental values. Germany derives its most important foreign policy goal in the 21st century from all of this:

> preserving this order and system and making them fit for the future ... In my opinion, Germany should make a more substantial contribution, and it should make it earlier and more decisively if it is to be a good partner.[7]

The president's call for a more substantial contribution was echoed by Steinmeier, who added that 'a culture of restraint must not turn into a culture of refraining from engagement. Germany is too big to comment on global policy from the side-lines.'[8] Von der Leyen declared that 'indifference is not an option for Germany. As a major economy and a country of significant size we have a strong interest in international peace and stability.'[9]

Two years later, the Munich consensus has not radically transformed German foreign and security policy, but it has certainly propelled the debate forward. It represents a deliberate attempt to reconcile adaptation pressures and policy, an attempt that will remain flawed as long as German policymakers shy away from substantiating it with an underlying strategic purpose: to contribute to reforming and actively defending the liberal international order, the basis for Germany's prosperity.

The spectrum of leadership

The link between material power and international responsibility rests on the notion of political leadership: the calculated act of launching calibrated political initiatives, based on forward-looking grand strategy.[10] Leadership is the practical expression of the purpose behind a country's vital interests, and how it wants to promote and defend them. Leadership is not, of course, crisis-independent. Sometimes the need to fight fires, real and political, will dominate agendas for extended periods of time, and it would be futile to suggest that these are occasions where no leadership is on display. Even crisis leadership, however, should have a broader purpose, lest it disintegrate into a purely tactical approach, with no sense of direction and little connection to vital interests. Put briefly, it is purpose that defines political leadership.

To what extent, then, has Merkel's government demonstrated security-policy leadership?[11] Five examples can help us understand Germany's choices and actions. Firstly, Russia's seizure of Crimea fundamentally challenged the post-Cold War settlement in Europe, and put Berlin's rhetoric to the test. While Ukraine was not a NATO member, some of President Vladimir Putin's messages vis-à-vis the Baltic states turned the occupation into a test of Western military credibility. With the United Kingdom, at that time, essentially dropping out of the management of the crisis, Berlin, in close coordination with France and strategically reassured by the US, positioned itself at centre stage. Merkel led all of the discussions with Putin. While Russia could not be expelled from Crimea, she succeeded in signalling that the supposedly morally corrupt West was ready to contest Putin's strategic calculations. Consequently, Merkel became the driving force behind an increasingly piercing set of economic sanctions against Russia, only stopping short of Moscow's exclusion from the lifeline of international financial transactions, SWIFT (the Society for Worldwide Interbank Financial Telecommunication).

The Merkel government went even further. Notwithstanding Germany's persistent problems in military capacity, the Bundeswehr formed the backbone of NATO manoeuvres held in eastern Europe, and accepted responsibility for setting up the Very High Readiness Joint Task Force (VJTF), a core measure agreed at NATO's 2014 Wales Summit, and a commitment recently reinforced when Berlin accepted the rotating framework-nation responsibility for the VJTF in 2019.[12] A renewed focus on collective defence triggered by Russian assertiveness might feel to some in the German armed forces to be leading the Bundeswehr back to its cultural comfort zone. This was never found in the expeditionary operations of the past two decades, focusing rather on high-intensity combined-arms warfare waged for existential purposes.[13] Recent plans to increase defence investment from 2016–30 to €130 billion, which would amount to an extra €3–4bn of investment per year, are focused on rebuilding the historically underfunded German army.[14] Whether a political initiative with a 15-year horizon will be implemented as advertised in early 2016 remains to be seen, of course, but it is clear that a shifting perception of the security environment is the core political driver. As von der Leyen explained when announcing her plans, 'if we want external security … then we have to invest.'[15]

Shifting to another area of intense diplomatic activity, thwarting Iran's nuclear ambitions has been a key concern for Western states ever since Tehran's development of uranium-enrichment capability was made public by an opposition group in 2003. Germany participated in the subsequent international negotiations, in both the 'EU3' (with France and the United Kingdom) and 'P5+1' (with, additionally, the United States, China and Russia) settings. By 2012, it had become clear that the talks had not halted Iran's nuclear plans. The US imposed tailored sanctions against the financial and economic sectors of Iran's heavily resource- and export-dependent economy, and the EU followed the American lead. An embargo on Iranian crude-oil imports, Iran's exclusion from SWIFT and sanctions on European-based insurers and re-insurers of oil tankers, struck Iran's domestic economy hard, coercing Iran's Supreme Leader, the key decision-maker in national-security-related issues, into serious negotiations.[16] In all, Germany was party to the negotiations on Iran's nuclear programme for more than a decade. Its financial and economic dominance in Europe gave it a role in imposing sanctions and promising relief from them in exchange for demands articulated by the P5+1, and, following the application of this coercive pressure, Berlin further helped to push Iran to adopt the comprehensive agreement reached in July 2015.

Requests for German hardware trigger public debate

The desire of Gulf states, such as Qatar, Saudi Arabia and the United Arab Emirates, to hedge against Iranian power has triggered intense debate in Berlin, given that Germany is seen by those governments as a potential provider of capable military hardware. Requests for German-made main battle tanks and other equipment tend to trigger public debates about the morality of German defence policy. The dominant narrative in German political discourse holds that arms exports are, by definition, destabilising, and likely to fuel either external conflict or internal repression in the receiving countries, when these are autocratic regimes. Saudi Arabia's growing security-policy assertiveness, for example, poses a difficult challenge. Pursuing regional stability requires cooperating with a number of actors, not all of whom are likely to be liberal democracies. To deny this implies a binary choice between security and freedom; Western governments are asked to provide both.[17] The controversy caused in late 2015 by a leaked German intelligence report, which suggested Saudi Arabia would develop an increasingly assertive foreign policy to counter Iranian influence and might turn into an 'impulsive interventionist', underscores the point. The German government was quick to point out the importance of Saudi Arabia as a partner in the development of solutions to conflicts in the region, but did little to engage with the substance of the report, most of which was not particularly surprising in substantive terms.[18]

Germany had no part in striking the 2013 US–Russian agreement that led Syria to sign the Chemical Weapons Convention and accept that its arsenal would be taken out of the country for destruction. After the deal was made, however, Berlin played a useful role in supporting the negotiated outcome by assisting in the destruction of some of the stockpile, which was shipped to Germany for this purpose between September 2014 and April 2015. Syria was at that point already well on its way to turning into what *The Economist* recently called 'a nasty complex of wars within a war'[19] with clear regional and international dimensions. Berlin then took a decision that had until then been a taboo for German policymakers: namely, to supply lethal aid to an active conflict zone. In the summer of 2014, Germany might not have acted first, but over the space of several weeks it moved from supplying humanitarian aid, to non-lethal aid, to tactical support: it equipped and trained what amounts to a light-infantry brigade of Kurdish Peshmerga in northern Iraq to fight the Islamic State (also known as ISIS or ISIL). Deliveries included machine guns and ammunition, anti-tank missiles and a small number of armoured vehicles. Up to 150 German personnel were deployed to northern Iraq in support. The rationale was threefold: ISIS was causing a humanitarian catastrophe; it poses an existential threat to the people in the areas it controls; and it attracts foreign fighters, a significant number of whom have EU passports, and might turn into a direct terror threat once they return from the battlefield.[20]

In broader diplomacy, Germany insisted that there had to be a negotiated solution but did not actively shape the agenda. Berlin was by no means the only Western government that woke up late to the fact that the options for its preferred outcome, a negotiated settlement, were being shaped by

Russian military intervention. In the end, it was the terrorist attacks on Paris in November 2015 that triggered more direct German involvement after a week of reluctant deliberations. Berlin decided to provide a solidarity package based around reconnaissance missions with six *Tornado*s for the air forces already fighting over Syria, a frigate to join the French carrier group in the eastern Mediterranean and an increased deployment to Mali in order to provide relief for French forces on operations there. The possibility of a concrete threat to Western societies and, in particular, the perception of an immediate threat to its own population, apparently changed the German position within those seven days.[21] It used to be that Germany would insist on a UN resolution to sanction military action, but the pressure of French, British and American expectations, and domestic threat perceptions, persuaded Berlin to do something to demonstrate its commitment in the fight against ISIS.[22]

A final case of German evolution concerns China's efforts to carve out a sphere of influence in the East and South China seas. Germany's export-driven economy has benefited hugely from the openness of international shipping lanes, in no small measure based on the protection and presence of the US Navy. Yet Berlin has never bothered to think systematically about the preconditions of its economic wealth with regard to the Asia-Pacific. As recently as 2010, a sitting federal president, Horst Köhler, resigned after being heavily criticised for suggesting that military means might sometimes be needed to protect trade and sea lines of communication.

Since then, there have been signs that Germany is rethinking its approach to the region, and hence to China. The strongest signal is the German government's support to Thyssen-Krupp Marine Systems, among others, in their bid for contracts relating to Australia's planned new $50bn submarine force.[23] India, Indonesia, Singapore and South Korea have been German customers in the past. To suggest that Germany does not have a direct stake in the regional security dynamics that affect these states would be short-sighted. Regardless of the future success of the Australia bid,[24] the sheer size of the potential contract, Australia's geostrategic position and the way Germany's move has been perceived by others in the region make it almost inconceivable that key officials have not thought about the political rationale behind their support for German businesses.

* * *

The overall picture is mixed, but is not one of policy failure. In some cases, Germany is beginning to show significant signs of leadership. When Russia invaded Crimea, red lines were drawn immediately. Support for the Australian submarine fleet is a sign of strategic decisions being made with regard to a distant, but crucially important, region. A combination of negotiations and sanctions proved ultimately useful in reaching a nuclear deal with Iran, and Germany did its fair share. Yet the conflict in Syria seems to suggest that Germany is still partly undecided about the core purpose of its power.

For better or worse, relationships between major powers determine international politics. The first half of the twenty-first century will, essentially, settle the question of whether China and Russia can be accommodated into the existing Western liberal order without war.[25] Neither Beijing, since the 1970s, nor Russia, since defeat in the Cold War, has had a major say in the political settlement that underlies today's order, which, in turn, has tremendously benefited Germany. The current major-power peace, which has allowed much of the world to prosper, might disintegrate quickly unless influential states focus their diplomatic efforts on preserving it. Deeply anchored in the West, Germany is one of those states.

The key will lie in standing up to challengers to liberal order in a way that combines firmness on principle with flexibility over details. This is an easy approach to prescribe, and a very difficult task to achieve in practice. Should Germany and other Western powers tacitly concede some of China's territorial claims? Would such accommodation satisfy China's ambitions or would it merely encourage China to go more aggressively after other and more comprehensive claims? A conversation with Russia about rebuilding Europe's security order should start with a clear-eyed assessment of which principles can be saved, and which need to be adjusted to reflect new realities. Yet giving Putin a major part of what he apparently wants, a veto on

NATO and EU expansion, requires giving up on the idea that European countries are free to choose their own alliances. The goal of negotiations about order would not be to socialise Russia into something that it is not – a liberal democracy interested in strategic partnership – but to identify ways to work out a compromise between Western and Russian interests.

Western powers must also be ready, on occasion, to throw an elbow. One potential way in which Germany could apply pressure to Russia and China, if it chose to do so, would be to take advantage of both countries' heavy dependence on oil and gas – for Russia, the most important source of external revenue, and for China the fuel for economic growth. Both Russia and China succeed in exploiting divisions over energy policy among Europeans, who seek economic and commercial rather than strategic gains. Germany could send a strong political signal by obstructing Russia's pipeline plans,[26] and could begin conversations aimed at shifting China's interest away from Russia's oil and gas supplies.

All such choices, however, come with serious costs. In order to judge which costs are worth paying, Germany's sense of purpose will be crucial. And aligning power, responsibility, leadership and purpose will be a tall order for Berlin. The way in which the Munich consensus emerged – a slow-burning, reflective response to external expectations, rooted in long-term domestic debates about Germany's role in the world – is something of a hindrance. Germany was asked to do more, and so it has, but that is only a first step. One key issue will be whether Berlin's new approach receives recognition and encouragement from other important European states, drawing Berlin into the closest circle of their trusted relationships. An early indicator might be a remarkable interview the British defence secretary, Michael Fallon, gave at the end of January 2016, suggesting Germany had finally been elevated to the status of a 'top tier ally', which from now on would place it alongside France and the United States, and would require significantly deepened exchanges of intelligence.[27] Rather than an invitation to a newcomer, this elevation is closer to an acknowledgement of Berlin's growing influence in international-security affairs, where previously it had been passive. The task now is to continue to define what 'doing more' with that influence means, and which German interests it is meant to serve.

Notes

1 Karl Vick with Simon Shuster, 'Chancellor of the Free World', *Time*, December 2015, http://time.com/time-person-of-the-year-2015-angela-merkel/?iid=coverrecirc.

2 'The Indispensable European', *The Economist*, 7 November 2015, http://www.economist.com/news/leaders/21677643-angela-merkel-faces-her-most-serious-political-challenge-yet-europe-needs-her-more.

3 See Adrian G.V. Hyde-Price, 'The "Sleep-Walking Giant" Awakes: Resetting German Foreign and Security Policy', *European Security*, vol. 24, no. 4, 2015, pp. 600–16; and Liana Fix, 'Eine deutsche Metamorphose. Vom unsicheren Kantonisten zur europäischen Führungsmacht', *Internationale Politik*, November/December 2015, pp. 56–9.

4 Timothy Garton Ash, 'The New German Question', *New York Review of Books*, 15 August 2013, http://www.nybooks.com/articles/2013/08/15/new-german-question/.

5 See Radoslaw Sikorski, 'I Fear Germany's Power Less Than Her Inactivity', *Financial Times*, 28 November 2011.

6 Stiftung Wissenschaft und Politik and German Marshall Fund of the United States, 'New Power, New Responsibility: Elements of a German Foreign and Security Policy for a Changing World', 2013, https://www.swp-berlin.org/fileadmin/contents/products/projekt_papiere/GermanForeignSecurityPolicy_SWP_GMF_2013.pdf.

7 Joachim Gauck, speech at the opening of the Munich Security Conference, 31 January 2014, http://www.bundespraesident.de/SharedDocs/Downloads/DE/Reden/2014/01/140131-Muenchner-Sicherheitskonferenz-Englisch.pdf;jsessionid=9FFBCE935EA18E7094771188719F5164.2_cid379?__blob=publicationFile.

8 Frank-Walter Steinmeier, speech to the Munich Security Conference, 1 February 2014, http://www.auswaertiges-amt.de/DE/Infoservice/Presse/Reden/2014/140201-BM_M%C3%BCSiKo.html. Authors' translation.

9 Ursula von der Leyen, speech to the Munich Security Conference, 31 January 2014, https://www.securityconference.de/fileadmin/MSC_/2014/Reden/2014-01-31-Speech-MinDef_von_der_Leyen-MuSeCo.pdf.

10 Mlada Bukovansky et al., *Special Responsibilities. Global Problems and American Power* (Cambridge: Cambridge University Press, 2012).

11 Axiomatically, German leadership perceives itself as the reflection of Franco-German consultations. See Ulrich Krotz and Joachim Schild, *Shaping Europe. France, Germany, and Embedded Bilateralism from the Elysee Treaty to Twenty-First Century Politics* (Oxford: Oxford University Press, 2013).

12 Claudia Major, 'NATO's Strategic Adaptation: Germany is the Backbone for the Alliance's Military Reorganisation', *SWP Comments*, no. 16, March 2015, https://www.swp-berlin.org/fileadmin/contents/products/comments/2015C16_mjr.pdf.

The demand for a visible German role in these manoeuvres was nicely captured by the Estonian defence chief, Lieutenant General Riho Terras: 'We need to see the German flag here … Leopard tanks would do very nicely.' See Charlemagne, 'On a Wing and a Prayer', *The Economist*, 3 May 2014, p. 26.

13 For the argument that Germany's military culture does not provide a well-developed frame of reference beyond the core task of high-intensity warfare, see Eric Sangar, 'The Weight of the Past(s): The Impact of the Bundeswehr's Use of Historical Experience on Strategy-Making in Afghanistan', *Journal of Strategic Studies*, vol. 38, no. 4, 2015, pp. 411–44.

14 See 'Ombudsman: German Army Is "Short of Almost Everything"', Deutsche Welle, 26 January 2016, http://www.dw.com/en/ombudsman-german-army-is-short-of-almost-everything/a-19005841.

15 Interview with Ursula von der Leyen, *ARD-Morgenmagazin*, 27 January 2016, http://www.ardmediathek.de/tv/Morgenmagazin/Bundeswehr-Verteidigungsministerin-wirb/Das-Erste/Video?documentId=33002044&bcastId=435054.

16 Maximilian Terhalle, 'Why Revolutionary States Yield: International Sanctions, Regime Survival and the Security Dilemma: The Case of the Islamic Republic of Iran', *International Politics*, vol. 52, no. 5, 2015, pp. 594–608.

17 Géza Andreas von Geyr, 'Mit Autokratien umgehen', in Josef Braml, Wolfgang Merkel and Eberhard Sandschneider (eds), 'Außenpolitik mit Autokratien', *DGAP-Jahrbuch Internationale Politik*, vol. 30, pp. 379–84.

18 Stefan Braun and Paul-Anton Krüger, 'Bundesregierung empört sich über BND', *Süddeutsche Zeitung*, 3 December 2015, http://www.sueddeutsche.de/politik/saudi-arabien-bundesregierung-empoert-sich-ueber-bnd-1.2765939.

19 'War in Syria: The Peril of Inaction', *The Economist*, 20 February 2016, http://www.economist.com/news/leaders/21693208-russian-daring-and-american-weakness-have-changed-course-warfor-worse-peril.

20 Bertold Kohler, 'Berlin will Kurden aufrüsten. Waffen für die Infanterie des Westens', *Frankfurter Allegemeine*, 20 August 2014, http://www.faz.net/aktuell/politik/ausland/naher-osten/berlin-will-kurden-aufruesten-waffen-fuer-die-infanterie-des-westens-13108327.html.

21 58% of Germans support the decision to provide military reconnaissance in the fight against ISIS. See Klaus-Dieter Frankenberger, 'Wer soll's richten?', *Frankfurter Allegemeine*, 5 December 2015, http://www.faz.net/aktuell/politik/kampf-gegen-den-terror/wer-kuemmert-sich-um-die-sicherheitspolitik-13948722.html.

22 It should also be noted, however, that an increased Mali engagement had been in the works before the Paris attacks, thus more directly supporting the argument that Germany had looked at this particular case from a strategic, and not just a crisis-driven, perspective. See Michael Hanisch, 'Eine neue Qualität des Engagements.

Deutschlands erweiterter militärischer Einsatz in Nord-Mali', *Arbeitspapier Sicherheitspolitik*, August 2015, Federal Academy for Security Policy (BAKS), Berlin.

23 Christoph Hein, 'Deutsche Waffen fuer Australien', *Frankfurter Allegemeine*, 13 November 2015, http://www.faz.net/aktuell/wirtschaft/unternehmen/ruestungsexporte-deutsche-waffen-fuer-australien-13909187.html.

24 *Ibid*. The likeliness of success appears high, because Thyssen Krupp has offered to build and maintain the submarines in Australia.

25 Maximilian Terhalle, *The Transition of Global Order: Legitimacy and Contestation* (New York: Palgrave Macmillan, 2015).

26 Hendrik Kafsack, 'Streit um Nord-Stream-Ausbau. Gegen den Gasstrom', *Frankfurter Allegemeine*, 3 December 2015, http://www.faz.net/aktuell/politik/ausland/europa/osteuropa-wehrt-sich-gegen-bau-von-nord-stream-pipeline-2-13944914.html.

27 Jochen Buchsteiner, 'London will Deutschland als "Hauptsicherheitspartner"', *Frankfurter Allegemeine*, 24 January 2016, p. 6, http://www.faz.net/aktuell/politik/ausland/europa/f-a-z-exklusiv-london-will-deutschland-als-hauptsicherheitspartner-14031723.html.

Who's Arming Asia?

Jonathan D. Caverley and Ethan B. Kapstein

In the international arms trade, as in any industry, market share is power. But unlike most other products, when it comes to the sale of weapons, power is not limited to economics. Arms exports not only benefit producers (and, sometimes, defence ministries) financially; they also cement relationships (often asymmetric, and occasionally coercive) between seller and client.

As the world's leading producer and consumer of high-end weaponry, the United States has long used arms sales to influence smaller states, manage regional arms races, encourage allies' inter-operability and contain rivals' capabilities, as well as to support its own defence-industrial base and broader economy. Arms sales are a crucial component of the United States' revitalised effort to 'train and equip' other military forces to more effectively pursue joint security interests around the world.[1] Any loss of market share therefore puts several aspects of the United States' political–economic order at risk, and nowhere is this risk more apparent and more consequential than in Asia.[2] Even those who care little about American influence in the region should recognise the potential for increased proliferation of sophisticated conventional weapons in an already tense region.

In Giuseppe Tomasi di Lampedusa's great Sicilian novel *The Leopard*, the young aristocrat Tancredi, intent on preserving his privileged position in

Jonathan D. Caverley is a Fellow at the Woodrow Wilson International Center for Scholars and a Research Associate in Political Science and Security Studies at the Massachusetts Institute of Technology. **Ethan B. Kapstein** is Arizona Centennial Professor of International Affairs at the McCain Institute and School of Public Affairs, Arizona State University, and Associate Director of the Empirical Studies of Conflict Program at Princeton University (esoc.princeton.edu).

Survival | vol. 58 no. 2 | April–May 2016 | pp. 167–184 DOI 10.1080/00396338.2016.1161911

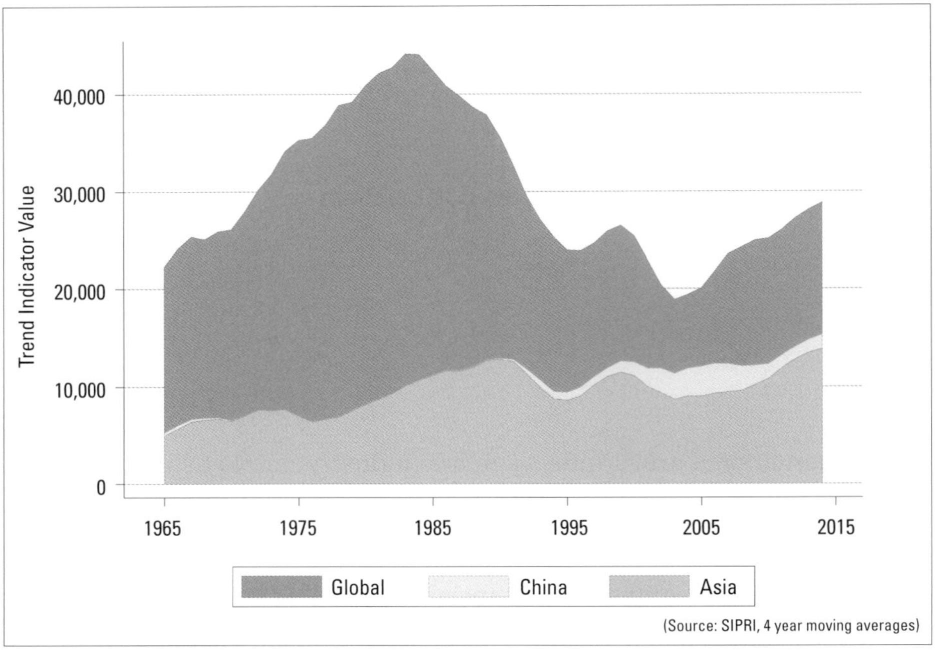

Figure 1: **Arms imports for the world, Asia and China**

fast-changing Risorgimento Italy, famously observes, 'If we want things to stay as they are, things will have to change.' If the United States is to continue to enjoy its own dominant status, it must do likewise.

Much of the growth in global arms sales over the past decade has occurred in Asia. Figure 1 uses data on arms deliveries from the Stockholm International Peace Research Institute (SIPRI) to show overall levels of arms imports for the world, for Asia and for China alone.[3] In 2010–14, Asia accounted for 48% of all imports (compared to the Middle East's 22%).[4] This represents a 37% increase in imports over 2005–09 (Middle East imports rose 25% over this period). Perhaps surprisingly, Beijing is not directly driving Asian arms imports. China actually makes up a smaller percentage of the import market than it did earlier this century, largely because it manufactures more weapons domestically now.

Figure 2 presents trends in market share within Asia (again excluding China). Clearly, US market share has plummeted from historic post-Cold War heights. Even as the Asian arms trade enjoys a decade-long boom, American market share is near its historically lowest point. Russian market share

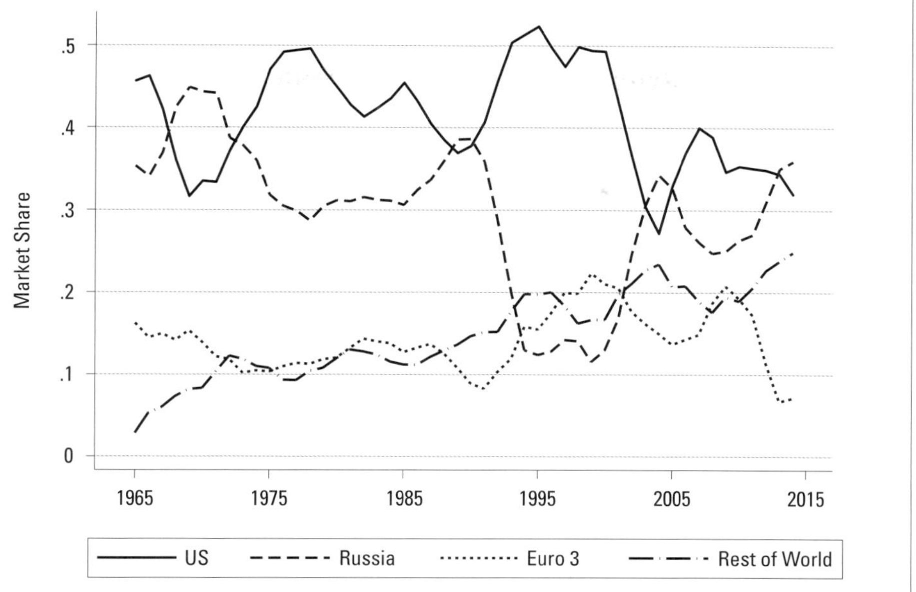

Figure 2: **Market shares of major arms exporters**

moves inversely to the United States' and indeed has recently outstripped its former Cold War rival (even when Chinese imports are excluded). This recovery is remarkable, given that Russia does not have nearly the same capacity as the Soviet Union had in the 1980s. The traditional friendly rivals to the United States – Germany, France and Britain – have seen their already weak position in Asia deteriorate further. The graph also shows the steady march of less traditional sellers of weapons, scrappier competitors like Israel, South Korea and China (which currently holds about a 10% share), to unprecedented highs.

Figure 2 might suggest that the current market is largely a duopolistic competition between the United States and Russia. But there are enough exporting countries with large enough sales that the market is now more competitive than ever. Figure 3 shows the trends in the Asian market's Herfindahl–Hirschman Index (HHI, a measure of market competitiveness), which takes into account both the number of exporting states in a market and the size of their shares. The HHI is used by US federal agencies to evaluate mergers for potential anti-trust implications, where any value above

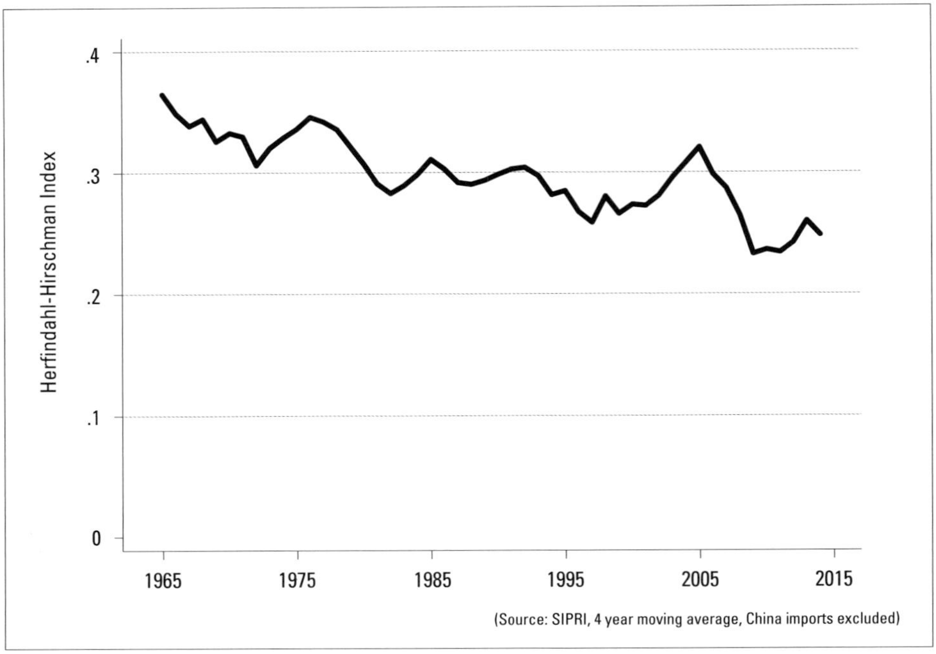

Figure 3: **Asia market concentration by exporting state**

0.25 is considered highly concentrated. The HHI shows a steady decline in concentration over the past several decades. The past ten years have seen a significantly lower level of concentration compared to the Cold War or the American-dominated 1990s.

Given the expense of producing major conventional weapons, a massive defence budget and America's tremendous international influence, how did the United States lose so much so quickly? The drop seems regionally specific; the US market share in the Middle East remains much higher. Over the past ten years, and despite its 'pivot' in strategic focus, America's share of the Asian defence market has hovered at around 35%, much smaller than its current 44% in the Middle East. When Asian states feel the need to arm themselves, they are not nearly as likely to turn to the United States as are their Middle Eastern counterparts.

With great market power comes greater responsibility

Basic economic logic and the historical data would suggest that American defence spending and the country's share of the global arms market should be positively correlated.[5] The unmatched size of its economy and defence budget provides massive economies of scale and learning effects in the production of armaments compared to any other country, where relatively small production runs drive up unit costs.[6] As a consequence, US weapons should be relatively cheap given the marginal costs of production, making it easy to win foreign sales. Moreover, these weapons are combat-proven and pitched by an aggressive sales force: the US State Department.

Compared to most other suppliers, the United States attaches many conditions to its sales.[7] It has strict technology-transfer controls and relatively comprehensive anti-corruption standards, and makes onerous demands on importing states to ensure that weapons do not get transferred to third parties. Moreover, the US has in the past cut off countries over policy differences, such as the sanctions that crippled India's *Tejas* light-combat-aircraft programme following that country's testing of nuclear weapons. The United States has historically forgone exporting its highest-capability weapons to a region until a viable competing product emerges. For example, the US refused to deliver AMRAAM missiles to Asian states until China purchased the Russian AA-12 *Adder*.[8]

Firms in the US defence base may blame such restrictions for undermining US competitiveness, but they are more a sign of market power than a cause of its decline.[9] Lower levels of conventional-weapons proliferation, technology diffusion and corruption in contracting arrangements result from US power not because it is a particularly responsible or moral country, but because it can afford to use its competitive advantage to restrict these nuisances (and still take care of its industrial base). Less powerful, second-tier exporting states are too constrained by the economics of production to pursue any goals besides increased arms sales.[10] A more competitive market will place pressure on this robust regulatory environment. The recent removal of many technologies from the United States Munitions List was driven in part by American industry convincing the government that it is losing competitive advantage abroad. Consequently, many weapons transfers may no longer be subject to rigorous human-rights vetting and end-use monitoring by the State Department.[11] In short, eroding American market dominance of higher-end weapons makes it less likely that it will exercise its traditional policy of 'unilateral restraint' in their sale.[12]

Despite the many strings attached, the United States has traditionally been adept at convincing countries to buy American, for which it provides compensation by delivering a better product at a lower, often subsidised, price relative to comparable products. At $5 billion, the US Foreign Military Financing programme is larger than the entire military budgets of Venezuela, Kuwait and Denmark. The sum of US foreign military assistance for 2015, $19.3bn, would amount to the 18th largest military budget in the world (slightly less than Canada's), much of which can fund arms purchases through disparate programmes such as the Global Security Contingency, Peacekeeping Operations, Section 1206 Train and Equip, and Counter-Narcotic funds.[13]

The controversial F-35 Joint Strike Fighter, so expensive that one critic has dubbed it the 'jet that ate the Pentagon', illustrates both American advantages and weaknesses in the arms market.[14] Ostensibly developed within a multinational collaboration, the United States has been very protective of the plane's major components, to the point that other countries will be unable to modify or even maintain the plane without American permission and input. Yet despite its costliness and lack of technology transfer, the US has successfully sold the plane abroad though a combination of industrial incentives, the promise of increased security cooperation and diplomatic arm-twisting.[15] International procurement decisions for the F-35 have been unusually fractious and controversial, yet the plane has not lost an international contract to a rival.[16] On the other hand, the visible losses of American aircraft in major competitions, such as in India and Brazil, have been in markets where cheaper planes (F-16s and F/A-18s) than the F-35 were on offer. What accounts for the differences in American competitiveness among these different weapons?

Disruption and hegemony

We argue that, while the US defence industry excels at producing the type of arms that its principal client (the Pentagon) wants, it does not produce cheaper variants of items well suited for the missions that much of the world, particularly in Asia, currently demands. The United States' privileged position in the world and the ambition of its foreign policy have ensured that it produces the materiel necessary for what the American political scientist Barry Posen calls 'command of the commons': the ability to operate at will in sea, air and space around the globe, as well as to prevent others from doing likewise. The requirements for this capability are extremely demanding and are unlikely to be matched, Posen suggests, by any other state in the near to medium term.[17] Posen describes at length the massive physical- and organisational-infrastructure requirements for such a mission and the consequently enormous barriers to entry for other states. Building cutting-edge weapons is hard: former Lockheed Martin CEO Norm Augustine famously observed that 'the last 10 percent of performance generates one-third of the cost and two-thirds of the problems'.[18]

On the other hand, what Posen describes as the 'weaponry of the close fight' is cheaper to purchase, simpler to operate and easier to develop.[19] The more ready supply of potential exporters for these types of weapons helps contribute to a 'contested zone' that demarcates the limits of American (or any other state's) hegemony.[20] In American parlance, these products are designed for anti-access/area denial (A2/AD). They include diesel submarines, anti-submarine-warfare aircraft, anti-ship cruise missiles and mines, as well as air and missile defences.[21] The US defence industry does not bother to produce many of the weapons required for such counter-intervention operations, and indeed in many cases has not done so for decades. Since the 1950s, the US Navy has deliberately refused to procure diesel submarines in favour of nuclear-powered, ocean-spanning undersea capital ships.[22] Nor does the American defence industry build ground-based anti-ship missiles, leaving this rapidly growing export market to smaller producers such as France, Russia, Sweden, Norway and Italy.[23]

Even when the United States develops weapons ostensibly for both export and domestic consumption, they rarely strike potential buyers as a particularly good deal. Seeking a flexible, multipurpose plane that could fulfil a variety of missions satisfactorily, Brazil recently chose the lighter, less sophisticated, but much less expensive *Gripen* (made by Sweden's Saab) over prominent competitors that included Boeing's F/A-18, a cheap plane by American standards. In terms of performance, the *Gripen* is the inferior plane in nearly every way, but, as one analyst pointed out, it is perfectly serviceable 'if you are not a country that wants to bomb areas with really strong air defences on day one of a war'.[24] Israel considered buying Littoral Combat Ships, developed by the United States to serve as affordable, coast-hugging vessels. Small by American standards but larger than anything the Israelis have owned to date, their spiralling costs proved too much. As one Israeli admiral noted, 'As much as we sought commonality with the U.S. Navy … we had no choice but to face the fact that, for us, it was unaffordable.'[25]

Sovereignty protection, rather than power projection, appears to be the primary purpose of contemporary arms purchases in Asia. Territorial defence not only for a state's major landmass, but also for smaller islands and more tenuous sovereignty claims, underpins much Asian strategic planning.[26] As an example, Indonesia aspires to build a 'green water navy', quintupling its diesel-submarine inventory to ten by 2024. In the past five years it has acquired four Dutch missile frigates as well as four Landing Platform Dock ships (licensed from South Korea), each carrying up to 400 troops and five helicopters.[27]

To put it in the famous terms of business guru Clayton Christensen, American defence firms are unlikely to produce such weapons because the demand for them is unlikely to come from their principal customer. Christensen observed that truly 'disruptive' innovations often result in reduced performance, but at a greatly diminished price. Established firms do not invest in these simpler, cheaper products due to their lower margins and smaller profits. Disruptive innovations thus tend to be first commercialised in emerging or seemingly insignificant markets, where 'good enough' performance is sufficient. Over time, new entrants can use the resulting revenue and experience to work their way up the quality ladder. Honda initially gained a foothold in the US motorcycle market not by building powerful, luxury products like those of Harley–Davidson and BMW, but by selling cheap, fun *Super Cub* bikes to an entirely different set of customers. Honda now competes effectively at every level of this and many other markets.[28] Korea Aerospace Industries (KAI) has built on its experience producing licensed versions of Lockheed Martin's F-16 to produce a trainer aircraft (the T-50) sufficiently capable and affordable for the Philippines to have purchased it for combat missions. KAI now seeks to develop a higher-end aircraft comparable to current versions of the F-16 to supply Korea, Indonesia and other potential export clients by 2023.[29]

What is Asia buying? And from whom?

To illustrate this disruptive process, we turn to deliveries in Asia of the types of weapons broadly necessary for an A2/AD strategy: aircraft, ships and missiles. Missiles, in particular, represent a major global proliferation problem, as well as a threat to the air superiority of the United States and its allies.

To do this requires making an important technical distinction between two types of data published by SIPRI. The first is the raw number of units delivered. For missiles, this covers a broad range of not-very-comparable weapons. The more complicated, but often more useful, SIPRI measurement of exports is the 'Trend Indicator Value' (TIV), designed to measure 'transfers of military capability rather than the financial value of arms transfers', which allows for the distinction between weapons of various levels of sophistication. An American SM-3 anti-ballistic-missile weapon has a TIV of 7, while a Chinese *Red Arrow* 73 anti-tank missile is valued at 0.02. Comparing the two measurements helps give a sense of US market share in terms of quality and quantity. If the TIV share is much higher than the unit share, it suggests that the United States is selling higher-quality weapons than its competitors.

Figures 4a–c (for aircraft, missiles and ships, respectively) present both the overall imports by Asian states as well as US market share in terms of both units and TIV. Even in a sector where the United States remains the dominant provider, supplying 42% of the region's value in aircraft, it only supplies 30% of the region's aircraft in unit terms. Looking at Figure 4b, after 15 years of essentially steady demand, the number of missiles being imported into Asia has increased by about 40%. Yet US share has remained relatively stagnant and has even dropped in terms of units. Turning to ships (Figure 4c), there does not seem to be much difference between the United States' TIV and unit shares, indicating that the United States is not export-

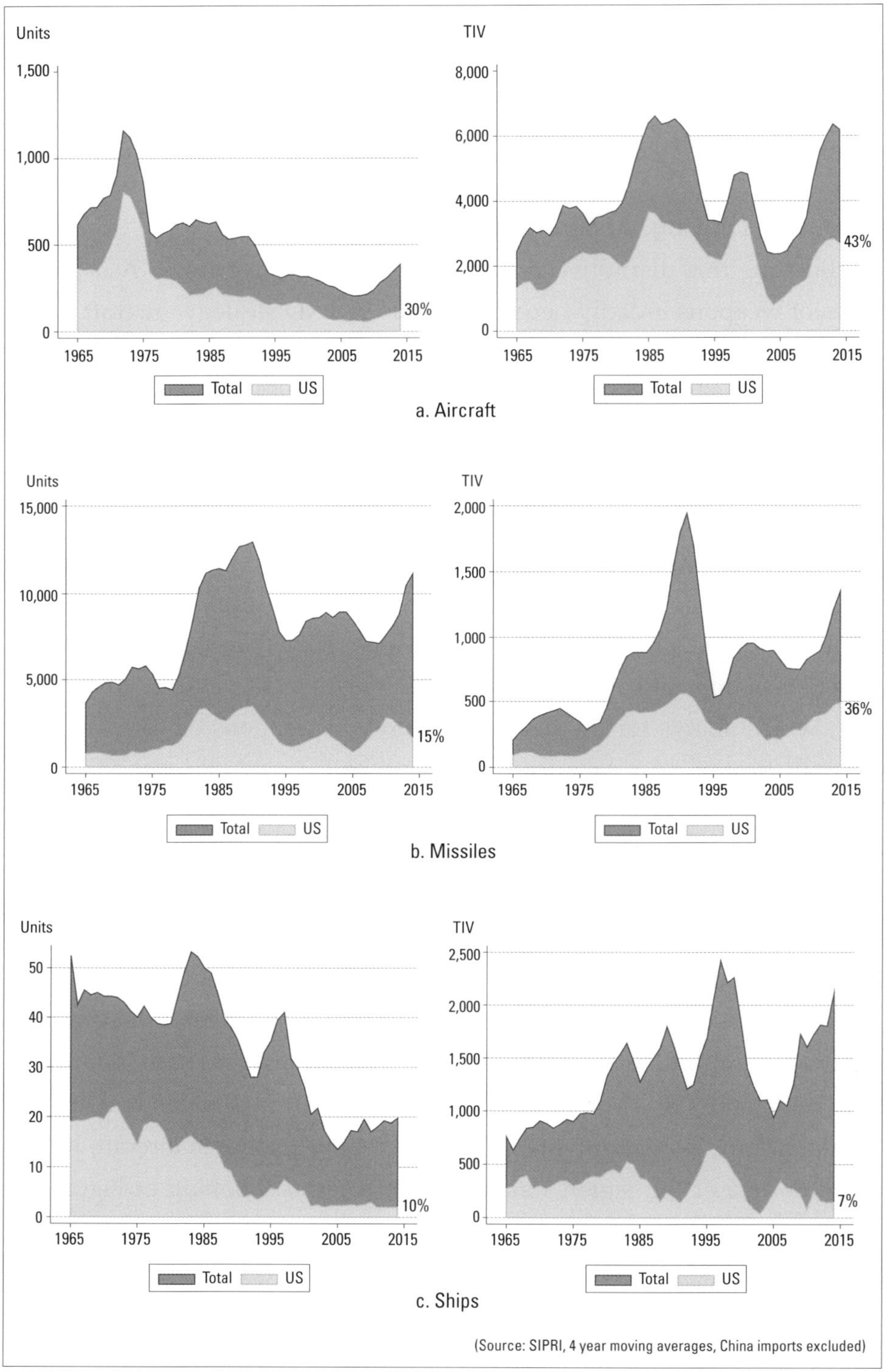

Figure 4: **Numbers and value of Asian arms imports, total and US, by category**

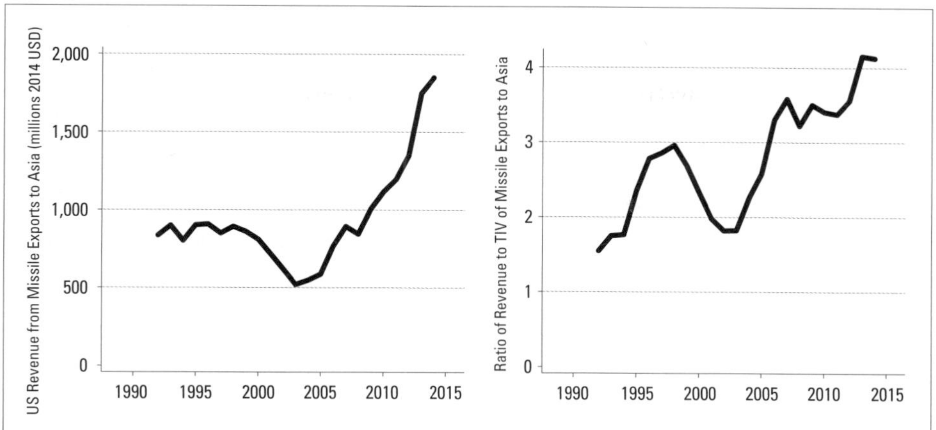

(Sources: USITC and SIPRI, 4 year moving average)

Figure 5: **United States revenue from Asian missile exports and ratio of revenue to TIV**

ing more sophisticated systems than the market demands. But that might be because the United States, with a 7% market share in terms of value, simply does not export these products.[30]

Christensen argues that disruption occurs when the market-leading firms concentrate on supplying the needs of their most profitable clients. Figure 5 depicts US International Trade Commission data on Asian export revenue for the category of guided missiles, and then graphs the ratio of revenue over SIPRI's TIV. Despite the decline in market share, revenues have never been higher. Between 2011 and 2014, the United States exported $6.2bn-worth of missiles, a 63% increase over 2007–10.[31] Moreover, the steeply climbing ratio shows that revenue is rising faster than the military capability exported, providing further evidence that the United States remains focused on (and successful in) selling to its most profitable customers. This may make sense for domestic firms, but in terms of international politics, as Stalin supposedly remarked, quantity has a quality all its own.

* * *

The massive American military-acquisition budget should provide economies of scale that enable the United States to shape the international arms trade, and consequently the international security environment, to suit its interests. Yet countervailing forces seem to have undermined this advantage. The quest for primacy, which correlates to both the size of the defence budget and the type of weapons acquired with it, undermines the effectiveness of a classic tool of great-power management: the sale of arms to client states. Ironically, as the US government aims to both pivot to Asia and train and equip its allies, its defence-industrial efforts are focused on building weapons that many in Asia, both friend and foe, are trying to defeat. This does not bode well for either US influence or regional proliferation. More disturbingly, uncompetitive American weapons may undermine regional stability, given Asia's large number of maritime disputes.

Among the benefits provided by arms exports is the ability to manage clients' excess aggressiveness – the so-called 'drunk tank' approach to alliance politics, which involves restraining an intoxicated actor until tensions have calmed.[32] While the regional spread of anti-access weapons may appear to favour the defence, there are consequences to small states being able to use them unilaterally. In 2010, then-secretary of state Hillary Clinton claimed an American 'national interest in freedom of navigation, open access to Asia's maritime commons, and respect for international law in the South China Sea'.[33] The interests of Indonesia, Malaysia and the Philippines are much more parochial. Vietnam, in particular, is a small, strategically located country that historically has not avoided conflicts with superpowers. Over the past two decades, it has also doubled its outposts in the disputed Spratly Islands to 48, compared to China's eight.[34] The acquisition of anti-access weapons such as *Kilo* diesel submarines and *Yakhont* anti-ship missiles will not only enable Vietnam and other countries to defend themselves against Chinese revisionism, it will also allow them to threaten the freedom of navigation of China – and other states – through vital sea lines of communication in the South China Sea, through which about 30% of the world's trade passes.[35] This could lead to more arms racing and regional crisis instability.[36]

That said, like the aristocratic Tancredi, the United States can adapt to a changing environment and preserve its privileged position. The US will continue to aggressively sell advanced products to wealthy allies such as Japan, Australia and South Korea. Japan and South Korea's participation in the *Aegis*-based missile-defence system, for example, pulls two states

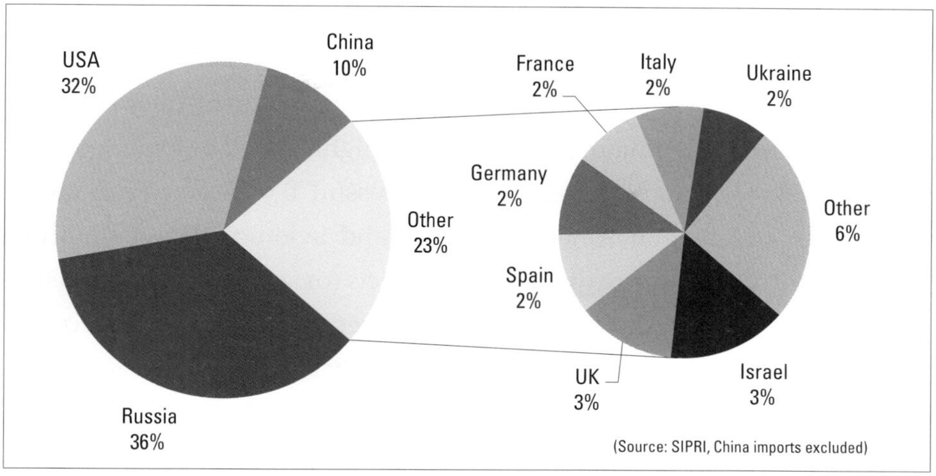

Figure 6: **Asia export market share of ten largest exporters, 2011–14**

unlikely to cooperate with each other bilaterally into something resembling a collective-security network. The United States remains the unrivalled producer of certain systems and services that make existing weapons more capable, and which even less-powerful states want. It still enjoys unmatched expertise in intelligence collection and information management. Even the anti-access weapons discussed above require significant upgrading in terms of both the human capital and the information-intensive C4SIR capability of small states' militaries.[37] As with the larger US economy, providing military software and services may not bring with it the domestic employment advantages of bending metal, but it can still enhance American interests.

Figure 6, which shows the market shares of the top ten exporters to Asia for 2011–14, tells a more subtle (and important) story than Figure 2. The countries that make up the 'rise of the rest' in the Asian arms market are not the emerging markets that Fareed Zakaria had in mind when he coined the term.[38] Brazil and India are nowhere to be found, despite several decades of concerted effort at developing arms exports. Other than China, there are no Asian exporters, despite that region's growing demand for weapons. With the exception of Ukraine, until recently a subsidiary to Russia's defence industry, the other arms suppliers are moderately sized liberal states with sophisticated economies. Perhaps more importantly, almost all of them are either formal or de facto allies of the United States.

Thus, even if the United States will not produce many weapons smaller states need, it can still encourage sales within a larger arms network that it continues to dominate. Sweden's *Gripen* contains so much American technology that, from a regulatory standpoint, it might as well be exported from the United States.[39] South Korea's quite successful T-50 *Golden Eagle* multi-role trainer contains an American engine and avionics. These countries would be hard pressed to export these products (or service the ones already in operation) without American approval; indeed, the United States recently vetoed the export of a fighter variant of the *Golden Eagle* to Uzbekistan.[40] Sale of these weapons to other countries unwilling to buy American arms would still provide a large measure of indirect influence for the United States relative to the weapons coming from Russia or China. Moreover, keeping Russian and Chinese hardware out of such export markets will inhibit the development of the economies of scale that the two countries require for a healthy and technologically advanced defence industry.

In one sense, India's 2004 purchase of the *Phalcon* airborne-warning and control system from Israel represents a billion-dollar loss to the US defence industry, which is largely responsible for the technology transfer that helped build the thriving Israeli arms-export sector. But the deal still required American approval, which it had withheld in 2000 for a similar sale to China. Such an arms network can be designed to keep China down, Russia out and friendlier states in, and the American defence industry will still make more money through these 'non-American' sales compared to Russian or Chinese products. Choking off as large a percentage of the Russian export market as possible, starting with India, in favour of the products of more closely aligned countries appears to be in the United States' interest. In terms of both American influence and curbing proliferation, it is better for Asian states to buy German or South Korean submarines than Russian. This will have the added benefit of diminishing the quality and raising the price in the long run of the products Russia will export to states, such as Syria, that cannot buy arms from anywhere else.

The United States will need to take advantage of this network if it sticks to its current grand strategy. As it pivots towards Asia, the US appears to be contemplating intensification and hardening of its power-projecting military, even as that region acquires weapons designed to deter such a force.[41] An ironic consequence of the US focus on 'anti-anti-access' weapons will be an increasingly competitive market in counter-intervention capabilities, largely beyond American control. Anti-access will grow cheaper, while power-projecting strategies such as Air–Sea Battle will grow more expensive.[42] America's acquisition of powerful weapons is leading to a market that makes balancing against them increasingly cheap.

Notes

1 Department of Defense, 'Sustaining US Global Leadership: Priorities for 21st Century Defense', Defense Strategic Guidance, January 2012, http://archive.defense.gov/news/Defense_Strategic_Guidance.pdf.

2 Here, we use the Congressional Research Service's regional categories. Asia encompasses Afghanistan, Australia, Bangladesh, Brunei, Burma, Cambodia, China, Fiji, India, Indonesia, Japan, Kazakhstan, Kyrgyzstan, Laos, Malaysia, Nepal, New Zealand, North Korea, Pakistan, Papua New Guinea, Philippines, Pitcairn, Singapore, South Korea, Sri Lanka, Taiwan, Tajikistan, Thailand, Turkmenistan, Uzbekistan and Vietnam. See Richard F. Grimmet and Paul K. Kerr, 'Conventional Arms Transfers to Developing Nations, 2004–2011', Congressional Research Service, 24 August 2012, available at https://www.fas.org/sgp/crs/weapons/R42678.pdf; and Catherine A. Theohary, 'Conventional Arms Transfers to Developing Nations, 2007–2014', Congressional Research Service, 21 December 2015, available at https://www.fas.org/sgp/crs/weapons/R44320.pdf.

3 Stockholm International Peace Research Institute (SIPRI), 'SIPRI Arms Transfers Database', 2016.

4 Siemon T. Wezeman and Pieter D. Wezeman, 'Trends in International Arms Transfers, 2014', SIPRI Fact Sheet, 2015, pp. 1–8. For simplicity we combine SIPRI's 'Asia' and 'Oceania' categories. For the rest of the paper we use the CRS definitions cited above.

5 Keith Krause, *Arms and the State: Patterns of Military Production and Trade* (Cambridge: Cambridge University Press, 1995).

6 See Ethan B. Kapstein, 'Capturing Fortress Europe: International Collaboration and the Joint Strike Fighter', *Survival*, vol. 46, no. 3, Autumn 2004, pp. 137–60; Jonathan D. Caverley, 'United States Hegemony and the New Economics of Defense', *Security Studies*, vol. 16, no. 4, 2007, pp. 598–614; and Andrea Gilli and Mauro Gilli, 'The Diffusion of Drone Warfare? Industrial, Infrastructural and Organizational Constraints', *Security Studies*, vol. 51, no. 1, 2016, pp. 50–84.

7 Transparency International, 'Watchdogs: The Quality of Legislative Oversight of Defence in 82 Countries',

Government Defence Anti-Corruption Index, September 2013, http://government.defenceindex.org/.

8 'Three Asian Countries to Get U.S. Missiles', *Arms Control Today*, vol. 33, no. 7, 2003. For a recent restatement of this policy, see Gregory M. Kausner, 'Conventional Arms Transfer Policy: Advancing American National Security through Security Cooperation', remarks to IISS, Washington DC, 23 April 2014, http://www.state.gov/t/pm/rls/rm/2014/225118.htm.

9 Coalition for Security and Competitiveness, 'Eight Associations Urge President Bush to Implement Modern Export Control System to Enhance U.S. Security, Competitiveness', 6 March 2007, http://securityandcompetitiveness.org/resources/show/2243.html.

10 Krause, *Arms and the State*, pp. 29–32.

11 Government Accountability Organization, 'Export Controls: U.S. Agencies Need to Assess Control List Reform's Impact on Compliance Activities', 23 April 2012, http://www.gao.gov/products/GAO-12-613.

12 White House, 'Presidential Policy Directive: United States Conventional Arms Transfer Policy', PPD-27, 15 January 2014, https://www.whitehouse.gov/the-press-office/2014/01/15/presidential-policy-directive-united-states-conventional-arms-transfer-p.

13 See IISS, 'Chapter Ten: Country Comparisons – Force Levels and Economics', *The Military Balance 2016* (Abingdon: Routledge for the IISS, 2016), pp. 481–92; and Security Assistance Monitor, 'Military and Police Aid (Programs)', database, accessed 22 February 2016, http://www.securityassistance.org/data/program/military/country/2010/2017/is_all.

14 See Winslow Wheeler, 'The Jet that Ate the Pentagon', *Foreign Policy*, 26 April 2012, http://foreignpolicy.com/2012/04/26/the-jet-that-ate-the-pentagon; and Kapstein, 'Capturing Fortress Europe'.

15 Srdjan Vucetic and Rebecka S. Rydberg, 'Remnants of Empire: Tracing Norway's F-35 Decision', *Contemporary Security Policy*, vol. 36, no. 1, 2015.

16 The plane has been selected by Australia, Israel, Italy, Japan, Netherlands, Norway, South Korea, Turkey and the United Kingdom. Some of the initial orders have been reduced, however. Canada's and Denmark's competitions are ongoing.

17 Barry R. Posen, 'Command of the Commons: The Military Foundation of US Hegemony', *International Security*, vol. 28, no. 1, 2003, p. 7.

18 Norman R. Augustine, *Augustine's Laws* (New York: Penguin Books, 1987), p. 103.

19 'Close' is, of course, a relative concept. China, for example, is seeking to develop missiles (and nuclear submarines) that can threaten American aircraft carriers at a range of 2,000km from its coast. China's neighbours, to which the United States seeks to sell weapons, have much less ambitious ranges in mind for their militaries.

20 Posen, 'Command of the Commons', p. 24.

21 Andrew J. Krepinevich, 'Strategy in a Time of Austerity: Why the Pentagon

Should Focus on Assuring Access', *Foreign Affairs*, November/December 2012.

22 Richard G. Hewlett and Francis Duncan, *Nuclear Navy: 1946–1962* (Chicago, IL: University of Chicago Press, 1974).

23 Terrence K. Kelly et al., 'Employing Land-Based Anti-Ship Missiles in the Western Pacific' (Santa Monica, CA: RAND Corporation, 2013).

24 Sash Tusa, quoted in Carola Hoyos, 'Gripen Outmanoeuvres Bigger Rivals in Brazilian Dogfight', *Financial Times*, 13 December 2013, http://www.ft.com/cms/s/0/7ed4123a-68d1-11e3-bb3e-00144feabdc0.html.

25 Barbara Opall-Rome, 'Israel Eyes Locally Built Warship, Drops LCS in Favor of German Design', Defense News, 29 June 2009. One LCS ship-builder claimed in 2006 that 'A reported 26 potential buyers exist worldwide for the ship and its companion equipment with two near-term contenders and four others that have expressed active interest'. See http://www.austal.com/en/media/media-releases/06-12-11/Austal-Wins-Second-Littoral-Combat-Ship-Order.aspx. Not one LCS has been exported to date.

26 Many of the White Papers of states in the region contain similar language to Japan's, which describes its security environment as 'becoming increasingly tangible, acute, and serious'. See Japan Ministry of Defense, 'Digest: Security Environment Surrounding Japan', in 'Defense of Japan 2013', 2013 defence White Paper, http://www.mod.go.jp/e/publ/w_paper/2013.html. See also Vietnam Ministry of National Defence, 'Vietnam: National Defence', 2009 defence White Paper, pp. 9–12; South Korea Ministry of National Defense, '2012 Defense White Paper', pp. 142–3; and Philippines Department of National Defense, 'Transforming the Department of National Defense to Effectively Meet the Defense and Security Challenges of the 21st Century', 2012, pp. 13–15.

27 Andrew T. H. Han, 'The Emergence of Naval Power in the Straits of Malacca', *Defence Studies*, vol. 12, no. 1, 2012. The American equivalent, the *San Antonio* class, is three times the size and five to 11 times more expensive. See http://www.navy.mil/navydata/fact_display.asp?cid=4200&tid=600&ct=4.

28 Clayton M. Christensen, *The Innovator's Dilemma: When New Technologies Cause Great Firms to Fail* (Cambridge, MA: Harvard Business Review Press, 2013), pp. 149–52.

29 Richard Weitz, 'South Korea's Defense Industry: Increasing Domestic Capabilities and Global Opportunities', Korea Economic Institute of America, 7 November 2013, http://www.keia.org/sites/default/files/publications/kei_aps_richard-weitz_final.pdf.

30 And, of course, if one looks at the diesel-submarine market, the other anti-access weapon par excellence, one sees that the United States has zero market share.

31 U.S. International Trade Commission, 'HTS: 9306900020 Guided Missiles', https://dataweb.usitc.gov. Revenue was converted to constant 2014 US dollars using a Department of Defense procurement deflator. See Office of the Under Secretary of Defense

(Comptroller), 'National Defense Budget Estimates for FY 2014', May 2013, pp. 65–6, http://comptroller.defense.gov/Portals/45/Documents/defbudget/fy2014/FY14_Green_Book.pdf.

32 See Stephen Van Evera, 'Primed for Peace: Europe after the Cold War', *International Security*, vol. 15, no. 3, 1990–91; and Jeremy Pressman, *Warring Friends: Alliance Restraint in International Politics* (Ithaca, NY: Cornell University Press, 2008).

33 Hillary Rodham Clinton, 'Remarks at Press Availability', Hanoi, 23 July 2010, http://m.state.gov/md145095.htm.

34 David Shear, 'Statement of Assistant Secretary of Defense for Asian & Pacific Security Affairs Before the Senate Committee on Foreign Relations', 13 May 2015, http://www.foreign.senate.gov/imo/media/doc/051315_Shear_Testimony.pdf.

35 'The South China Sea: Sunnylands and Cloudy Waters', *The Economist*, 20 February 2016.

36 Nor can the possibility of conflict between these small countries be dismissed.

37 C4ISR stands for command, control, communication, computers, intelligence, surveillance and reconnaissance.

38 Fareed Zakaria, *The Post-American World and the Rise of the Rest* (New York: Penguin Books, 2009).

39 Hans G. Andersson, *Saab Aircraft Since 1937* (London: Putnam, 1997), p. 181.

40 See Catherine Putz, 'US Stops Export of Korean Fighter Jets to Uzbekistan', *Diplomat*, 27 October 2015, http://thediplomat.com/2015/10/us-stops-export-of-korean-fighter-jets-to-uzbekistan/. Exports to Indonesia, the Philippines, Thailand and Iraq have been allowed.

41 See Abraham Denmark and Hames Mulvenon, *Contested Commons: The Future of American Power in a Multipolar World*, (Washington DC: Center for a New American Security, 2010); and Evan Braden Montgomery, 'Contested Primacy in the Western Pacific', *International Security*, vol. 38, no. 4, 2014.

42 US Department of Defense Air–Sea Battle Office, 'Air-Sea Battle: Service Collaboration to Address Anti-Access & Area Denial Challenges', May 2013.

Review Essay

History and Policy: Please Think Responsibly

Russell Crandall and Wade Leach

The Power of the Past: History and Statecraft
Hal Brands and Jeremi Suri, eds. Washington DC: Brookings Institution Press, 2015. $32.00. 300 pp.

Orange flames and smoke lit up Baghdad's silhouetted skyline. It was 17 January 1991, and the Gulf War was finally under way. Five months earlier, in the early hours of 2 August 1990, Iraqi president Saddam Hussein's forces had invaded Kuwait. After several days of deliberation and diplomacy, United States secretary of defense Dick Cheney and King Fahd of Saudi Arabia, meeting in the Kingdom, agreed that Washington would rush US forces to Saudi Arabia in order to prevent what appeared to be Saddam's next conquest.[1] For George H.W. Bush, this military response did not yet mean war. It was time, the US president and decorated Second World War veteran said on 5 August, to 'push forward on diplomacy'.[2] Yet, three days later, needing to convince a public and Congress fearful of any war's protracted consequences, Bush's tone had changed. For support, he turned to history: 'Appeasement does not work ... As was the case in the 1930s, we see in Saddam Hussein an aggressive dictator threatening his neighbors.'[3]

As American military assets began to gather in the Gulf, Bush's foreign-policy team worked to assemble an international coalition. When Saddam

Russell Crandall is a Professor of American foreign policy at Davidson College in North Carolina and a contributing editor to *Survival*. His latest book is *The Salvador Option: The United States in El Salvador, 1977–1992* (Cambridge University Press, 2016). He served as a national-security aide to presidents George W. Bush and Barack Obama. **Wade Leach** is a Davidson undergraduate writing his political-science honours thesis on American intellectual conservatism's role in public policy since 1980.

 DOI 10.1080/00396338.2016.1161912

ignored repeated calls for Iraq to leave Kuwait, Bush's secretary of state James Baker helped broker UN Security Council Resolution 678. Backed by Washington, Moscow and Paris in a surprising demonstration of post-Cold War international cooperation, the UN resolution authorised coalition members 'to use all necessary means' to remove Iraqi forces from Kuwait if Saddam did not withdraw by 15 January 1991.[4] Saddam's forces remained in Kuwait, and with diplomacy exhausted, it was time to unleash the (overwhelming) military option. After weeks of relentless bombing, and four days of a massive ground invasion, the US-led campaign liberated Kuwait, trouncing the vaunted Iraqi military in the process. The coalition stopped short, however, of marching on Baghdad.

This was America's first real war of the post-Cold War era – not counting the late-December 1989 invasion to oust Panamanian narco-strongman Manuel Noriega – and it had precipitously ended in the West's favour. The Gulf War was the most significant foreign-policy event of Bush's presidency. It came to define the character of the post-Cold War international system, eclipsed only by the post-9/11 'war on terror' that included another invasion of Iraq in 2003, this time with calamitous consequences. The latter invasion arguably owed something to the limits of the former; had Saddam been removed from power, George W. Bush would have been left with a different Iraq to deal with. But the elder Bush could not have known what would follow. He was guided not by a prediction of the future, but by the past: specifically, the duelling historical memories of appeasement at Munich that had failed to check fascist expansion, and quagmire in Vietnam that had ruined the presidency of Lyndon B. Johnson and torn America apart.

Long shadows

In their stellar edited collection *The Power of the Past: History and Statecraft*, the prolific young diplomatic historians Hal Brands and Jeremi Suri attempt to foster 'a more fruitful interaction' between the production of historical knowledge in academia's cloistered ivory towers and the making of American foreign policy (p. 2). A manual on the use and abuse of history, it should be kept, well-thumbed, on desks in the White House, Pentagon and State Department, and on Capitol Hill. *The Power of the Past* provides a much-needed reminder that events cannot be separated from their historical context, even if it is politically convenient to do so. In a polarised Washington, of course, this is easier said than done. But in collecting contributions from a who's who of historians, former policymakers and hybrids of the two, Brands and Suri are leading by example.

The Power of the Past tells us what we already know, but seem often to forget: applying history to policy via analogy can be useful, but is often misleading or worse. This is not to suggest, Brands and Suri clarify, that policymakers should avoid drawing on historical examples – simply that examples need context. This is a truism, but the book provides plenty of evidence to suggest that weak historical analogies abound.

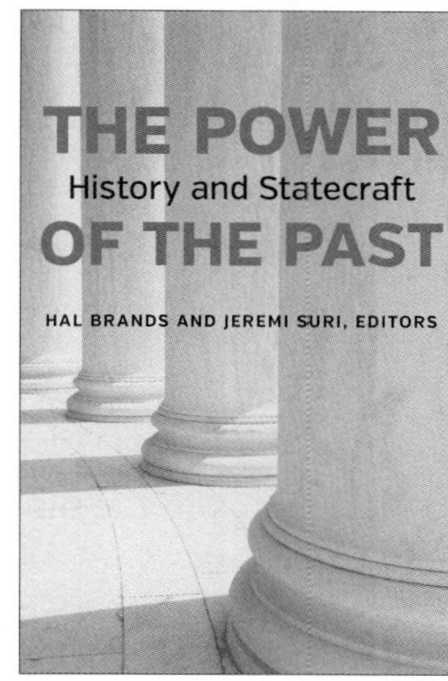

Brands and Suri also remind us that the study of history is the study of uncertainty, and is short on easy answers. Different observers can draw completely different, and sometimes conflicting, lessons from the same historical event. 'Vietnam' is a powerful analogy, acknowledges the historian Mark Atwood Lawrence in his chapter, but it can be used to support an 'extraordinarily wide array of policy options' (p. 65). Proponents of the idea that the United States must recognise the limits of its global power – and not become bogged down abroad – cite the inability to win the 'hearts and minds' of the South Vietnamese as evidence that the United States failed to understand Vietnamese politics (pp. 53–4). Supporters of the American mission in Vietnam find that the gradual build-up of forces, and a 'failure to commit fully to the war', led to the United States' defeat (p. 60). To them, Vietnam is a lesson in the importance of American decisiveness and resolve. In large part, Lawrence contends, the different conclusions are drawn from different periods of the war, which provided enough historical ammunition to fill any politician or policymaker's rhetorical arsenal in the ensuing decades. Lawrence notes various political uses of the Vietnam analogy, raised by congressional Republicans in the debate over sending troops to Kosovo in 1999, and by Democrats in the run-up to the 2003 invasion of Iraq. The length and the significance of America's wars in Afghanistan and Iraq may make their histories similarly malleable.

Bringing the Vietnam War to a close was but one of the tasks assigned to national security advisor and later secretary of state Henry Kissinger, of whom Suri contends that 'no American figure in the last century has used historical analysis more explicitly to formulate policy'. Yet Kissinger did not have the 'training or inclination' to be a historian (p. 29), and with a formal education in philosophy and politics, he often used historical research carelessly. This is a trait, Suri suggests, which he continues to exhibit. Kissinger's weighty tomes bolster his reputation as a grand strategist by offering 'coherent and actionable frameworks to explain the options available for policymakers today' (p. 32). Kissinger's is a philosophical approach to history, allowing the former Harvard faculty member to define global conflicts as he sees them – and, by extension, to encourage American leaders to do the same. And, not a little self-servingly, as Suri points out, Kissinger's world view has plenty of room for the power of great men: 'Metternich and Bismarck in the nineteenth century, Mao and Anwar Sadat in the twentieth century' (p. 39).

Such explanatory frameworks can, of course, be helpful, but they do not necessarily make the application of historical 'lessons' any easier. In his astute chapter on the Persian Gulf War, historian H.W. Brands (the co-editor's father) analyses the analogies applied to the Gulf War. Bush's appeal to remember Munich, Brands argues, 'was always suspect, for it extrapolated from one person, Hitler' (p. 93). Nor was the causal logic clear: did Bush go to war 'because he recalled the consequences of Munich, or did he use the language of Munich to justify a decision that he would have made anyway?' (p. 93). Brands finds the Vietnam analogy 'more solidly grounded, for it dealt not with the character of individual foreign rulers but with the American body politic' (p. 93). For this respected historian, 'the lesson of Vietnam ... was that the United States should not initiate wars it was not willing to fight to the finish' (p. 93). Bush saw to it that American forces were in the Middle East for a limited time, fighting a limited war. He wrote in his diary of his determination to avoid 'another draw, another Vietnam, a sloppy ending' (p. 91). Yet Brands's chapter might have benefited from looking past Munich and Vietnam to include other historical influences. The cold calculation of American interest in the Gulf, based in large part on access to oil, and the exercise of personal diplomacy, had a hint of the Kissinger to it, and, indeed, Kissinger called Bush after the war started to congratulate him on standing up to the Iraqi dictator. Brands might also have added that Bush cribbed from some of the military lessons learned in Grenada in 1983 and Panama in 1989, which installed a preference for swift, and politically and strategically expedient, operations over a gradual increase in commitment.

The corollary of George H.W. Bush's decision not to depose Saddam was the adoption of a strategy with its own historical overtones: containment. Saddam Hussein was not a Soviet general secretary or a bearded Third World guerrilla revolutionary, but he was, for approximately a decade, successfully contained. The continuing relevance of containment is argued in an excellent chapter by former George W. Bush official and current Naval War College professor Thomas Mahnken. Containment was 'arguably the most influential national security concept of the twentieth century' (p. 133), but, Mahnken warns, is thought of properly as a strategy with defined ends, rather than as a vague 'surrogate for policy' (p. 147). Yet Mahnken also attributes American victory in the Cold War to president Ronald Reagan's 'break with containment' (p. 137): a strategic adjustment to apply increasing pressure to the Soviet Union.

That shift in strategic direction, in turn, is attributed by University of Texas scholar William Inboden to Reagan's National Security Council (NSC), on which Inboden served as a senior director. 'Incandescent strategic insights and innovations by themselves make for good reading', Inboden argues, 'but unless married to effective implementation are of little use in the realm of statecraft' (p. 153). The Reagan NSC's reputation for organisational dysfunction, according to Inboden, obscures its effectiveness in turning the president's vision into policy reality. Reagan 'knew what he wanted' (p. 154), and 'policy entrepreneurs' in tune with the president's thinking, such as national security advisor William Clark, helped Reagan to get it (p. 174). Instead of acting as an 'honest broker' – the NSC's conventional role – the Reagan NSC took the initiative. Inboden concludes that an effective leader should be willing to impose his principles on a 'recalcitrant bureaucracy' (pp. 173–4). The lesson is worth learning even if one believes that it is a stretch to attribute the end of the Cold War to the Reagan NSC's gusto.

* * *

Directly and indirectly, *The Power of the Past* makes clear that once you have picked your policy, a historical analogy will always be on hand to back it up. This is not, it should be noted, a testament to policymakers' historical understanding. 'Few policymakers come into office with rich education in history, especially with respect to parts of the world that are not a mainstream part of the educational curriculum for the typically well-informed nonspecialist', observes former senior Clinton official James Steinberg (p. 239). Steinberg argues that this led policy towards the Balkan crises of the 1990s to be shaped by two 'competing paradigms' (p. 242). The first, drawn from the experience of the late nineteenth and early twentieth centuries, was that the messy conflicts in the Balkans were not worth an investment of American blood and treasure. The second, at odds with the first, was 'the Munich/Holocaust analogy' (p. 242), demanding prompt action to prevent genocide. More recent events lent credence to both: misadventure in Somalia in 1993 boosted isolationism, while the failure to stop the Rwandan genocide strengthened the case for intervention (p. 244). In turn, intervention in Kosovo inspired varying conclusions. The pre-Iraq-invasion George W. Bush administration treated Kosovo as an example of the dangers of nation-building (p. 245). A decade later, the example of Kosovo was used to bolster the Obama administration's case for intervention in Libya (p. 246).

Even where clear precedent is unavailable, historical experience can still be used to guide policy. Inboden and Duke University's Peter Feaver, both former members of the George W. Bush administration, consider this issue in a chapter on the post-9/11 'war on terror'. They conclude that officials reached for the analogy they knew best – the waging of the Cold War. The administration defined the conflict as a generational and ideological struggle that would last well beyond the existence of Bush's presidency, and cast it in 'Trumanesque' terms – that is, in the manner of Harry Truman's effort to define the communist threat (p. 261). Inboden and Feaver argue that this kind of 'historical thinking' improved the Bush administration's foreign-policy performance (p. 273). Given that this was a presidency to which history has so far not been kind, the observation is somewhat ironic.

If it is so easy for history to hurt, how can we find history that helps? Reading through the many fine contributions in this volume, it is depressingly apparent how loosely political leaders use history, intentionally and unintentionally. One cure may be to focus on accessibility. The tendency of smart and highly trained academic historians to research arcane topics and write for narrow audiences is a key part of the problem. Admittedly, there is no way for even the most accessible historian to prevent a politician from using history expediently. But, over time, policymakers' history will only get better if historians provide more useful inspiration. This exceptional volume is a sober wake-up call.

Notes

1 See Jon Meacham, *Destiny and Power: The American Odyssey of George Herbert Walker Bush* (New York: Random House, 2015), pp. 423–31.

2 President George H.W. Bush, remarks to the press, Washington DC, 5 August 1990, available at http://www.margaretthatcher.org/document/110704.

3 President George H.W. Bush, address from the Oval Office on Iraq, quoted in Meacham, *Destiny and Power*, p. 436.

4 UN Security Council Resolution 678, 'Iraq–Kuwait', 29 November 1990, http://daccess-ods.un.org/access.nsf/Get?Open&DS=S/RES/678%20(1990)&Lang=E&Area=RESOLUTION. Yemen and Cuba voted against the resolution, and China abstained.

Book Reviews

Politics and International Relations

Gilles Andréani

The Mediator: A Biography of Martti Ahtisaari
Katri Merikallio and Tapani Ruokanen. London: C. Hurst & Co., 2015. £25.00. 420 pp.

Martti Ahtisaari was born in 1937 in Viipuri, or Vyborg, a town on the Karelian isthmus which Finland had to cede to the Soviet Union as a result of the 1939–40 Winter War. From a relatively modest family background, he was trained as a primary-school teacher. His first exposure to international affairs came through development aid: in 1960 he went to Karachi to run a physical-education training centre, and in 1965 he joined the development-aid bureau of the Finnish Ministry for Foreign Affairs. He later served as Finnish ambassador to Tanzania, and eventually became a UN diplomat, serving as the commissioner for Namibia, a position he held until the country achieved its independence. He also served as UN under-secretary for management.

Elected president of Finland in 1994, he participated, along with Russian premier Viktor Chernomyrdin, in the mediation with Slobodan Milosevic which put an end to the war in Kosovo in 1999. Following his term as president, he continued to take part in diplomatic missions, the most important of which was the negotiation of peace terms between Indonesia and insurgents in that country's Aceh region. A second round of negotiations on Kosovo failed to produce an agreement with either Moscow or Belgrade on the independence of the country, but detailed arrangements aimed at turning it into a stable, multi-ethnic democracy. (The independence of Kosovo has since been widely acknowledged, though it is still opposed in principle by many countries.) In recognition of his long career as a peacemaker,

 DOI 10.1080/00396338.2016.1161915

which continues to this day, Ahtisaari was awarded the Nobel Peace Prize in 2008.

The Mediator, by Katri Merikallio and Tapani Ruokanen, two senior editors of Finnish magazine *Suomen Kuvalehti*, is a vivid biography providing a fairly complete narrative of Ahtisaari's remarkable diplomatic feats, as well as a portrait of the statesman himself. Two episodes stand out. The first is Namibia, a defining experience in Ahtisaari's career, in which he demonstrated his resolve, clarity of purpose and ability to respect his interlocutors (and to gain their respect in turn), all while delivering clear and unambiguous messages, which were to be his hallmark throughout his career. The second is the original negotiation on Kosovo, perhaps Ahtisaari's diplomatic masterpiece, during which he clearly understood that the key to success was first to devise a solution that was mutually agreeable to the Americans and the Russians, and then to have Chernomyrdin join him in presenting it to Milosevic, thereby depriving the Serbian leader of any illusion that he could appeal to Russia to help him out. Even so, the book rightly stresses that the ease with which Milosevic capitulated remains something of a mystery, one which Ahtisaari has sought to explain by pointing to an agreement between the Russian military and the Serbian leader that the Russians would occupy Pristina and the north of Kosovo as a separate sector, which would allow Milosevic to hedge against the possible independence of the country (p. 230).

In the second Kosovo negotiation, Ahtisaari was unable to forge a Russian–American agreement, an essential ingredient of his success in 1999. According to the book, Ahtisaari believes that, in 2006, a year after the negotiation started, the Russians could have accepted the notion of an independent Kosovo (p. 371), and that the hardening of Russian President Vladimir Putin's stance towards the West is mostly to blame for the lack of an agreement. Be that as it may, Kosovo is a subject about which Ahtisaari had strong feelings, even arguing that he knew what it meant to have to leave one's native town (his family fled Viipuri before Soviet troops). From the outset, he made clear to his interlocutors, including the Russians and the Serbs, that the end result of the process would be an independent Kosovo. According to him,

> negotiations never start from a neutral position [...] For me it is essential that the negotiating parties know who I am, what I stand for, and where I draw the red line. The more mediators try to hide their aims, the greater risk that they are seen as manipulators. And the more mediators cultivate harmony, the more they distance themselves from neutral territory. (pp. 332–33)

In this sense, Ahtisaari belongs to that class of diplomats for whom strength of character, clarity of mind and openness of purpose are indispensable elements of diplomacy.

The only shortcoming of this excellent book is that it lacks an in-depth description of another masterpiece of Finnish diplomacy, the process by which the country, from 1991 to 1994, dismantled the remnants of Finlandisation, its former special relationship with the Soviet Union, becoming fully integrated with the West (except NATO, which Ahtisaari himself, as president of the country, did not want Finland to join). One might argue that this falls outside the subject of Ahtisaari as mediator, but it nonetheless belongs, at least in part, to his accomplishments as a statesman and a diplomat, and could have been accorded more space.

Foreign Policy Breakthroughs: Cases in Successful Diplomacy
Robert Hutchings and Jeremi Suri, eds. Oxford and New York: Oxford University Press, 2015. £19.99/$29.95. 304 pp.

Like the preceding book, *Foreign Policy Breakthroughs* is about diplomacy and those responsible for it. It presents nine case studies of diplomatic endeavours that had positive outcomes. These include chapters by Christopher J. Lee on the operations of the UN Relief and Rehabilitation Administration (UNRRA) after the Second World War, and by Paula R. Newberg on the provision of humanitarian assistance in Afghanistan under Taliban rule. Other chapters describe diplomatic moves which unquestionably qualify as breakthroughs, such as Washington's engagement of China, symbolised by US president Richard Nixon's visit to Beijing in 1972; Egyptian president Anwar Sadat's visit to Jerusalem and speech to the Knesset, and the following peace process up to the Camp David accords; and the actions of US diplomacy in managing German reunification and the end of the Cold War. Contributions by Mark Dawson on the European Community as a 'community of law', Jonathan Hunt on the negotiation of the Non-Proliferation Treaty (which he emphatically describes as 'the birth of an international community'), and co-authors Rafael Fernández de Castro and Beatriz Leycegui on Mexican diplomacy within NAFTA and the Pacific Alliance describe processes which are less justifiably labelled as breakthroughs, although they certainly qualify as successful diplomacy. Each of the chapters is of high quality and worth reading in itself.

In their well-crafted introduction and conclusion, the editors present an analytical framework which seeks to identify key factors that can account for success in diplomacy. Their findings will come as no great surprise: Hutchings and Suri stress the importance of a patient, competent and determined leadership, of empathising with friends and adversaries alike, of planning and proper timing, of carrying out domestic negotiations at the same time as international ones, and, most importantly, of accepting that the measure of success for diplomacy is not victory but compromise.

All in all, this excellent book is more about good diplomacy in general than it is about breakthroughs. Yet breakthroughs are undeniably useful in helping us to understand success, as well as failure, in diplomacy. In this respect, there are questions which the book does not exhaustively address: are breakthroughs simply to be equated with initiatives that worked? Do they not more frequently occur when one has a problem to solve from which escape is not possible?

Consider, for example, the case of the European Community. Faced in 1950 with the prospect of the imminent end of Allied control over West Germany, Robert Schuman and Jean Monnet had to devise a way to restrict the resurgence of German power, while allowing for Germany's equality within the new Europe. The result was the Schuman Declaration and European integration. By the same token, the pace of emigration from East to West Germany after the fall of the Berlin Wall prompted first Helmut Kohl, then George H.W. Bush, then everyone else to address German reunification as an urgent matter, even though it was an outcome that some wished to avoid. Even François Mitterrand came to accept the inevitable, contrary to Hutchings's simplified narrative that he 'colluded' with Margaret Thatcher and that both 'conspired' with Mikhail Gorbachev to oppose unification (p. 163). In this instance, American management of the problem was brilliant, but the timing and inescapable character of that problem were the product of unforeseen events, not of diplomacy.

In their conclusion, Hutchings and Suri argue that 'procrastination can pay off'. It certainly can, but only up to a point. Refusing to face a difficult problem when there is reason to believe that time will only make things worse has paved the way to some of history's most abject diplomatic failures, from the Munich Agreement to the current state of the Palestinian question. Short of being forced to act by events, having the courage to determine that a question cannot be left unanswered and acting accordingly can also be a kind of breakthrough, perhaps the most demanding kind of all.

The Globalization of Inequality
François Bourguignon. Thomas Scott-Railton, trans. Princeton, NJ: Princeton University Press, 2015. £19.95/$27.95. 210 pp.

François Bourguignon is a professor at the Collège de France and a leading French economist. He was chief economist of the World Bank from 2003 to 2007, before becoming director of the Paris School of Economics. *The Globalization of Inequality* is the translated and expanded version of a book he published in 2012 for the République des idées, a centre-left French think tank, in which he sought to provide an overview of the rise of inequality and its relationship with globalisation.

The result is a clear, rigorous and stimulating book, which describes a continuous increase in inequality from the beginning of the nineteenth century to the 1990s, followed by a reversal in the last two decades. The latter trend has two components: a decrease in inequalities among countries, along with a rise in inequality within countries, globalisation being a key factor for both.

Bourguignon goes on to address the forces behind rising inequality, some of which are market forces, while others are more institutional or political in character, such as the deregulation of labour markets and structural-adjustment policies. He also deals with the rising costs of inequality, and offers policy prescriptions to reduce these costs and provide for a fairer globalisation.

At first glance, the book would seem to confirm the wisdom of Harry Truman's quip that he wished he knew a one-armed economist, because such a person would never say, 'on the other hand'. Bourguignon is a serious, meticulous and cautious economist. He explores all the facets of his subject with care, reviewing the existing literature and consistently offering balanced and considered conclusions. For instance, his discussion of the relationship between inequality and economic efficiency concludes with his judgement that the former can be detrimental to the latter. This suggests a need for redistribution policies, of which Bourguignon observes:

> Is redistribution economically efficient? To the extent that it requires increased tax pressure it could lead to a distortion of incentives and could be inefficient over the short term; but to the extent it equalizes the chances of developing the talents of all, it contributes to efficiency over the medium to the long term. (p. 143)

A dispassionate book on an issue which inflames passions, *The Globalization of Inequality* is nonetheless a determined and convincing plea for curbing inequality within countries, and managing more collectively the consequences of their evolution among countries. Bourguignon argues that, as with climate change, there is an inequality 'threshold' beyond which its adverse societal and economic effects will become unsustainable. It is a conclusion he arrives at with caution, but sustains convincingly.

How Propaganda Works
Jason Stanley. Princeton, NJ: Princeton University Press, 2015.
£19.95/$29.95. 376 pp.

At first sight, propaganda appears to be mainly a twentieth-century phenomenon. It flourished mostly in times of war, and under now-discredited regimes: Nazi Germany had a Reich Minister of Propaganda (Joseph Goebbels), while the Communist Party of the Soviet Union had a Department for Agitation and Propaganda, which came to be known as Agitprop. Should any of this concern us today?

Very much so, says Jason Stanley, a professor of philosophy at Stanford University and author of *How Propaganda Works*. In this brilliant and incisive book, he makes the case that propaganda poses a direct challenge to a central requirement of liberal democracy: that political decisions should be arrived at through rational deliberation in the public sphere. Propaganda's objective is to appeal directly to the emotions and beliefs of the public in order to sidestep the deliberative phase of democratic decision-making, or at least to subvert and neutralise it. It is thus a perversion of democracy as much as it is a feature of non-democratic regimes, a view epitomised by an epigraph attributed to Goebbels at the outset of the volume, which states, 'one of the best jokes of democracy is that it gave its deadly enemies the means by which it was destroyed'.

As a result, warns Stanley, propaganda is not confined to authoritarian or totalitarian regimes. It can flourish in democracies, where it represents a different kind of danger. In authoritarian regimes, where propaganda is acknowledged, the danger is not to take it seriously. To illustrate the point, Stanley draws heavily on *LTI: Lingua Tertii Imperii*, Victor Klemperer's masterful analysis of the language of the Third Reich (which Klemperer commented on daily in a notebook which he hoped the Gestapo would believe to be about a Latin subject), in which he recalls how people were initially dismissive of Hitler's anti-Semitic speeches ('it is only propaganda'). In democracies, the danger is not to recognise propaganda for what it is, although there is plenty of it, according to Stanley, who analyses a wide range of examples, including what he describes as subliminal racial slurs in American political discourse and the Bush administration's misleading messages during the Iraq War.

These examples underscore the point that Stanley mostly approaches his subject from a liberal standpoint, reflecting his acceptance of Karl Marx's famous view, as expressed in *The German Ideology* (which Stanley quotes), that 'the ideas of the ruling class are in every epoch the ruling ideas'. While Stanley makes his case persuasively, he thus narrows the scope of his subject: propaganda does not come only from elites, governments or large corporations. The experience of the twenty-first century shows that it can also be effectively used by fringe or extremist movements that have been empowered to an unprecedented degree by the revolution in information technology, jihadist terrorism being a tragic case in point.

Middle East

Ray Takeyh

The Other Saudis: Shiism, Dissent and Sectarianism
Toby Matthiesen. Cambridge: Cambridge University Press, 2015. £19.99/$29.99. 292 pp.

The academy has often been censured for its esoteric preoccupations and abstruse offerings. Still, there are occasional gems, and Toby Matthiesen's *The Other Saudis* is clearly one of them. With this book, the author has managed to shed much light on an important subject that is not easily accessible: the predicament of the Shi'ites in a country that professes an intolerant branch of Sunnism. Matthiesen's mastery of primary sources and keen eye for detail makes his account an indispensable work of historical scholarship.

The Kingdom of Saudi Arabia is the product of a peculiar marriage between religious orthodoxy and tribal ambition. The Saud warriors were adept at conquest, but required a rationale for their rule. The Wahhabi clerics offered the legitimacy of Islam, but at a price: a nation that safeguarded religion, imposed onerous cultural restrictions on its citizens and discriminated against the Shi'ites. A certain narrative evolved, in which the Shi'ites were not just heretics, but also suspect as citizens. The monarchs on occasion proved more pragmatic than the clerics, since the clerics sought to preserve their religious monopoly, while the rulers sought to pacify their country. At times, Saudi leaders seemed open to accommodating the Shi'ites, only to be pushed back by the religious guides.

For their part, the Shia population has historically sought integration and a measure of respect for its religious rituals and traditions. This is not to suggest that there has been no opposition to the House of Saud, or that violence has never been embraced by Shia political parties. The revolution in Iran and the rise of Shi'ites in Iraq in the aftermath of the American invasion had an emotive appeal for a segment of the Shia community. Those excluded from the corridors of power and disclaimed as heretics have at times looked abroad for redemption. The example of Iranian mullahs overthrowing a monarchy and Iraqi Shi'ites reigning over one of the seats of Arab civilisation inspired activism and even violent resistance. But the history of Saudi Shi'ites has generally been defined by a peaceful quest for acceptance and respect.

At times, astute Saudi rulers have recognised the need for treating all their citizens with a measure of equality. No one exemplified this tradition better than King Abdullah. As both crown prince and monarch, Abdullah led the way in conducting an interfaith dialogue, meeting with and hearing the grievances of Shia delegations and conceding some of their ritualistic observations. It is this noble legacy that is being squandered by Abdullah's successors, who seem more interested in waging sectarian conflicts and propitiating aggrieved Sunnis than maintaining a project of national reconciliation.

The Other Saudis is an important, if not indispensable, guide to one of the least understood but most influential countries of the Middle East, a region that is coming apart in the midst of sectarian conflicts and civil wars.

The Iran–Iraq War
Pierre Razoux. Nicholas Elliott, trans. Cambridge, MA: Harvard University Press, 2015. £29.95/$39.95. 688 pp.

The Iran–Iraq War is the longest inter-state conflict in the history of the modern Middle East, yet it is one of the least assessed by historians. Pierre Razoux steps into this vacuum with a solid but curiously uneven account of the war. Although billed as a comprehensive study, it is basically a military history that often ignores the international diplomacy surrounding the conflict. The domestic politics of both Iran and Iraq are also treated in a casual manner. After pages and pages of detail on military campaigns, one would have appreciated an accounting of the intricate domestic policies of both combatants.

The Iran–Iraq War was an unusual conflict. It marked the first time that Saddam Hussein's impetuous behaviour and lack of strategic planning became apparent. To the extent that the Iraqi strongman had a plan, it was to dismember the eastern portion of Iran and hope that the vengeful mullahs would fail to react. For Iran, the war was not fought for reasons of territory, but for spiritual redemption. This was not a nation fending off an invader, but a theocracy spearheading the cause of righteousness. It was difficult to craft a compromise solution between the warring parties given that both sides seemed committed to their maximalist goals. Iraq invaded Iran, but Iran undeniably prolonged the war. The military history of the war is a story of misjudgements, misperception and amateurish planning by both Iraq's military brass and Iran's Revolutionary Guard. Iraq's behaviour violated the canons of war with its relentless use of chemical weapons, the targeting of civilians and attacks on neutral ships in the

Gulf. Iran was in many ways a victim, but its revolution was so alarming and its leaders so appalling that it was hard to grant it any leeway. The war eventually ended when Iran grew exhausted, its revolution imperilled and its people weary of war. In the end, a conflict that had lasted so long and cost so many lives achieved nothing. The countries' boundaries remained essentially unchanged, and both sides continued to be ruled by the same reckless actors who were there at the beginning.

A curious omission of this book is the absence of any Persian sources. There is an attempt by the author to engage the recently published record of Iraq's deliberations, but even that is tentative. The United States itself is in the process of publishing the record of the Reagan years, which the author largely ignores. Such a massive book should rely on more than just old newspaper stories.

The Arab Gulf States and Reform in the Middle East
Yoel Guzansky. Basingstoke: Palgrave Macmillan, 2015.
£47.00/$70.00. 147 pp.

The Persian Gulf is one of the most volatile regions of the world, simmering with sectarian and strategic tensions. The oil-rich sheikhdoms, such as Saudi Arabia and the United Arab Emirates, keep a wary eye on Iran and Iraq. Iraq is mired in attempts to reconstitute its power, while Iran is intent on expanding its influence. The region's complexities mandate a long-overdue examination of its politics and alignments.

This slim volume provides a useful introduction to the changing politics of the region. It begins with a historical survey of the Gulf sheikhdoms and their ceaseless attempts to secure a steady foundation for their rule. Iran has always been an outlier in the region as a Persian state that has attempted to exert its influence in an Arab arena, and a Shia country swimming against the tides of Sunni opinion. The Gulf Cooperation Council came into existence to fend off Iran's revolutionaries, only to find itself befuddled first by Iraq and then by a succession of American administrations whose policies ranged from intrusion to indifference.

Guzansky then proceeds with an assessment of the individual Gulf states, their history and evolution during the past century. The individual cases will be familiar to the specialist, and the material can be repetitious, if not tedious. Given the author's reliance on secondary literature, he seldom breaks new ground, and the book's rapid march through decades of history can seem unedifying. The narrative stretches all the way to the Arab Spring, with a discussion of how the Saudis tried to fend off the forces of history through a clumsy but ultimately successful intervention in Bahrain.

Among the most interesting parts of the book is its chapter on Israel's newfound allies in the Gulf, particularly its unstated but all too visible cooperation with Saudi Arabia. Common fears of a surging Iran are pushing Jerusalem and Riyadh into an unusual alliance in a region famous for its amoral politics. Still, the two powers have different concerns regarding Iran. The Saudis fear a prospective US–Iran detente, while the Israelis are much more focused on how to tame an Iran with an enlarging and empowering nuclear programme. For now, tactical considerations have drawn these two states closer together. Yet the barriers of ideology remain. A Wahhabi state that seemingly champions the cause of the Palestinians and has indulged in its own share of the demonisation of Israel makes an odd partner for the Jewish state.

The Arab Gulf States and Reform in the Middle East is a useful introduction to the complexities of the Gulf. As with most introductory works, however, it engages in simple analyses that raise questions not always answered by the book itself.

Saudi Arabia in Transition: Insights on Social, Political, Economic and Religious Change
Bernard Haykel, Thomas Hegghammer and Stéphane Lacroix, eds. Cambridge: Cambridge University Press, 2015. £19.99/$32.99. 357 pp.

Three of the most astute observers of Saudi Arabia have assembled a collection of first-rate essays that cover a wide range of topics, from domestic politics to oil policy, and from the dogma of development to religious orthodoxy. Unlike some edited volumes, which suffer from a lack of cohesion and contain essays that are limited in scope and casual in their treatment of subjects that merit a deeper dive, the skilful editors of this volume have filled it with important offerings by expert authors.

Saudi Arabia is often said to model a transactional relationship between the state and society. The public is offered a generous welfare state and reciprocates with political passivity. Gregory Gause challenges this received wisdom by suggesting that the Kingdom's stability is less contingent on the fluctuations of the oil market than the vagaries of regional politics. According to this view, the Iranian Revolution and the post-9/11 convulsions had more to do with the monarchy's stability than the price of oil, the impact of which has usually been mitigated by reliance on reserve funds. This portends poorly for a monarchy that today is surrounded by civil strife and failed states, and that relies on a staple crop that is becoming less relevant. The advent of alternative fuels means that oil will slip from its commanding position as the firewood of the industrial world.

Toby Jones follows this with an equally impressive essay on how development has become one of the defining principles of the Kingdom, and the hazards and promises that such dogma entails. The country has done much to weave together a nation and develop its infrastructure, but such projects inevitably come with costs. A cluster of essays on religion chart the unusual rise of a monarchy tied to the religious sector, and the opportunities and restraints that such an association entails. The monarchy's schemes require religious approbation, while the country's religious leaders cannot sustain their power without the muscle of the House of Saud. At times, both parties suffer from this relationship, as excessive reliance on political power has compromised the Saudi clerical estate and opened up possibilities for Islamist opposition. Paradoxically, a state that relies on religion is increasingly open to an Islamist critique that seems persuasive to a significant segment of the population.

Politics, oil and social change are all thoughtfully assessed in this timely book. It is a must-read for anyone wishing to come to terms with a kingdom known for its opacity.

Behind the 1953 Coup in Iran: Thugs, Turncoats, Soldiers, and Spooks
Ali Rahnema. Cambridge: Cambridge University Press, 2015.
£60.00. 320 pp.

Ali Rahnema is the latest historian to venture into the contested literature of the August 1953 Iranian coup, a historiography that has been badly deformed by the ongoing tensions between the United States and Iran. Rahnema's book is the latest victim of this conflict, as the evidence he presents and the judgements he proffers are at times at odds with one another. The fact is that, in August 1953, there were not one but two coups in Iran. The first, which attempted to replace the government of prime minister Mohammad Mossadegh with one led by Fazlollah Zahedi, had the unmistakable imprint of the United States and Britain. Once that failed, prompting Shah Mohammad Reza Pahlavi, who had signed off on Mossadegh's dismissal, to flee the country, a second coup followed. This one was successful, allowing the shah to return to Iran. The question that has divided historians is who was primarily responsible for the execution of the second coup. Rahnema does a good job of detailing the alliance of mullahs, merchants and military men that supported the shah and feared the chaos that Mossadegh's premiership was causing. This was not just a manufactured American coalition, but one populated by real Iranians, with real power, who had genuine concerns about the direction their country was taking. In Rahnema's unfair and unflattering characterisation, if a military officer supported the shah, he was a collaborator; if he supported Mossadegh, he was a nationalist. Such a dichotomy distorts more than it informs.

A review of some basic facts is in order. The shah had the right to dismiss his prime minister. Mossadegh's rejection of that dismissal was unconstitutional and illegal. The prime minister was an honourable patriot and a monarchist (yes, a monarchist) who seemed incapable of resolving his country's oil dispute with Britain, and whose obduracy was crippling Iran's economy, creating an opening for radical forces of both left and right. The institution of the monarchy was still popular, and the shah was held in high esteem by his citizenry. The role of Western intelligence agencies in conspiring against Mossadegh is undeniable, but eventually of minimal importance. In the end, Iran's fate was decided by a fight between two coalitions, with the shah's proving more capable than Mossadegh's narrow grouping of disgruntled intellectuals and leftist politicians.

Rahnema has done impressive research in various Iranian depositories, and his use of Persian memoirs is impeccable. Yet, despite the fact that his thesis relies on American complicity, he evidently did not visit the relevant US archives, such as the Truman and Eisenhower presidential libraries, or the National Archives. There are three internal CIA studies of the coup available to scholars; he selectively cites only one. And, as mentioned, there is often a disturbing mismatch between the evidence presented and the conclusions offered. In the end, the author plants a lot of trees, but then gets lost in a forest of his own making.

United States
David C. Unger

Liberty and Coercion: The Paradox of American Government from the Founding to the Present
Gary Gerstle. Princeton, NJ: Princeton University Press, 2015.
£24.95/$35.00. 472 pp.

This is a powerful and important book that will reshape the way most readers think about United States history and governance. Gary Gerstle, who teaches American history at the University of Cambridge, has drawn on a lifetime of reading and teaching to produce this masterwork. Gerstle's thesis is that the US constitution erected a classically liberal (in the eighteenth-century sense) central government with very little authority over economics, society and individual rights. This was superimposed on a pre-existing system of state governments empowered to act robustly in all of these fields. He then proceeds to show how this formula was all but reversed over the course of the next two-and-a-quarter centuries. It is a work of ambitious scope, and Gerstle, a clear thinker and gifted writer, makes it work.

Moving through successive phases of American history, Gerstle shows how Washington used three basic techniques of constitutional construction (or perhaps misconstruction) to aggregate powers to the centre that the constitution never intended, until a conservative reaction gathering force over the past 30 to 40 years started stripping some of those powers back. He identifies these three techniques as *exemption, surrogacy and privatisation*. Exemption works through proclaiming that broad areas of policy, such as national security, are exempt from the normal constitutional checks and balances. Surrogacy means stretching actual constitutional language, such as the commerce clause, to enable federal regulation of activities the founders never intended, such as economic activity within states. Privatisation involves contracting private firms to perform governmental functions the federal government has no clear constitutional authority or capacity to carry out on its own, such as building transcontinental railroads. Each of these techniques has significantly distorted the intended constitutional balance through the course of American history, and each continues to do so.

To these three techniques can be added the vastly superior taxing power the federal government originally acquired to fight the Second World War, and which it used in later decades to encroach on policy areas reserved to the states by conditioning federal revenue flows on state compliance with federally approved policies. Add, too, the powerful mid-twentieth-century assist provided by the Supreme Court when it systematically applied the protections of the federal Bill of Rights to limit the previously unchecked police powers of state governments. Yet even as the Warren Court extended the reach of individual rights at the expense of state governments, it took a permissive attitude toward the expanding reach of the national-security state at the federal level.

Gerstle is particularly good at showing how the semi-privatisation of policies not clearly assigned to the federal government has helped lead to Washington's characteristic iron-triangle alliances of corporations, federal bureaucrats and interested members of Congress. And he makes a strong argument that the privatisation of election finance (or, rather, the failure to provide for public financing of an extremely expensive and extensive campaign and election process) has seriously undermined American democracy. Though well aware of how intentionally difficult it is to amend the US constitution, he suggests that may be the only viable way to reassert democratic accountability over some of these excessively privatised functions.

Taken together, these arguments provide a powerful analytical frame that makes broader constitutional sense of policy shifts that are usually considered separately, including Reconstruction, the New Deal, the national-security state, the Warren Court and the Reagan reaction. *Liberty and Coercion* has the further virtue of extending its analysis into the present, showing these forces at work in real time and reminding us of the historic significance of today's fights over gun control, the commerce clause and federal-budget sequestering. All this is accomplished in a highly readable, deeply sourced, magisterial narrative. Readers may quarrel with some of Gerstle's specific contentions, but it would be difficult to deny the overall thrust of his argument.

Deceit on the Road to War: Presidents, Politics, and American Democracy
John M. Schuessler. Ithaca, NY: Cornell University Press, 2015.
£18.95/$27.95. 176 pp.

Democracy is supposed to serve as a check on unwise wars. But does it? Or do the requirements of winning democratic assent for war actually give political leaders incentives to deceive? And is deceit on the road to war always a bad thing, particularly when it rallies a reluctant public to support military actions later vindicated by history, or at least by victory? John M. Schuessler, who teaches strategy at the Air War College in Alabama, has produced a well-written book that thoughtfully examines core questions of war and peace, the quality of American democracy and the definition of national interests. Schuessler explores these questions through well-documented case studies of three episodes of presidential deception: Franklin Delano Roosevelt's undeclared naval war against Germany in the North Atlantic before Pearl Harbor, Lyndon Johnson's secret preparations for escalation in Vietnam while running for president as a peace candidate in 1964, and George W. Bush's use of exaggerated threat assessments to mask a war of choice in Iraq. Schuessler divides patterns of deceit into two broad categories. The first, 'blame shifting', typically occurs when public opposition to war is strong. The aim is to make it appear as though war or escalation is inevitable because of enemy action, not US presidential volition – think Gulf of Tonkin. 'Overselling' is more common when public opinion is receptive to war but needs a push – think the 2003 US invasion of Iraq. As the examples suggest, there can be considerable overlap between the two.

Franklin Roosevelt, faced with the deepest and broadest anti-war opposition of the three cases, engaged in what Schuessler shows to have been a sustained and sophisticated pattern of deceit, especially in the North Atlantic theatre, to allow him to deploy US naval escorts for British cargoes. He makes a less convincing case for Roosevelt having tried to provoke Japan into providing a 'back door' route into the European war. A stronger case can be made that Washington miscalculated its tactics on oil and other economic sanctions that were intended to contain Japanese expansion without war.

Lyndon Johnson also faced public scepticism, including strong doubts among leading Democratic senators, over escalating US military involvement in Vietnam. He followed, probably knowingly, the deceitful precedents set by Roosevelt, his early political icon. But, while Schuessler does not emphasise the point, Johnson's motives for deceit were markedly different from Roosevelt's. Roosevelt believed that a British defeat would endanger the very survival of the United States, and that only direct US military intervention could prevent this. Johnson worried less about the military survival of the United States than about the political survival of his party and his presidency, recalling the political cost Harry Truman and the Democrats had paid for 'losing China' a decade and a half earlier.

Unlike either of these predecessors, George W. Bush faced an American public shocked, frightened and enraged by the 9/11 terrorist attacks and eager for greater military catharsis than it had so far achieved in Afghanistan. But that did not translate into public eagerness to launch an unprovoked war of choice – Americans do not like to see themselves behaving that way in the world. So the Bush administration orchestrated a deliberate campaign of threat inflation to make its invasion of Iraq look like a pre-emptive, or at least preventive, war. Particularly interesting in this case study is Schuessler's explanation of why the supposed marketplace of ideas failed to subject a pro-war campaign based on often flimsy evidence to a sterner test. He chiefly blames congressional Democrats, who knew better but thought it politically safer to remain silent.

Are these three case studies sufficiently representative to justify the author's conclusion that democracy often spurs deceit? Probably. Together, they encompass a fair portion of US wartime experience over the past 75 years. Schuessler further strengthens his case with a useful concluding chapter testing his hypothesis against an additional set of well-chosen examples from the US and abroad. More open to question is his conclusion that deceit is sometimes justified – for example, in the case of Roosevelt's behaviour before Pearl Harbor. Even when such deception seems justified in hindsight, it can carry corrosive costs in terms of public trust and understanding of international reality. And one can only speculate about whether it might have been possible for a politician as gifted and popular as Roosevelt to have achieved his interventionist goals without, or at least with less, deceit.

American Pendulum: Recurring Debates in U.S. Grand Strategy
Christopher Hemmer. Ithaca, NY: Cornell University Press, 2015. $29.95. 224 pp.

In this engaging book, Christopher Hemmer takes a usefully atypical approach to familiar debates in American grand strategy. He considers four perennial polarities. Should the United States engage the world mainly on the basis of its unilateral strength, or proceed only when it can mobilise multilateral support? Must Washington defend a global security perimeter, or should it focus its finite resources on its most vital national interests? Should America seek to spread its values by peaceful example, economic pressures or military force, or should it put those values to the side and pursue a strategy based on the realpolitik of state interest? Finally, should US policymakers act as if time is on their side, or is working against them?

Instead of arguing for particular answers to these questions, Hemmer acknowledges that these debates have recurred for good reason: there is truth on each side of all these questions. Grand strategies, he points out, should serve as aids to strategic judgement, not rigid instruction manuals. Hard choices need to be made, of course, but wise choices are not preordained by ideological predilection. Rather, they are arrived at by carefully weighing available alternatives.

Hemmer, who is dean and a professor of international security at the Air War College, writes largely jargon-free prose that allows him to frame clear and rigorous arguments unencumbered by academic obscurantism. Using well-chosen examples mainly from the past 100 years of US foreign policy, he marshals convincing evidence for his arguments. American policymakers are most likely to stumble, he notes, not when these recurring domestic debates are at their fiercest, but when a particular set of answers to the above questions becomes dogma, with criticism discouraged and possible alternatives ignored. Such self-induced stumbles have been unfortunately frequent in American history, often leading to a pendulum swing toward some other insufficiently scrutinised set of answers.

Hemmer's earliest examples reach back to the founding years of the republic. Along the way, he highlights an interesting parallel between the way in which the multiple security shocks of 1949 consolidated America's commitment to a containment strategy, and the way the similarly seismic shocks of 1979 derailed Jimmy Carter's efforts to move beyond containment. He shows an equally sure hand carrying the argument forward to the present day, capturing the essential dynamics of the most recent administrations, even those not yet exposed to the full light of archival research. He thus delineates the Obama administration's preference for multilateralism, its distaste for military crusading on behalf of American values, its efforts to define a more geographically limited security perimeter – yet also to expand its threat assessment beyond the previous administration's heavy and almost exclusive focus on terrorism – and, finally, its optimistic belief that time is generally on America's side.

Oil, Illiberalism and War: An Analysis of Energy and US Foreign Policy
Andrew T. Price-Smith. Cambridge, MA: The MIT Press, 2015.
£19.95/$28.00. 210 pp.

The central argument Andrew Price-Smith sets out to make in *Oil, Illiberalism and War* is that neither what he calls archetypal liberal-internationalist theory, nor the various schools of modern realist thought, can provide an accurate or complete description of US foreign policy on energy issues. Realists, he argues, are undone by their state-centric mode of analysis, given that non-state actors are sometimes significant players in the energy world. Liberal internationalists fall short, he says, because they fail to take account of Washington's political and economic entwinement with large private oil companies at home, or of its promiscuous use of force and alliances of convenience with illiberal autocrats in the non-Western world. Thus, while Washington has acted the part of benign hegemon in its post-1945 dealings with Europe and Japan, helping to provide energy security for its economically developed allies, it has only been able to do so through the periodic, illiberal use of force in its dealings with weaker states in oil-producing regions, and by using oil provided by illiberal regimes, such as the Saudi monarchy, that oppress their own people.

As an alternative analytical frame, Price-Smith, who teaches political science at Colorado College, proposes something he calls 'shadow liberalism', combining benign hegemony and market relations in dealings with the developed world with illiberal uses of force, autocracy and non-market-based deals with national oil companies in the less-developed world. His analysis of the substantial role of military power in the international political economy of oil is persuasive, and he usefully points to the energy-related issues underlying many modern wars, from the world wars to more recent American wars in the Persian Gulf. He might have made even more of a point of Washington's commitment, for reasons of world order, to assure not just its own domestic energy security, but also that of energy-poor allies. Without this commitment, Washington would have little, if any, need for oil from sources outside the Western hemisphere.

It is not clear, however, that Price-Smith's findings require or justify an entirely new theoretical frame, as opposed to more nuanced versions of liberal internationalism or realism. Those doubts are compounded by his overemphasis on oil as a primary cause of wars that, in reality, had multiple causes, such as those over Georgia and Afghanistan. Realists might overemphasise state interests, but Price-Smith sometimes seems to underemphasise them. Another problem is what sometimes comes across as the unnecessary flaunting of international-relations jargon. Social-science concepts and vocabulary can add precision and rigour, but when a thought can just as easily be presented in plain language, it probably should be.

While Price-Smith's political–economic model predicts highly volatile oil prices, his book, published in mid-2015, understandably failed to anticipate the extremely low prices of early 2016. These have at least temporarily called into question the profitability of recently exploited unconventional-energy deposits such as Alberta's oil sands and North Dakota's Bakken Formation. Without continued investment in further developing such unconventional sources, some of the book's geopolitical prescriptions, such as reduced US attention to the Persian Gulf, make less sense. And while climate change is acknowledged, the book's underlying assumption seems to be continued large-scale reliance on petroleum for industry, power and transport. That may well be a realistic assumption, but other possibilities might also have been given more serious consideration.

Superpower: Three Choices for America's Role in the World
Ian Bremmer. New York: Portfolio, 2015. £14.99/$27.95. 226 pp.

Ian Bremmer, president and founder of the global-risk consultancy Eurasia Group, chose an interesting way to organise his book on America's strategic choices in the coming decades. In successive chapters, he presents the case for three very different approaches to the world, which he calls 'Independent America', 'Moneyball America' and 'Indispensable America'. In each chapter, he presents the strongest arguments he can summon for the named approach. Obviously, these arguments are not consistent from chapter to chapter; much of the time they are diametrically opposed. At the end of the book, Bremmer reveals his own position, but also invites the reader to form different conclusions based on his exposition. This is healthy and useful. American democracy can only benefit from people engaging in this kind of systemic thought about US foreign policy.

At times, however, *Superpower* can be a frustrating read. Bremmer's argumentation can be sharp and original, but it can also be superficially glib. His greatest strengths are on policy issues involving Russia and China, about which he knows a great deal. Elsewhere, he seems to have spread himself too thin, or maybe set himself an impossible task by trying to keep his prose engaging for the widest possible audience.

The Independent America approach consists mainly of leading by example, perfecting democracy at home and becoming John Winthrop's shining 'city upon a hill'. It draws its strength from the perception, shared in part by President Barack Obama, that American policy has become overextended and insolvent, forcing a choice between fulfilling the country's democratic vocation or its globalist ambitions. Some might label this approach isolationist, at least in comparison to the almost indiscriminate globalism which has characterised American policy for the past 75 years. But labels should not decide the case; the real challenges to Independent America are substantive. Critics will rightly rejoin that international problems such as climate change, refugees and the Zika virus will not ignore the United States, even if the country chooses to ignore them. And are Americans truly ready for the emergence of competing national powers such as Germany, Russia and China, the likely geopolitical result of Independent America?

Moneyball America takes its name from Michael Lewis's 2003 book detailing how the Oakland Athletics became a winning baseball team despite limited financial resources. In Bremmer's foreign-policy version, leaders in Washington work to make the US an international winner while minimising taxpayer costs. A Moneyball foreign policy would be driven by shrewd opportunism rather than democratic or any other kind of values. It would act when it saw opportunities for gains on the cheap and leave it to others to bear global costs and burdens when they could be induced to do so. In that sense, it is a caricature of the kind of national-interest policy that almost every administration believes it is pursuing. Pushed to its limits, it has more than a faint resemblance to some of Donald Trump's foreign-policy nostrums.

Indispensable America is summed up by the familiar phrase 'America must lead'. In this approach, the fact of American leadership seems almost more important than the direction in which the country might lead. It postulates spreading freedom, by whatever means necessary, as America's national mission. Yet this is the mindset that has produced every recent US foreign-policy disaster.

In the end, Bremmer reluctantly chooses Independent America. He acknowledges that paring down America's foreign commitments will have costs, but concludes that America's endlessly expanding commitments have become fiscally and politically unsustainable. At least as important, he sees them as coming at the expense of the quality of American society and democracy at home.

Is it really necessary to choose just one of these foreign-policy visions, all of which have deep roots in the American experience and psyche? Bremmer says yes, arguing that the current eclectic mixture is unsustainable. But choosing one, and only one, seems artificially confining, denying policymakers the kind of leeway needed to make wise choices in unexpected or fluid situations. With that in mind, continuing to mix and match American policies to its real-world needs and capabilities does not seem such a bad approach.

War, Conflict and the Military

H.R. McMaster

ISIS: Inside the Army of Terror
Michael Weiss and Hassan Hassan. New York: Regan Arts, 2015. £16.99/$22.95. 270 pp.

Events at the end of 2015, including the mass murder of Parisians in November, the refugee crisis in Europe, mosque bombings in Yemen, attacks on tourists in Tunisia, suicide bombings in Ankara and Beirut, the destruction of a Russian airliner over the Sinai Peninsula, and the San Bernardino shooting in December, led many to conclude that the Islamic State, also known as ISIS or ISIL, cannot be merely contained. As Michael Weiss and Hassan Hassan point out in *ISIS: Inside the Army of Terror*, 'enduring and expanding' is not just the group's motto; it is their ambition. In attempting to explain where ISIS came from and how it has managed to do so much damage in such a short time, the authors have produced a readable and sound description of the group's rise and defining characteristics.

The first four chapters tell the story of how an old US enemy, al-Qaeda and its associated groups, became a new enemy after the United States and its coalition partners toppled Saddam Hussein's Ba'athist regime in Iraq in 2003. The authors describe the rise of Abu Musab al-Zarqawi's al-Qaeda in Iraq (AQI) in the context of that group's relationship with Osama bin Laden's original al-Qaeda organisation, as well as with former Ba'athists. They recount how al-Zarqawi and AQI used an apocalyptic ideology, assassinations and mass-murder attacks against Iraq's Shia population to spark a sectarian civil war, one that would allow the terrorist group to portray itself as the patron and protector of the Sunni population. By 2006, the chaos of civil war had strengthened the influence of Iranian-sponsored Shia militias and accelerated the cycle of violence. AQI, along with the Shia militias and their Iranian sponsors, were the only winners of that contest, while the majority of Iraqis suffered the disintegration of their country's social and political order.

In chapter 5, Weiss and Hassan tell the story of how a change in US strategy, a reinforced security effort and the Sunni tribal 'awakening' against AQI defeated that terrorist organisation and nurtured a fragile political accommodation that isolated not only AQI, but also Shia militias, from popular support. In the authors' telling, '[General David] Petraeus' army ... administered the powerful drug of counterinsurgency warfare, which helped Iraq's own antibodies in turn to destroy a foreign and deadly pathogen' (p. 81). Chapter 6 recounts how that opportunity was then squandered due to a failure to consolidate military gains in the political realm, or to contest the Iranian-led effort to hand the 2010 Iraqi national election to Prime Minister Nuri al-Maliki. The authors argue that it was Washington's political and diplomatic withdrawal, as much as its military withdrawal in 2010, that set up the conditions for a return to large-scale communal conflict in Iraq. This violence, along with the associated alienation of Iraq's Sunni population, Iran's subversion of the Iraqi state and the effects of the Syrian civil war, propelled the rise of ISIS.

Chapters 7 through 9 examine in detail the origins of the Syrian civil war and its relationship to the rise of ISIS. This sectarian conflict helped Syrian President Bashar al-Assad maintain his power base, as well as his support from Iran, while at the same time murdering and repressing his own citizens. The Assad regime facilitated AQI activities while portraying itself as a victim of the very terrorists it supported. This allowed it to use the terrorist threat to maintain support among non-Sunni Syrians at home, and to extort resources from Western nations interested in stabilising Iraq and in protecting their own nations from groups associated with al-Qaeda. As Syria descended into chaos, a small cohort of terrorists from the Islamic State of Iraq developed a clandestine jihadist network in Syria that prepared the way for the rapid rise of ISIS. The authors also expose the hand of Iran's Revolutionary Guard Corps in perpetuating the conflict and in propping up the weak Assad regime, describing the Iranians as an occupying force in Syria.

The book's closing chapters cover the rise of ISIS in Syria and Iraq as a terrorist organisation, propaganda machine, organised-crime network and proto-state. The authors note that recruits come from a variety of backgrounds and possess diverse motives for joining the group. Its control over territory, populations and resources permits it to generate revenue through a wide range of criminal activities, including illicit trafficking (mainly of oil), theft and extortion. ISIS competes on the battlegrounds of information and perception with its slick marketing of its cruel exploits, its interpretation of Islamic eschatology and its mastery of social media. It has sought to consolidate control not only through intimidation and coercion, but also through the establishment of governance, the provision of basic services and the pre-emption of internal threats by a sophisticated internal-security organisation, Amniyat. The final chapter describes Islamic State 'sleeper cells' abroad, such as those that planned and conducted recent attacks in Lebanon, Tunisia and Paris (the book's publication predated those attacks). These cells perform both counter-intelligence and offensive missions while avoiding detection through encrypted communications and the compartmentalisation of people and information.

The authors' analysis reveals the importance of a safe haven and support base to ISIS's psychological and physical strength. Its control over territory, resources and populations represents not only a present-day international security problem, but also a multi-generational threat to all civilised peoples. After all, it was in Pakistani safe havens that the 'alumni' of the resistance to Soviet occupation in Afghanistan and the Afghan civil war learned the skills and were indoctrinated with the ideology that would later give rise to the transnational terrorism of al-Qaeda and ISIS. The threat from ISIS alumni is already orders of magnitude larger. Although the group has recently begun to lose ground, it endures. The analysis presented by Weiss and Hassan suggests that denying ISIS its territorial base ought to be its enemies' most urgent priority. Breaking up the would-be caliphate militarily would destroy the perception of its invincibility and reduce the associated attraction to potential recruits. That said, a sustainable outcome that prevents successor groups from emerging with the same ideology will require a multinational and sustained effort to consolidate gains politically. The authors express no confidence that this will take place, predicting instead that 'the Army of terror will be with us indefinitely' (p. 242).

Since the publication of this book in 2015, the suffering in Syria and Iraq, along with the complexities of the problems there and of the attendant refugee crisis, have only increased. Coping with the catastrophe in the greater Middle East and beyond will require an effort consistent with that complexity. The tendency, however, will be to simplify the situation and to act based on a reductive definition of the problem, assuming that what nations would prefer to do – as opposed to what they *need* to do – is relevant and helpful. Guarding against this requires an examination of ISIS not as the disease itself, but as a symptom of a disease that will require not only military operations, but also a long-term, multinational effort combining political, social, diplomatic, intelligence, communications, law-enforcement and economic projects aimed at both denying ISIS its safe haven and support base, and at healing and strengthening fragmented societies so that ISIS or its next manifestation is unable to regenerate.

ISIS: Inside the Army of Terror represents a useful corrective to the kind of flawed thinking that precludes such badly needed efforts.

The Future of Land Warfare
Michael E. O'Hanlon. Washington DC: Brookings Institution Press, 2015. $32.00. 254 pp.

Declining defence budgets and self-declared 'conflict fatigue' have spurred a return of the belief, last widely held among Western defence communities in the 1990s, that investments in stand-off technological capabilities (such as long-range missiles, advanced aircraft and autonomy-enabled systems) are the best way to promote national defence. To pay for expensive hardware in a period of austerity, most Western militaries have cut the manpower of their land forces. The reductions have continued (with the exception of the French and Polish armies) despite recent and ongoing events that highlight the need for ready land forces to deter, respond to and resolve crises. Even now, Russia is using unconventional land forces under the cover of conventional forces in an effort to change the geopolitical landscape and overturn the post-1991 security order in Europe. Meanwhile, more than 18 months' worth of air-force and special-operations bombings and raids against the Islamic State have failed to end its control over territory, people and resources.

In *The Future of Land Warfare*, Michael O'Hanlon, research director at the Brookings Institution and author of many books on defence issues, argues against the conventional wisdom that large-scale ground warfare is passé. Instead, he concludes that 'ground warfare does have a future and a significant one at that' (p. 3). Moreover, because land warfare is likely to 'get messier and harder rather than easier, simpler, or somehow less central to human security' (p. 167), he argues that maintaining ready land forces capable of operating at sufficient scale and duration will remain essential for 'deterring conflict, partnering with allies and others abroad, resolving conflicts when necessary, and helping keep the peace in general' (p. 172). His analysis focuses on the US military, particularly the army, but is relevant to other Western militaries as well.

While acknowledging that future conflicts or catastrophes are difficult to predict, O'Hanlon envisions plausible scenarios that could necessitate the commitment of significant numbers of US ground forces. These include deterring Russia from attacking the Baltic states; deterring China from intervening in a crisis on the Korean Peninsula; protecting the Philippines or other regional allies from Chinese aggression; maintaining a ceasefire and providing humanitarian relief in South Asia after a potentially nuclear war between India and Pakistan; deterring Iran from using weapons of mass destruction through the ability to mount a ground invasion; restoring order in the Middle East after a destructive sectarian conflict; coping with a severe Ebola outbreak and related violence in a large, populous state such as Nigeria; and addressing deteriorating security conditions in Central America. What these scenarios have in common is that, in every case, the commitment of land forces in considerable magnitude would be necessary to achieve sustainable outcomes. The mere deployment of advanced technological capabilities would not suffice. Consequently, O'Hanlon argues that US ground forces should be sized for a combination of these scenarios involving a 'single decisive war' and a 'possibly prolonged U.S. role in two simultaneous, multilateral missions, which could involve counterinsurgency, stabilization, deterrence, or a major disaster response' (p. 7).

O'Hanlon acknowledges a reluctance among some decision-makers to prepare for such scenarios due to a belief that this might lead to ill-advised, costly and protracted commitments. He contends, however, that unpreparedness for wars has, across US history, posed a greater risk to national security than the unwise or capricious use of force. He observes further that inadequate preparation for certain types of fighting increases the cost and duration of conflicts while reducing prospects for success. His findings should be of particular interest to defence officials charged with the development of planning scenarios and the design of future forces. It might also help military and civilian officials examine critically the assumptions on which defence priorities and spending are based.

Ghost Fleet: A Novel of the Next World War
P.W. Singer and August Cole. New York: Houghton Mifflin Harcourt, 2015. $28.00. 416 pp.

Good science fiction allows us to imagine the future in ways that can help us understand the present. In *Ghost Fleet*, P.W. Singer, a strategist at New America, and August Cole, a senior fellow at the Atlantic Council, imagine a world war between the United States and a Russo-Sino alliance. While many readers will be interested in the new technologies they describe and the way these influence the conflict, the authors' depiction of the interaction between people and technologies in the context of a high-stakes competition is arguably the most compelling feature of the book.

In the war that Singer and Cole imagine, technology enables both villains and heroes. Robots and autonomy-enabled systems range across battlegrounds on the land and sea, and in the air. Hackers infiltrate and take control of weapon systems with counter-hackers in pursuit. Drugs are used to enhance human performance. Yet, men and women – thinking opponents who operate in environments of complexity and uncertainty – remain central to the contest of wills that defines the conflict. Because its authors weave facts (and include over 400 footnotes to document those facts) into their story, *Ghost Fleet* is both imaginative and connected to the real world.

Singer and Cole highlight several imperatives for developing and integrating new military technologies. These include emphasising the integration of people with technology; designing systems that degrade gracefully; hardening systems against cyber and electronic attacks; ensuring sufficient capacity (in terms of size and numbers) and redundancy to build depth and resilience; and considering enemy countermeasures in the design phase. Perhaps the greatest lesson of the book, however, is to caution against the assumption that technological superiority guarantees victory in war, much as Arthur C. Clarke's 1951 science-fiction essay 'Superiority' did back in 1951. In the novel, investments in a range of technological capabilities in the aerospace and maritime domains are initially assumed to provide a differential advantage over potential enemies. Yet these same technologies, when subjected to enemy technological countermeasures, asymmetric operations and deception, fail catastrophically.

The book also contains a geopolitical warning, confirming that a Russo-Sino alliance would indeed be dangerous to Western interests. In *Ghost Fleet*, America's allies actually reach an accommodation with its enemies. The novel appears to depict a plausible extension of Russia's annexation of Crimea and invasion of Ukraine, and its sophisticated strategy to undermine the post-Cold War security order in Europe. Meanwhile, the kind of Chinese aggression imagined in *Ghost Fleet* appears consistent with recent Chinese actions in the South China Sea, as well as with Chinese defence strategists' tendency to bemoan the 'peace disease' that they believe has weakened their military's ability to fight and win wars. Clearly, the scenario presented in *Ghost Fleet* is one to be avoided, possibly through the methods the story itself endorses, including by strengthening alliances and maintaining modernised naval, air and land forces capable of operating at sufficient scale and duration to reassure allies and convince adversaries that they cannot accomplish their objectives through the use of force.

Because it is a well-told story, *Ghost Fleet* will attract general readers as well as those with a more specialised interest in international security. It is the latter type of reader, however, that will benefit most from this cautionary, sobering and instructive tale. As Western militaries pursue technological 'offsets' while reducing the manpower and capacity of their armed forces, one might hope that books such as *Ghost Fleet* will inspire efforts to uncover and examine the implicit assumptions underpinning those efforts, and defence strategy more generally. *Ghost Fleet* warns that strategies dependent on a narrow range of technological capabilities are likely to fail when confronted by determined enemies who emulate, evade and disrupt them. To paraphrase the science-fiction writer Raymond Bradbury, Singer and Cole might not have predicted the future, but the story they tell might help defence officials and senior military leaders prevent it.

Red Team: How to Succeed by Thinking Like the Enemy
Micah Zenko. London and New York: Basic Books, 2015.
£17.99/$26.99. 336 pp.

In *Red Team*, Micah Zenko, a fellow at the Council on Foreign Relations in New York, sets out to explain how leaders might improve institutional performance. According to him, 'an astonishing number of senior leaders are systemically incapable of identifying their organization's most glaring and dangerous shortcomings' (p. xix). Red-teaming, which encompasses simulations, vulnerability probes and alternative analysis, overcomes that deficiency by helping leaders to see themselves, evaluate plans, identify opportunities to improve performance, and spot vulnerabilities or weaknesses in their organisations and strategies. Simulations, of which military war games are an example, replicate the motivations and capabilities of key actors and the interaction between them. Vulnerability probes involve red teams assuming the role of surrogate adversaries and attempting to breach defensive systems, thereby exposing weaknesses. To carry out alternative analysis, red teams employ new people or processes to overcome cognitive or institutional biases.

According to Zenko, an effective red-teamer must be willing to learn from others; possess sufficient empathy to assume the motives and values of an adversary; and be able to transcend a particular discipline to view problems from a broad perspective. Red-team members must also possess the necessary social and communications skills to allow them to work well with others. In delivering their assessments, effective red-teamers present their findings through compelling stories that resonate with their audience.

Following a detailed examination of red-teaming in the US military, intelligence community, Department of Homeland Security and private sector, Zenko identifies six best practices for red teams. These include 'getting the boss to buy in' and ensuring that the host institution 'is willing to accept bad news and to act on it'. His valuable analysis and advice will be of particular interest to executives, and anyone charged with strategic planning.

21st Century Sims: Innovation, Education, and Leadership for the Modern Era
Benjamin F. Armstrong, ed. Annapolis, MD: Naval Institute Press, 2015. $21.95. 176 pp.

In *21st Century Sims*, Lieutenant Commander Benjamin Armstrong has made accessible selected papers by Admiral William Sims, an officer of extraordinary vision who drove US naval modernisation in the early twentieth century. As Armstrong points out, Sims's writings provide today's military and defence leaders with an opportunity to learn from an exemplary leader. The book comes as part of a series by the Naval Institute Press meant to communicate to today's officers how leaders of previous generations learned from operational experience, thought about the problem of future armed conflict and contributed to military innovation. Very early in his career, Sims demonstrated mastery of his profession and a determination to lead change, overcoming considerable bureaucratic and cultural obstacles to advance his ideas. Armstrong concludes that 'the foundation of much of Sims's writing and thinking is the idea that asking questions, and doing the work of research and reflection necessary to find the right questions, is at the heart of being a professional' (p. 146). The qualities that made Sims an effective leader included intellectual courage (he wrote directly to the US president as a lieutenant commander), his commitment to the development of professional knowledge, and his ability to develop fact-based, logical arguments.

The speeches and essays included in this book contain lessons for military officers that are as relevant today as they were in the early twentieth century. These include the importance of participating in professional debates and learning from recent conflicts. Sims opposed the famed naval theorist and historian Alfred Thayer Mahan concerning the design of battleships. He studied the Russo-Japanese War to identify harbingers of change in naval warfare. Perhaps most importantly, he urged officers to take initiative, pursue self-development and avoid the kind of 'military conservatism' that stifles innovation. He urged junior officers to prepare for strategic leadership early in their careers through the study of military history and theory. Should an officer fail to possess the intellectual curiosity or discipline necessary for self-study, Sims warned, he 'may be highly successful, and even brilliant, in all grades up to the responsible positions of high command, and then find his mind almost wholly unprepared to perform its vitally important functions in time of war' (p. 99).

Military officers might read *21st Century Sims* to sharpen their ability to think about the problems of future war and how to make the most out of limited defence resources. Defence officials might use Sims's discussion of wargaming and the effect of aircraft and submarines on naval warfare to consider the implications of today's emerging capabilities, such as long-range missiles and autonomy-enabled systems. Sims's emphasis on people, especially in times of austerity, seems particularly relevant as Western militaries shrink and threats to international security grow. He urged the graduates of the US Naval War College in 1922 to focus on the 'condition of training and morale as to make the best of any material conditions that may be imposed upon us' (p. 134). In democracies, generals and admirals get the militaries that their citizens are willing to pay for. As Sims advised, it is their job to do the best they can with what they are provided.

Closing Argument

Donald Trump's America

Dana H. Allin

I

'There are some things that you just can't imagine happening in your life. This is one of them.' So spoke Mitt Romney on 2 February 2012, at the Trump International Hotel Las Vegas. We can reasonably infer that his statement of disbelief contained some recognition of the situation's inherent absurdity. The leading candidate for the Republican presidential nomination had flown to Las Vegas to receive the blessing of a famous hotel and casino mogul, tabloid king, marketer of eponymous steaks, vodka, a university, and a reality-TV programme in which he intoned 'you're fired', from a leather armchair, for 14 seasons.

At the time, however, Donald Trump was also associated with an important political idea: that Barack Obama did not legitimately occupy the office of the presidency. The reason, never coherently stated, was nonetheless obvious. Trump mouthed functional gibberish about a missing birth certificate, but the only salient truths about the president were that his skin was black and his African father had been born a Muslim. Romney's own father, George, had been governor of Michigan, had allied himself with Martin Luther King, Jr, had refused to support Barry Goldwater in 1964 because of Goldwater's opposition to the Civil Rights Act, and ran for president in 1968 as a representative of the liberal-to-moderate Republicanism that used to thrive in the North. Mitt clearly

Dana H. Allin is Editor of *Survival*, and Senior Fellow for US Foreign Policy and Transatlantic Affairs at the IISS. Portions of this closing argument previously appeared on the *Survival* editors' blog, 'Politics and Strategy'.

Survival | vol. 58 no. 2 | April–May 2016 | pp. 221–228 DOI 10.1080/00396338.2016.1161919

revered his father and has striven to emulate his essential decency, and so we should charitably assume that, in embracing the endorsement of a noxious purveyor of racist conspiracy theory, he had decided that there are trade-offs in life necessary for advancing the conservative political ideals in which he believes.

Four years later, on 3 March 2016, Romney delivered a speech in Salt Lake City, Utah. This time he called Donald Trump a 'con man, a fake … a phony, a fraud'.[1] Now something unimaginable really was happening. Trump had won ten out of 15 state nominating contests, and looked well on his way to winning the Republican Party nomination for president. Leading Republicans were speaking seriously of the end of the party of Abraham Lincoln – not just an aesthetic or moral demise, but its actual collapse. The night of Romney's speech, on the Republican candidates' debate stage in Detroit, Trump assured his supporters and other viewers that there was 'no problem' with the size of his penis.[2] This was in the first ten minutes of the proceedings, which did not become more edifying as the night progressed.

II

In the film of national life, this is the dream sequence. It is a dream from which America has been struggling, in leaden panic, to wake itself since sometime last summer. Or it is the reality-TV version of *The Great Gatsby* – except that F. Scott Fitzgerald's Gatsby was truly, if shadily, self-made, not the mediocre steward of an inherited fortune; Gatsby's strivings for lost love and green-light redemption followed a lyrical trajectory; and he was a character in a novel. As a third alternative, Robert Kagan, the neoconservative historian and public intellectual, proposes Greek myth. 'Today's Republican Party is our Oedipus', Kagan wrote in late February. 'A plague has descended on the party in the form of the most successful demagogue-charlatan in the history of U.S. politics.'[3]

For all of his unusual success, however, Trump is a known character in history. His American antecedents include Henry Ford, Charles Lindbergh, Father Coughlin and George Wallace. In contemporary Europe, the late Jörg Haider of Austria's Freedom Party offered a similar mixture of xenophobia, media savvy, appeal to middle-class anxieties, and attacks on the complacency and corruption of establishment political parties. Haider's successor, Heinz-Christian Strache, ploughs the same swampy fields, as have France's Jean-Marie Le Pen and his daughter-successor Marine.

The big difference is that the European far-rightists are mainly third-party forces, challenging but not supplanting the establishment parties. Italy's Silvio Berlusconi, a Trump-like demagogue, was an exception, and both Poland and Hungary are today governed by rightist, illiberal parties. The general pattern in Western Europe, however, is that while far-right parties pose significant dangers, the mainstream has a way of uniting to fight back, as in 2002, when French socialists fell behind Jacques Chirac in the second round of voting for president rather than risk a Le Pen victory.

In an entrenched two-party system like America's, radicalism is more likely to take hold if it takes over one of the parties. Here, too, there is prologue. The writer Peter Beinart has compared the Tea Party conquest of the Republican Party to what had happened to Democrats after vice president Hubert Humphrey lost narrowly to Richard Nixon in the 1968 presidential election.

> Between 1968 and 1972, grassroots activists—many of them incubated in the anti-war movement—took over the Democratic Party, state by state. In 1970, activists rewrote Michigan's party platform so that it advocated reparations to North Vietnam. In Washington state, they demanded amnesty for draft evaders and a ban on the building of missiles.[4]

George McGovern, the Democratic nominee in 1972, was really a conventional, Midwestern liberal in the mould of Humphrey – and a Second World War hero to boot – but he was driven left by the zeal of this movement and his own anger about the truly senseless war in Vietnam. My own most vivid memory of the campaign is how the McGovern team lost operational control of the Democratic nominating convention; the candidate had to deliver his acceptance speech well after midnight, a time when few Americans were awake to hear a message that they would have tuned out anyway. Nixon, running for re-election, trounced the hapless Democrat, who lost every state except Massachusetts.

Yet the Democrats quickly re-centred themselves. Their next nominee, Jimmy Carter, came from the right of his party, although from the left of the great civil-rights struggle in his native South. After Carter lost his re-election bid to Ronald Reagan, his party put forward two sedate Northern liberals, Walter Mondale and Michael Dukakis. And after both lost, the southerner Bill Clinton led his party in accepting that it would have to engage the national debate on terms that had been set by Reagan. This meant taking more seriously middle-class anxieties about urban crime, and it meant purging the party of residual pacifism. Clinton was lucky on both counts. Crime fell sharply for reasons mainly unrelated to policy, and he inherited a uniquely benign international environment.

It was arguably under Clinton that Republican right-wing radicalism took off. 'Movement conservatism' had started with Goldwater. Reagan was a creature of it, but his presidency was pragmatic. So was that of the classic New England moderate, George H.W. Bush. During Clinton's presidency, however, the Newt Gingrich 'Contract with America' became the foundational text of the first Republican majority in the House of Representatives since the 1950s, promising a 'historic change [that] would be the end of government that is too big, too intrusive, and too easy with the public's money … the beginning of a Congress that respects the values and shares the faith of the American family'.[5] Gingrich had already promised a 'civil war' against liberals, saying in a 1988 speech to the Heritage Foundation that it 'has to be fought with a scale and a duration and a savagery that is only true of civil wars'.[6] In 1990, his political action committee advised Republican candidates to 'speak like Newt', by describing Democrats with words such as 'decay, traitors, radical, sick, destroy, pathetic, corrupt and shame'.[7] It was an approach that gave spirit to the later impeachment proceedings against Clinton.

For their presidential nominees, Republicans still put forward conventional conservatives, if not moderates: Bob Dole, George W. Bush, John McCain and Mitt Romney. Bush as president presided over the radical misadventure of Iraq, and he authorised forms of torture for terrorist suspects. Yet he later appeared, in behaviour if not words, to recognise that the torture was a mistake, and he remained faithful to other fundamental liberal principles. Paramount among these, he recognised and worked against the danger of an anti-Muslim backlash after 9/11.

III

Barack Obama was the first Northern liberal since John F. Kennedy to win the presidency. He came to office in a time of economic crisis and near catastrophe, and with brief Democratic majorities in both houses of Congress he was able to apply the traditional liberal remedy of stimulus spending, together with financial and industrial rescue packages. In enacting expanded access to health insurance, he completed a liberal agenda that Harry Truman had proposed six decades earlier. He used his executive powers to regulate carbon emissions and to exercise considerable discretion regarding the status of illegal immigrants. All of these measures offended the philosophical principles of a Republican Party that had moved significantly to the right.

And yet – it is impossible to ignore the racial divide that coincides with these ideological disagreements and which has constituted the central drama of American history. To the poisonous legacy of slavery there is now added the cultural, economic and religious panic induced by Hispanic immigration and growth, and the association of Islam and jihadist terrorism. With credit to George W. Bush, the anti-Muslim backlash did not occur on his watch, but it started darkly, almost inexplicably, with the 2010 proposal in New York City for a 'Ground Zero Mosque' that was not really a mosque and was definitely not at Ground Zero. (Gringrich, again, took an agitating lead.) Net immigration from Latin America has, since the economic crisis, become negative, but the growth of Hispanic populations continues. Lower-middle-class whites are stuck in an economy of stagnant real wages, even as the wealth of the rich multiplies prodigiously; they have experienced an increase in mortality reminiscent of post-Soviet Russia; and they are watching their country's complexion, and even its language, change around them.

And so Republicans have had a lot of anger to ride. The right–populist Tea Party faction advanced impressively in Congress two years after Obama's election, and two years after his re-election, installing some very right-wing representatives and senators, including Marco Rubio and Ted Cruz. But the Tea Party has proven an inadequate vessel to contain the anger – fear and loathing, really – which has now metastasised into the phenomenon of Donald Trump.

Robert Kagan argues that his party, like Oedipus, brought the plague upon itself. Trump, he insists, is the natural consequence of the 'party's wild obstructionism — the repeated threats to shut down the government over policy and legislative disagreements, the persistent calls for nullification of Supreme Court decisions, the insistence that compromise was betrayal, the internal coups against party leaders who refused to join the general demolition'. Trump's bigotry has also been 'enabled', Kagan insists, by the party's attacks on immigrants, its trafficking in Islamophobia, and by its drumbeat of 'Obama hatred, a racially tinged derangement syndrome that made any charge plausible and any opposition justified'.[8]

Republican leaders, to their credit, are genuinely dismayed by Trump's reckless demagoguery, which could further poison America's already polarised politics and ruin America's reputation. But they are also worried about his heterodox opinions, which are attracting lower-middle-class whites who resent multi-racial liberalism but who also are unmoved by conventional conservative orthodoxies: low marginal tax rates; a decimated welfare state; unfettered free markets including free trade; and, at least implicitly, a large supply of cheap immigrant labour.

Trump thus threatens his party's orthodoxy and its decorum. Does he pose a broader threat? Elsewhere in this issue, Michael J. Boyle writes of a growing challenge to the post-war liberal order, citing politicians such as Trump and Hungary's Viktor Orbán, as well as the possible emerging illiberal alliance of such powers as Russia, China and even India and Brazil.[9] Anne Applebaum speculated recently that we could be two or three elections away from the demise of the West: with help of another terrorist attack or major scandal, Trump could become president of the United States and Marine Le Penn president of France. Britain could leave the European Union and commitment to alliances and principles could more generally fade away.[10]

Who knows? As Applebaum also notes, Europe came back from 'years of lead', terrorism from the Red Brigades, the Red Army Faction and the IRA without, in the end, sacrificing democracy or the rule of law. The United States around the same time overcame a fierce southern backlash against the enactment of civil rights for black people. If Trump wins the nomination, Hillary Clinton appears likely to defeat him.

Some heightened vigilance seems like a good idea, however. Kagan was among the 100 Republican foreign-policy analysts and operatives who signed an open letter, circulated on the same day as Romney's speech, vowing that they will not support a Trump campaign if he wins the nomination.[11] But Kagan in his February op-ed intimated strongly that this would not be enough. 'For this former Republican, and perhaps for others, the only choice will be to vote for Hillary Clinton. The party cannot be saved, but the country still can be.' On the reasonable, though by no means certain, assumption that Trump continues to be successful, the central drama of the next six months will be how many Republicans follow Kagan's renunciation. Some have spoken instead of backing a third-party candidacy, which would probably have the practical effect of ensuring a Democratic victory, and which also might split the Republican Party irrevocably. Trump's fellow candidates, however – Marco Rubio, Ted Cruz and John Kasich – were asked at the end of the 3 March debate whether they were still committed to supporting the party's nominee, even if it is Trump. They all said yes.

Notes

1 Mitt Romney, speech at the University of Utah, 3 March 2016, available at http://time.com/4246596/donald-trump-mitt-romney-utah-speech/.

2 Gregory Krieg, 'Donald Trump Defends Size of His Penis', CNN, 4 March 2016, http://edition.cnn.com/2016/03/03/politics/donald-trump-small-hands-marco-rubio/.

3 Robert Kagan, 'Trump is the GOP's Frankenstein Monster. Now He's Strong Enough to Destroy the Party', *Washington Post*, 25 February 2016, https://www.washingtonpost.com/opinions/trump-is-the-gops-frankenstein-monster-now-hes-strong-enough-to-destroy-the-party/2016/02/25/3e443f28-dbc1-11e5-925f-1d10062cc82d_story.html.

4 Peter Beinart, 'Palin is the New McGovern', Daily Beast, 20 September

2016, http://www.thedailybeast.com/articles/2010/09/20/palin-the-gops-mcgovern.html.

5 Newt Gingrich et al., 'The Contract with America', 27 September 1994, available at https://www.udel.edu/htr/Psc105/Texts/contract.html.

6 Sheryl Gay Stolberg, 'Gingrich Stuck to Caustic Path in Ethics Battles', *New York Times*, 26 January 2012, http://www.nytimes.com/2012/01/27/us/politics/the-long-run-gingrich-stuck-to-caustic-path-in-ethics-battles.html.

7 *Ibid.*

8 Kagan, 'Trump is the GOP's Frankenstein Monster'.

9 Michael J. Boyle, 'The Coming Illiberal Order', *Survival*, vol. 58, no. 2, April–May 2016, pp. 35–66.

10 Anne Applebaum, 'Is This the End of the West As We Know It?', *Washington Post*, 4 March 2016, https://www.washingtonpost.com/opinions/donald-trump-and-the-end-of-nato/2016/03/04/e8c4b9ca-e146-11e5-8d98-4b3d9215ade1_story.html.

11 'Open Letter on Donald Trump From GOP National Security Leaders', War on the Rocks, 2 March 2016, http://warontherocks.com/2016/03/open-letter-on-donald-trump-from-gop-national-security-leaders/.